The Life And Ministry of Jesus Christ:
The Greatest Story Ever Told

Don Stewart

The Life And Ministry Of Jesus Christ:
The Greatest Story Ever Told
© 2016 By Don Stewart

Published by EOW (Educating Our World)
www.educatingourworld.com
San Dimas, California 91773
All rights reserved

English Versions Cited

The various English versions which we cite in this course, apart from the King James Version, all have copyrights. They are listed as follows.

Verses marked NRSV are from the New Revised Standard Version, copyright 1989 by Division of Christian Education of the National Council of the Churches of Christ in the USA. Used by permission. All rights reserved

Verses marked NIV are taken from the HOLY BIBLE, New International Version 2011, Copyright 1973 1978, 1984, 2011 by International Bible Society. Used by permission of Zondervan Publishing House. All rights reserved

Verses marked ESV are from The Holy Bible English Standard Version™ Copyright © 2001 by Crossway Bibles, a division of Good News Publishers All rights reserved.

Scripture quotations marked (NLT) are taken from the Holy Bible, New Living Translation, copyright 1996. Used by permission of Tyndale House Publishers, Inc., Wheaton, Illinois 60189. All rights reserved.

Scripture quotations marked "NKJV" are taken from the New King James Version. Copyright © 1982 by Thomas Nelson, Inc. All rights reserved. Used by permission.

Scripture quotations marked CEV are taken from the Contemporary English Version (CEV) copyright American Bible Society 1991, 1995.

Scripture taken from THE MESSAGE: Copyright © 1993, 1994, 1995, 1996, 2000, 2001, 2002. Used by permission of NavPress Publishing Group.

Scripture quoted by permission. Quotations designated NET are from the NET Bible Copyright © 2003 By Biblical Studies Press, L.L.C. www.netbible.com All rights reserved.

Verses marked RSV are The Holy Bible: Revised Standard Version containing the Old and New Testaments, translated from the original tongues: being the version set forth A.D. 1611, revised A.D. 1881-1885 and A.D. 1901: compared with the most ancient authorities and revised A.D. 1946-52. — 2nd ed. of New Testament A.D. 1971.

Verses marked HCSB are taken from the Holman Christian Standard Bible® Copyright © 1999, 2000, 2002, 2003 by Holman Bible Publishers. Used by permission.

GOD'S WORD is a copyrighted work of God's Word to the Nations. Quotations are used by permission. Copyright 1995 by God's Word to the Nations. All rights reserved.

TABLE OF CONTENTS

THE WORLD INTO WHICH JESUS CAME
WHAT THE WORLD WAS LIKE IN THE FIRST CENTURY A.D. 7

QUESTION 1: WHAT WAS THE WORLD LIKE IN THE FIRST CENTURY AD? 9

QUESTION 2: WHAT WERE THE DIFFERENT POLITICAL DIVISIONS OF THE HOLY LAND WHEN JESUS CAME INTO THE WORLD? 17

QUESTION 3: WHAT LANGUAGE OR LANGUAGES DID JESUS SPEAK? 21

QUESTION 4: WHO WERE THE CAESARS MENTIONED IN THE FOUR GOSPELS? 25

QUESTION 5: WHO WAS PONTIUS PILATE? 31

QUESTION 6: WHO WERE THE HERODS? 39

QUESTION 7: WHAT WAS THE SANHEDRIN? 51

QUESTION 8: WHO WERE THE HIGH PRIEST'S ANNAS AND CAIAPHAS? 55

QUESTION 9: WHO WERE THE SCRIBES? (THE TEACHERS OF THE LAW) 63

QUESTION 10: WHO WERE THE PHARISEES? 69

QUESTION 11: WHO WERE THE SADDUCEES? 75

QUESTION 12: WHO WERE THE HERODIANS? 81

QUESTION 13: WHO WERE THE SAMARITANS? 85

QUESTION 14: WHO WERE THE ESSENES? 89

QUESTION 15: WHO WAS JOHN THE BAPTIST? 93

QUESTION 16: WHAT DO WE KNOW ABOUT THE TWELVE DISCIPLES? 103

QUESTION 17: WHO WAS MARY MAGDALENE? 123

QUESTION 18: WHAT WAS GOLGOTHA? (MOUNT CALVARY) 131

THE LIFE AND MINISTRY OF JESUS CHRIST
WHAT THE WORLD WAS LIKE IN THE FIRST CENTURY A.D. 135

QUESTION 19: WHY DID GOD THE SON, JESUS CHRIST, BECOME A HUMAN BEING? (THE INCARNATION) 137

QUESTION 20: WHY DID JESUS COME AT THAT PARTICULAR TIME IN HISTORY? 151

QUESTION 21: IF JESUS WAS WITHOUT SIN, THEN WHY WAS HE BAPTIZED? 155

QUESTION 22: DID JESUS FULFILL THE PROPHECIES ABOUT THE MESSIAH? 159

QUESTION 23: DID JESUS COME TO BRING PEACE ON EARTH? 171

QUESTION 24: DID JESUS GET INVOLVED IN THE CONTEMPORARY POLITICS IN ISRAEL? 177

QUESTION 25: WHAT WAS JESUS' RELATIONSHIP WITH THE LAW OF MOSES? 183

QUESTION 26: WHY WAS JESUS CALLED LORD? 189

QUESTION 27: WHAT WAS THE SIGNIFICANCE OF THE TRANSFIGURATION OF JESUS? 193

QUESTION 28: DID JESUS PERFORM MIRACLES? 201

QUESTION 29: WHAT WAS THE PURPOSE OF JESUS' MIRACLES? 209

QUESTION 30: WHY SHOULD ANYONE BELIEVE IN THE MIRACLES OF JESUS? 213

QUESTION 31: WHAT OBJECTIONS HAVE BEEN MADE TO JESUS MIRACLES? 239

QUESTION 32: WHY DID JESUS SPEAK IN PARABLES? 249

QUESTION 33: DID JESUS KNOW THE PEOPLE WOULD REJECT HIM? ... 253

QUESTION 34: WAS JESUS A PROPHET? 257

QUESTION 35: IN WHAT WAYS DID JESUS FULFILL THE PROPHETIC MINISTRY? 263

QUESTION 36: DID JESUS MAKE PREDICTIONS THAT HAVE COME TRUE DURING HIS LIFETIME? 271

QUESTION 37: DID JESUS MAKE PREDICTIONS THAT HAVE COME TRUE AFTER HIS LIFETIME? 281

THE BETRAYAL, TRIAL, AND DEATH OF JESUS
THE LAST DAYS OF CHRIST 289

QUESTION 38: WHAT WAS THE CHRONOLOGY OF THE EVENTS SURROUNDING THE DEATH OF CHRIST? 291

QUESTION 39: WHY WAS JESUS BETRAYED BY JUDAS ISCARIOT? 297

QUESTION 40: WHY DID THE RELIGIOUS LEADERS WANT TO KILL JESUS? 303

QUESTION 41: WAS THE DEATH OF JESUS PLANNED AHEAD OF TIME? 309

QUESTION 42: DID JESUS RECEIVE A FAIR TRIAL? 315

QUESTION 43: WHY DID JESUS DIE ON THE CROSS? 325

QUESTION 44: WHY WAS JESUS CRUCIFIED RATHER THAN BEING STONED TO DEATH? 333

QUESTION 45: WHAT IS THE SIGNIFICANCE OF THE WORDS JESUS SPOKE WHILE ON THE CROSS? 337

QUESTION 46: WHAT WAS RESPONSIBLE FOR THE DEATH OF JESUS? 345

APPENDIX 1: WHAT DAY OF THE WEEK WAS JESUS CRUCIFIED: WEDNESDAY, THURSDAY, OR FRIDAY? 349

ABOUT THE AUTHOR 365

PART ONE
The World Into Which Jesus Came
What The World Was Like In The First Century A.D.

What was the world like into which Jesus came? What were the different political and religious divisions of the Holy Land?

This first section will examine the historical background of the world that saw the coming of Christ as well as some of the important characters that were prominent in the four gospels.

QUESTION 1
What Was The World Like In The First Century A.D.?

It is important that we have some understanding of the world into which God the Son, Jesus Christ, came. Indeed, there are a number of things that are necessary for us to know to better appreciate the events in the life of Christ.

First, we need to know something about what happened during the four hundred years between the completion of the Old Testament and the beginning of the New Testament era.

Second, it is necessary to know the conditions in the world in which Jesus came. Understanding these things will help put the life and ministry of Christ in its proper historical context.

There is something else important we will learn from this. Indeed, we will find that the God of the Bible is truly controlling all things.

WHAT HAPPENED BETWEEN THE TESTAMENTS

There was a period of four hundred years of silence between the completion of the Old Testament and the birth of Jesus Christ. It is important to understand what occurred during these years as background to the coming of God the Son into the world. We will briefly sum up these four hundred "silent years."

1. THE PERSIAN PERIOD (430-334 B.C.)

When the Old Testament ended it was the Persians who were ruling. These silent years were relatively uneventful in Israel's history. However, two important events did occur. The High Priest began to exert political influence and the synagogue was used for Bible instruction and worship.

2. THE GREEK PERIOD (334-323 B.C.)

Alexander the Great and his Greek army conquered the Persians who were dominating the world at that time. History tells us that Alexander and his followers were friendly to the Jews. He spread both Greek culture (Hellenism) and established Greek as the international language. This would later set the stage for the proclamation of the gospel to all parts of the world.

3. THE PTOLEMAIC PERIOD (323-198 B.C.)

After the death of Alexander, his kingdom was divided into four parts. One of his generals, Ptolemy took Egypt and ruled from there. His kingdom included the Holy Land.

During this period, the translation of the Old Testament from the Hebrew into Greek occurred. This translation is known as the Septuagint. The knowledge of the Old Testament then became accessible to the Greek-speaking people—the language which Alexander had spread to all parts of his empire.

4. THE SELEUCID PERIOD (198-166 B.C.)

Syria eventually took over rule of the Holy Land. There was one particularly evil king, Antiochus IV, who gave himself the title Epiphanes "the coming one." He was the Nero of Jewish history. Antiochus slaughtered a pig on the altar in the temple in Jerusalem and brought idols into the Holy of Holies. This led to a number of things in response.

First, there was rise of Jewish resistance, and second the rise of the Hasideans and Hellenists. The Hasideans eventually became Pharisees, and the Hellenists became the Sadducees.

5. THE MACCABEAN PERIOD (166-135 B.C.)

The Jewish patriot, Judas Maccabaeus, led a revolt against Antiochus. After overcoming this enemy, he cleansed the defiled temple and established the Jewish state. The Maccabees revived a weak and lifeless people and allowed religious and civil freedom.

6. THE HASMONEAN PERIOD (135-34 B.C)

The Hasmoneans were the descendants of the Maccabees. They ruled as kings during this period—but they were not in rightful kingly line, the line of David.

This was also a time of the expansion of the Jewish state. It is also when the terms Pharisee and Sadducee were first used. It was during this period a rift grew between the Pharisees and Sadducees.

7. THE ROMAN PERIOD (34 B.C. TO A.D. 70)

Judah was made a province of Syria. Herod the Great was appointed ruler. He was not Jewish but Idumean. Herod was brilliant, but cruel. Much building occurred during his long reign including the expansion of the Temple and the Temple Mount. Herod treated the Jews fairly by giving them much civil and religious freedom.

This briefly sums up the various periods from the end of the Old Testament era leading to the time of Christ—as well as shortly beyond. This is the background of the world into which God the Son, Jesus Christ, came.

THE FIRST CENTURY WORLD

We also find that the world was prepared for the coming of Jesus Christ. This exact time in which Jesus came into the world did not happen by mere chance. Indeed, the Bible says that Jesus was born in the "fullness of time." Paul wrote the following to the Galatians.

> But when the fullness of time had come, God sent his Son, born of a woman, born under the law (Galatians 4:4 NRSV).

It was the fullness in God's timing when Jesus came.

The New Living Translation puts it this way.

> But when the right time came, God sent his Son, born of a woman, subject to the law (Galatians 4:4 NLT).

Jesus came as the "right time." This was "God's time."

We can make the following observations about the first century world in which God the Son entered.

1. THERE WAS POLITICAL UNITY

In the first century, Rome was ruling with absolute power. Indeed, they had united both the east and west. The Mediterranean Sea was known as the "Roman Sea." God used this political unity which Rome established for His own purposes.

Specifically, we find this in the enrollment ordered by Caesar that brought Joseph and Mary to Bethlehem. In fact, without that imperial order, there would have been no reason whatsoever for Joseph to bring his pregnant wife some eighty miles from Nazareth to Bethlehem to enroll his family.

However, the order of Caesar had to be obeyed. By obeying this order, Mary's Son, Jesus, was born in Bethlehem—the predicted birthplace of the Promised Messiah.

2. THE PEOPLE HAD A UNIVERSAL LANGUAGE

The culture that Alexander the Great had spread—Hellenism—led to one universal language in the empire, Greek. Greek was spoken everywhere in the Roman Empire. Communication, therefore, was easy between one part of the empire and another part.

This situation was used to immediately to spread the good news of Jesus Christ to all parts of the Empire. Again, we find that the Lord had set the stage for the spreading of the message of Christ by uniting the Roman Empire with the Greek language.

3. THE SCRIPTURE WAS IN THE UNIVERSAL LANGUAGE: THE SEPTUAGINT TRANSLATION

In fact, the Scriptures were already in all parts of the Roman Empire. One of the things that made the spread of the gospel easy was the Septuagint translation. The Hebrew Scriptures had been translated from Greek into Hebrew. This allowed the understanding of God's Word to be possible everywhere.

When the message of Jesus Christ was then proclaimed, it fulfilled the predictions of the Holy Scriptures—which were already in the possession of these people. In other words, the people were aware of the historical background of Israel as well as their expectation of the coming of the Messiah. Indeed, they were ready to hear the message of Christ.

4. WORLD TRADE WAS A REALITY

There was a signpost in the marketplace in each city that gave the distance to Rome. Great highways, easy travel, and easy shipping characterized this time. This allowed the good news about Jesus to travel quickly from one end of the empire to another.

5. THERE WERE SYNAGOGUES IN VARIOUS CITIES

There is also the fact that the synagogues were in major cities across the Roman Empire. Hence, the Hebrew Scriptures could be read and studied in various parts of the empire. Consequently, the people knew the promises of God which were yet to be fulfilled. In particular, there was the promise of a coming Messiah, or Christ.

6. THERE WAS WORLD PEACE

The *Pax Romana* (the peace of Rome) occurred in 29 B.C. The war temple was closed after 200 years of constant fighting. This further paved the way for the spread of the gospel. Nothing stopped people from moving from province to province. Consequently, the message could be quickly spread and indeed it was quickly spread.

7. MORAL DEGENERATION WAS RAMPANT

The moral climate was one of gluttony, infanticide, and gladiators. It was a time of decadence. However, great revivals occur in times of moral decay. Indeed, there was spiritual emptiness on the part of the people.

8. THERE WAS RELIGIOUS INADEQUACY AMONG THE PEOPLE

This brings us to our last point. There was lots of religion in the Roman Empire but there was no reality. The Greeks were lovers of wisdom. They worshipped a number of gods with a vague hint as to a chief god. The time was right for God to send His Son into the world.

CONCLUSION: GOD CONTROLS ALL THINGS

As we can observe from the above points, the timing of the coming into the world of God the Son, Jesus Christ, was certainly not accidental. Indeed, as we find throughout the Scripture, there is no such thing as coincidence or chance. The God of the Bible has a plan. Before His Son entered our world there were a number of things which had to be prepared for His arrival.

The Lord, therefore, made certain that everything was set for the coming of Christ and the spreading of His message to the known world. The "fullness of time" had indeed come!

SUMMARY TO QUESTION 1
WHAT WAS THE WORLD LIKE IN THE FIRST CENTURY AD?

To better appreciate the life and ministry of Jesus Christ it is important to have some understanding of the world in which He came.

For one thing, there were four hundred silent years between the time the Old Testament was completed and when God broke into the world again in the New Testament period. While these were silent years from God, they certainly were not uneventful.

The world in which Jesus came was well prepared for the promised Messiah. Indeed, when Alexander the Great conquered the world in 330 B.C. he established Greek as the international language. Thus, wherever one traveled in the Roman Empire they could communicate to others in the Greek language. This, of course, allowed the gospel message to be spread rapidly.

Furthermore, the Old Testament Scriptures had been translated into this universal language. The Septuagint translation allowed the people of the Roman Empire to read the Scripture in Greek—the Old Testament story was everywhere told.

Moreover, there were synagogues in the various cities around the Roman Empire where these Scriptures were read. Hence, the people were anticipating the coming of the Promised Messiah.

In addition, the Roman world was at peace at the time of Christ. This made travel from one area to the next that much easier—since there would not be the concern about entering an area of conflict.

Add to this, the Roman road system was remarkably efficient. This was another feature that allowed the gospel to be quickly spread to all parts of the empire.

The morality had also degenerated. Indeed, all sorts of distractions and perversions were part of life in the Roman Empire.

This led to the people having a deep spiritual need. Something was needed to fill their emptiness.

Therefore, the time was right for God to send His Son into our world.

QUESTION 2
What Were The Different Political Divisions Of The Holy Land When Jesus Came Into The World?

When Jesus Christ, God the Son, came into our world the land of promise, the Holy Land, was divided up into a number of different political divisions. The following is a simple breakdown of these various divisions in the Holy Land at the time when Jesus came.

JUDEA

This was the Greek and Roman designation for the land of Judah. After the Roman conquest in 63 B.C., the word was used in two senses: (1) denoting the entire Holy Land (2) the Holy Land minus Galilee and Samaria. Jerusalem is in Judea. This was the last part to fall into captivity and the first to be reclaimed by the people. The strict religious Jews lived there—the right wing.

SAMARIA

This was the dwelling place of poor Jews, and Samaritans (half-Jew and half-Gentile). They adopted a mixed form of religion. There had been a bitter rivalry between them and Jews from the time of Nehemiah (440 B.C).

We read about this in the Gospel of John where Jesus had an exchange with a Samaritan woman.

> The Samaritan woman said to him, "You are a Jew. How is it that you ask me, a Samaritan, for something to drink?"—Jews, of course, do not associate with Samaritans (John 4:9 NLT).

As this passage tells us, the Jews did not associate with the Samaritans.

Though traveling Jews often bypassed Samaria, Jesus took the shorter route through Samaria to Galilee despite the mutual antagonism. Luke explains the route He took.

> While traveling to Jerusalem, He passed between Samaria and Galilee (Luke 17:11 HCSB).

Jesus Himself had no problem being with the Samaritans.

GALILEE

Both Jews and Gentiles lived there. The Jews were loyal to the nation but they were not as fanatical as the Judeans. The Judeans considered Galileans as second class Jews. Most of Christ's ministry was in Galilee.

In fact, every one of His twelve disciples were Galileans (with the possible exception of Judas Iscariot). He may have been from Judea.

PEREA

This is a district beyond the Jordan (Transjordan). It is never mentioned by name in the New Testament (except in a variant reading of Luke 6:17).

However, the district is referred to several times—as the land beyond the Jordan. We read of this in Matthew.

> When Jesus had finished saying these things, he left Galilee and went to the region of Judea beyond the Jordan (Matthew 19:1 NRSV).

At the time of Christ's public ministry, it was occupied by Jews, and ruled by Herod Antipas. Geographically it was connected to both Galilee and Judea. Because it adjoined both these regions, one could pass from Judea to Galilee, and bypass the territory of the Samaritans.

DECAPOLIS

Decapolis was a league of ten cities founded by the Greeks. Its large territory was south of the Sea of Galilee and mainly to the east of Jordan. Inhabitants from Decapolis joined the great crowds that followed Jesus.

Matthew writes about Jesus' crowds from this geographical area following Jesus. We read.

> Large crowds followed Him from Galilee, Decapolis, Jerusalem, Judea, and beyond the Jordan (Matthew 4:25 HCSB).

When Jesus cast the demons out of the man in the land of the Gadarenes, they were sent into a heard of pigs. The presence of the swine in this area suggests that the population was primarily Gentile. These cities were not on good speaking terms with the Jews.

This gives us a basic idea of the political and geographical divisions of the land where Jesus ministered. These divisions are important to know for our understanding of the public ministry of Jesus.

SUMMARY TO QUESTION 2
WHAT WERE THE DIFFERENT POLITICAL DIVISIONS OF THE HOLY LAND WHEN JESUS CAME INTO THE WORLD?

When God the Son, Jesus Christ, came into our world, there were five basic political/geographical divisions in the Holy Land. We can simply explain them in the following manner.

Judea was the Roman name for the entire land. However, the term Judea was also used for the entire land—minus Samaria and Galilee. In other words, it referred to the area around Jerusalem. The context must determine what is meant by the use of this word.

Galilee was to the north where Jews and Gentiles lived together. This is the place where Jesus was raised, as well as the area where most of His public ministry took place. Each of His twelve disciples, with the possible exception of Judas, were Galileans.

Samaria was where the Samaritans, half-Jews and half-Gentiles, lived. They were not on good speaking terms with the Jews. Indeed, they had their own center of worship as well as their own translation of the first five books of Scripture, the books of Moses. While most Jews avoided Samaria, Jesus chose to travel through this area.

Perea was the area beyond the Jordan and was mostly inhabited by Jews. While not mentioned by name in the gospels, it is referred to several times as "the land beyond the Jordan." When Jews traveled from Galilee to Jerusalem and back, they would usually bypass Samaria and travel through Perea.

The word Decapolis means "ten cities." Mostly Gentiles inhabited this particular area which was south of the Sea of Galilee and east of the Jordan. Great crowds would come out from these cities and follow Jesus.

This gives us a brief idea of the various divisions of the Holy Land at the time of Jesus Christ. It is important to recognize these divisions because a number of events in the life of Christ have special significance due to where they took place.

Therefore, the more that we appreciate who lived in these particular areas, as well as their current religious and political situation, it will better help us understand the significance of Jesus' words and deeds.

QUESTION 3

What Language Or Languages Did Jesus Speak?

The language that the children of Israel spoke in the days of the Old Testament was a form of Hebrew. However, in 587 B.C., the entire nation went into the Babylonian captivity. In captivity, Aramaic was the main spoken language. Aramaic, a sister language to Hebrew, began to spoken by the Jews from the Babylonian captivity onward.

When Jesus came into the world the Greek language was spoken in all parts of the Roman Empire. There were however, both local and regional dialects. While there is still some question about this, it seems that Jewish people in Israel Jesus' day continued to speak Aramaic. There are a number of observations that should be made about this issue.

1. GREEK WAS THE INTERNATIONAL LANGUAGE

Greek became the international language through the conquests of Alexander the Great (330 B.C.). We know that Jesus was able to speak Greek because several of His conversations could have only taken place in the Greek language.

This includes the account of His speaking to the woman with the demon-possessed child (Matthew 14) as well as His conversations with Pontius Pilate. There is no indication in either of these instances that there was an interpreter present. Therefore, Jesus was able to converse with these individuals in their native language—Greek.

2. ARAMAIC WAS ALSO SPOKEN

Jesus also spoke Aramaic in His public ministry. We have several recorded sayings of Jesus in the Gospels that are transliterated from Aramaic to Greek. These include the words He uttered at the raising of Jairus' daughter. Mark records what occurred.

> He took her by the hand and said to her, "Talitha cum," which means, "Little girl, get up!" (Mark 5:41 NRSV).

Here Mark translates the Aramaic phrase for his readers. Other Aramaic words found in the New Testament are *abba*, translated as "Father," and *ephphatha*, which means "be opened." Consequently, we know that on certain occasions Jesus spoke Aramaic.

3. HEBREW MAY HAVE BEEN SPOKEN

There is the possibility that Jesus spoke in Hebrew at times. Indeed, some people argue that Hebrew was actually the main language that Jesus spoke. While this is a minority view among Bible scholars, there are a number of reasons given as to why this may have been the case.

Since the discussions can get highly technical and involved, we will not give the pros and cons for each side in this book. In a future work, we plan to look at this issue in more detail.

4. LATIN WAS NOT SPOKEN BY THE MASSES

Although Latin was the official language of the Roman Empire it was not spoken by the masses. Only the aristocracy would converse in Latin.

THE SIGN OVER THE CROSS WAS IN THREE LANGUAGES

The sign over the cross of Jesus illustrates the fact of the many languages spoken at that time. It reads as follows.

> Pilate also had a notice written and fastened to the cross, which read: "Jesus the Nazarene, the king of the Jews." Thus

many of the Jewish residents of Jerusalem read this notice, because the place where Jesus was crucified was near the city, and the notice was written in Aramaic, Latin, and Greek (John 19:19,20 NET).

This allowed everyone who had the ability to read, to read the charge or accusation against Jesus in their own language. It is clear that the sign was in both Greek and Latin. It is uncertain, however, whether the other language was Hebrew or Aramaic.

For example, many Bible translations translators understand Aramaic to be the third language such as the NET which we just cited. Other Bible translations agree with this.

However, a number of translations think the third language was Hebrew.

For example, the Holman Christian Standard Bible reads.

> Pilate also had a sign lettered and put on the cross. The inscription was: JESUS THE NAZARENE THE KING OF THE JEWS Many of the Jews read this sign, because the place where Jesus was crucified was near the city, and it was written in Hebrew, Latin, and Greek (John 19:19,20 HCSB).

Hence, there is no consensus as to whether the sign was in Hebrew or Aramaic.

CONCLUSION: JESUS SPOKE AT MORE THAN ONE LANGUAGE

Therefore, we can conclude that Jesus spoke more than one language. We know He spoke Greek and Aramaic, and possibly Hebrew.

SUMMARY TO QUESTION 3
WHAT LANGUAGE OR LANGUAGES DID JESUS SPEAK?

The world in which Jesus came had an international language—Greek. This language was spoken everywhere in the Roman Empire. When

Alexander the Great conquered the world, Greek became the international language.

We know that Jesus spoke Greek. Indeed, there are certain occasions that the New Testament records for us where Jesus would have had to have spoken Greek. This includes His dialogue with a Gentile woman from Syro-Phoenecia, as well as His exchange with Pontius Pilate. There is nothing in either context which would give us the impression that Jesus used an interpreter when He spoke to these people.

On other occasions the Lord probably spoke Aramaic. This seems to be the common language of those Jews of Jesus' time which lived in the Holy Land. Therefore, most of His teaching would have been in Aramaic.

However, it is possible that He spoke Hebrew on occasion. Some actually believe that Hebrew was the main language which Jesus spoke. However, this is debated.

We know that the sign over Jesus' cross was in Greek and Latin as well as one other language. It is debated as to whether it was Hebrew or Aramaic. Modern Bible translations are not in agreement as to which of the two languages it was.

What we can conclude from the evidence is that the Lord Jesus spoke in at least two different languages, Greek and Aramaic, and possibly a third, Hebrew.

QUESTION 4

Who Were The Caesars Mentioned In The Four Gospels?

In the four gospels, the name "Caesar" figures into the life of Jesus Christ. We find Caesar Augustus mentioned at the birth of Christ and Tiberius Caesar at the beginning of His public ministry. Who were these men? What importance do they have with respect to the life of Christ?

1. CAESAR AUGUSTUS

One of the prominent figures in the New Testament was the first Roman Emperor, Caesar Augustus. Augustus ruled from 27 B.C to A.D. 14. He was originally named was Caius Octavius Caepias. He was the grandnephew of Julius Caesar.

Caesar was murdered in 44 B.C. and Augustus eventually succeeded him without a rival. He refused to be called *rex* or *dictator*.

However, in 27 B.C, the Roman Senate called him "Augustus." This name gave the implication that he was to be venerated above all mortals.

HE GAVE A COMMAND TO ENROLL EVERYONE

It was Augustus who was ruling Rome when Jesus was born. He is the one who decreed that the entire world should be enrolled for the purpose of taxation. We read about this in Luke's gospel. It declares.

> In those days a decree went out from Caesar Augustus that all the world should be registered (Luke 2:1 ESV).

The command made each family member register for taxation. This is why Joseph had to leave the Galilee with Mary and go to Bethlehem.

CAESAR UNKNOWINGLY FULFILLED BIBLE PROPHECY

When Augustus made the decree that everyone in the empire should be enrolled in a census, he had no idea that this act would fulfill Bible prophecy. The decision he made, some fifteen hundred miles from the Holy Land, started a chain of events that led to the birth of the Messiah in the predicted city of Bethlehem.

The Bible says Joseph and Mary went from Galilee to Bethlehem to register in the census. The eighty-mile journey would have taken them four or five days. We read in Luke.

> All returned to their own towns to register for this census. And because Joseph was a descendant of King David, he had to go to Bethlehem in Judea, David's ancient home. He traveled there from the village of Nazareth in Galilee. He took with him Mary, his fiancée, who was obviously pregnant by this time. And while they were there, the time came for her baby to be born (Luke 2:3-6 NLT).

There would have been no reason for them to leave their hometown of Nazareth to have their child—except for this decree of Caesar.

Joseph was a descendant of King David. Consequently, they had to travel to the city of David, Bethlehem, to register or enroll. In going to Bethlehem, the prophecy regarding the city of the Messiah's birth was fulfilled. The prophet Micah wrote.

> But you, Bethlehem Ephrathah, though you are small among the clans of Judah, out of you will come for me one who

will be ruler over Israel, whose origins are from of old, from ancient time (Micah 5:2 NIV).

The irony is that Caesar Augustus, for whom deity was claimed, unwittingly fulfilled the prediction of Scripture of the birthplace of the true God who became a human being. This is a further indication how the God of the Bible is in control of all events.

THIS IS AN ACCURATE ACCOUNT OF A CENSUS

It had been charged by critics of the Bible that Rome never ordered its citizens to return to their ancestral homelands to enroll. However, the discovery in Egypt of a Roman census edict from A.D. 104 proved that those who lived elsewhere had to return to their original homes to register. Consequently, there is no reason to doubt the historical accuracy of the account.

Furthermore, we have the testimony of an accurate historian, Luke, as to what happened. This should settle the matter.

2. TIBERIUS CAESAR

The other Caesar mentioned in the New Testament was Tiberius. There is one specific reference to him as well as a number of references to Caesar in general.

HE IS MENTIONED AT THE BEGINNING OF JOHN'S MINISTRY

We find him mentioned at the beginning of the ministry of John the Baptist. This is recorded in the Gospel of Luke. It reads.

> In the fifteenth year of the reign of Emperor Tiberius, when Pontius Pilate was governor of Judea, and Herod was ruler of Galilee, and his brother Philip ruler of the region of Ituraea and Trachonitis, and Lysanias ruler of Abilene, during the high priesthood of Annas and Caiaphas, the word of God came to John son of Zechariah in the wilderness (Luke 3:1,2 NRSV).

It is interesting to note that the only importance Caesar had, as far as God was concerned, was to mark the time in history when the word of the Lord came to John the Baptist. Otherwise his life and rule was of no concern for the plan of God as recorded in Scripture.

This is the only mention of Tiberius by name in the four gospels. He is referred to as Caesar on two other occasions without being named—the poll tax question, and at Jesus' trial.

THE POLL TAX QUESTION WAS PUT TO JESUS

There was the question put to Jesus about the paying of the poll-tax. Should the people pay it or not? Jesus answered.

> Show Me a denarius. Whose image and inscription does it have? "Caesar's," they said. "Well then," He told them, "give back to Caesar the things that are Caesar's and to God the things that are God's" (Luke 20:24,25 HCSB).

The Caesar in question was Tiberius.

THERE WERE FALSE CHARGES THAT JESUS PLOTTED AGAINST CAESAR

There was also the charge that Jesus was plotting to overthrow Caesar. When Jesus was brought before Pontius Pilate, this charge was put forth. The Bible says.

> Then the whole multitude of them arose and led Him to Pilate. And they began to accuse Him, saying, "We found this *fellow* perverting the nation, and forbidding to pay taxes to Caesar, saying that He Himself is Christ, a King" (Luke 23:1,2 NKJV).

Again, this is a reference to Tiberius.

JESUS WAS CHARGED WITH OPPOSING CAESAR

The accusation by the religious rulers was that Jesus was opposing Caesar. We read in John's gospel.

From then on, Pilate tried to set Jesus free, but the Jews kept shouting, "If you let this man go, you are no friend of Caesar. Anyone who claims to be a king opposes Caesar" (John 19:12 HCSB).

The religious leaders had no love for Caesar. However, they hated Jesus all the more. This is why they made reference to Caesar.

SUMMARY TO QUESTION 4
WHO WERE THE CAESARS MENTIONED IN THE FOUR GOSPELS?

Only two Caesars are mentioned by name in the four gospels—Augustus and Tiberius. We can make the following observations about what Scripture says about these Roman leaders.

Caesar Augustus, the first Roman Emperor, made the decree that a census should be taken of everyone in the Empire. This caused Joseph and Mary to leave their home in Nazareth and go to Bethlehem. Her Son Jesus was born in Bethlehem—fulfilling the prediction of Micah the prophet with respect to the birthplace of the Messiah.

Therefore, unwittingly, this decree made by Caesar allowed God's Word to be fulfilled in a miraculous way. It is further confirmation that the God of the Bible is control of all things.

Tiberius Caesar is only mentioned in the New Testament to mark the time in history when the Word of God came to John the Baptist. He is referred to on two other occasions by his title "Caesar,"—but without his name.

We find that the only importance that these two world leaders had, as far as God was concerned, was in reference to the events around the life of Jesus Christ. Otherwise, the New Testament would not have mentioned them at all because they have no other relevance in God's great plan for our world.

QUESTION 5

Who Was Pontius Pilate?

One of the most notable of all the New Testament characters is the Roman Governor, Pontius Pilate. From the New Testament, as well as from secular history, we can determine a number of things about this man who sentenced Jesus Christ to be crucified.

Pontius Pilate was the fifth Roman governor of the province of Judea. His rule lasted from A.D. 26 to A.D. 36 or early A.D. 37.

Although Pilate's residence was in the Caesarea on the coast, he was in Jerusalem for the time of the Passover. It was at that time that Jesus Christ was brought before him.

From the four gospels we learn a number of things about Pilate and his part in the death of Jesus. We can make the following observations.

1. JESUS MADE NO DEFENSE BEFORE PILATE

The Bible says that Pilate marveled that Jesus did not attempt to defend Himself. We read the following in the Gospel of Matthew.

> "Don't you hear their many charges against you?" Pilate demanded. But Jesus said nothing, much to the governor's great surprise (Matthew 27:13,14 NLT).

Pilate was used to seeing prisoners protest their innocence. Jesus, a man who was innocent, said nothing.

2. PILATE ADMITTED JESUS WAS INNOCENT

Pilate told the large crowd that had gathered that Jesus was innocent of any crime. We read of this in the Gospel of John. It says.

> Pilate asked him, "So you are a king?" Jesus replied, "You're correct in saying that I'm a king. I have been born and have come into the world for this reason: to testify to the truth. Everyone who belongs to the truth listens to me." Pilate said to him, "What is truth?" After Pilate said this, he went out to the Jews again and told them, "I don't find this man guilty of anything. You have a custom that I should free one person for you at Passover. Would you like me to free the king of the Jews for you?" (John 18:37-39 God's Word).

Pontius Pilate realized that Jesus was not guilty for the crimes in which He was charged. He made this clear to the crowd.

3. PILATE TRIED TO RELEASE JESUS

Since he realized that Jesus was innocent of all charges, Pilate attempted to release Jesus. John writes.

> Then Pilate tried to release him, but the Jewish leaders told him, "If you release this man, you are not a friend of Caesar. Anyone who declares himself a king is a rebel against Caesar" (John 19:12 NLT).

Yet, the crowd was loudly calling for His death. They falsely claimed that Jesus was opposing Caesar.

4. PILATE DENIED RESPONSIBILITY IN JESUS' DEATH

Pilate tried to put the responsibility of Jesus' death onto others. He washed his hands of the matter thinking this would remove any responsibility from him. Matthew records what took place.

Pilate saw that he wasn't getting anywhere and that a riot was developing. So he sent for a bowl of water and washed his hands before the crowd, saying, "I am innocent of the blood of this man. The responsibility is yours!" (Matthew 27:24 NLT).

He believed this would absolve him of any role in this matter.

5. PILATE HANDED HIM OVER FOR DEATH

Pilate then handed Jesus over to be crucified—a man whom he, the governor of Judea, declared to be innocent.

> So Pilate, wishing to satisfy the crowd, released Barabbas for them; and after flogging Jesus, he handed him over to be crucified (Mark 15:15 NRSV).

Like so many politicians, Pilate wanted to satisfy the noisy crowd rather than do what he knew was right.

6. PILATE COULD NOT DENY HIS RESPONSIBILITY

Although Pilate wanted to absolve himself of responsibility for the death of Jesus, the Apostle Paul later emphasized that Jesus was tried before Pilate. We read what he wrote to Timothy.

> And I command you before God, who gives life to all, and before Christ Jesus, who gave a good testimony before Pontius Pilate (1 Timothy 6:13 NLT).

The statement of Paul seems to be part of a Christian creed—a statement of beliefs. Pilate was guilty with the rest of them.

7. PILATE IS ACKNOWLEDGED IN THE BOOK OF ACTS

In addition, Pilate's role in Jesus' death is also referred to in the Book of Acts. In fact, there are three separate statements about his involvement.

PILATES EFFORT TO RELEASE JESUS IS NOTED

First, the Book of Acts records Pilate's efforts to release Jesus.

> The God of Abraham, the God of Isaac, and the God of Jacob, the God of our fathers, glorified his servant Jesus, whom you delivered over and denied in the presence of Pilate, when he had decided to release him (Acts 3:13 ESV).

This again demonstrates to us that Pilate wanted to release Jesus but did not follow through on what he knew was right.

PILATE AND HEROD WERE CONNECTED

The early church also connected Pilate and Herod in their guilt for putting Jesus to death. We read in the Book of Acts.

> For in this city, in fact, both Herod and Pontius Pilate, with the Gentiles and the peoples of Israel, gathered together against your holy servant Jesus, whom you anointed (Acts 4:27 NRSV).

Pilate is linked with Herod in the death of Jesus. Both were guilty.

PILATE IS THE ONE WHO WRONGFULLY ALLOWED JESUS TO BE EXECUTED

Finally, Pilate is again mentioned as the one whom allowed Jesus to be wrongfully killed. We read the following.

> They found no just cause to execute him, but they asked Pilate to have him killed anyway (Acts 13:28 NLT).

The religious leaders could find no reason to execute Jesus so then sent Him to Pilate. He too could find no crime which Jesus had committed. However, Jesus was killed anyway.

8. THIS IS ALL THAT THE BIBLE HAS TO SAY ABOUT HIM

No other details are given about Pilate after Jesus' death. As is true with other secular and religious leaders mentioned in the gospels, his only importance is how he figured in the story of Jesus.

Scripture has no intent, whatsoever, to give us any details about him—or any of these other leaders.

9. THE TESTIMONY OF THE CHRISTIAN CREEDS

Pilate's role in the death of Jesus has never been forgotten. Whenever the Apostles' Creed is recited, the words, "crucified under Pontius Pilate" remind the world of his responsibility. Pilate can *never* escape his role in Jesus' death.

10. THERE HAS BEEN RECENT EVIDENCE FOUND CONCERNING PILATE

There is one interesting footnote to all of this. During the summer of 1961, Italian archaeologists excavated an ancient theater in Caesarea, in Israel. They discovered a two-by-three-foot inscribed stone. The inscription read:

Pontius Pilate, Prefect of Judea, has presented the Tiberieum to the Caesareans.

This was the first archaeological evidence of the existence of Pontius Pilate. Therefore, the authenticity of Pilate is found in written records, the New Testament, and the archaeological evidence. He truly was an historical character.

11. PROCURATOR OR PREFECT?

There is one other note of interest on Pilate. Traditionally he had been given the title "Procurator of Judea." This was based upon the writings of the early Roman historian Tacitus. However, the limestone inscription found in Caesarea called Pilate "Prefect." Why the difference?

Simply stated, the titles of the Roman governors during this period were varied. From A.D. 6 to A.D. 44 the title "Prefect" was used for them. After this time, they were known as "Procurators." Tacitus used the current title at his time to refer to Pilate's governorship.

Technically, he was in error because Pilate was a "Prefect" not a "Procurator." However, there was no difference in duties or rank between the Procurator and Prefect.

The New Testament uses a Greek word to describe Pilate which can be best translated as "governor" or "ruler." In other words, it is not a technical term like Procurator or Prefect. Therefore, we do not find the New Testament writers making the same mistake as Tacitus in giving the wrong title to Pilate.

PILATE'S LEGACY

In sum, Pontius Pilate is an historical figure who is remembered for one thing only. He was the Roman governor who sent Jesus Christ, a man he declared innocent, to His death on the cross. Unfortunately for him, Pilate will have all eternity to regret that decision. Indeed, he asked Jesus the question "What is truth?" Pilate now realizes that he was looking at "truth" when he asked that fateful question.

SUMMARY TO QUESTION 5
WHO WAS PONTIUS PILATE?

One of the most well-known figures of the New Testament is the Roman Governor Pontius Pilate. History tells us that he was the "Prefect" of Judea from A.D. 26 to A.D. 36. It was Pilate who sentenced Jesus Christ to death by crucifixion. Although he wished to set Jesus free, this weak politician gave in to the large crowd who wanted Jesus dead.

Pilate tried to absolve himself of any blame in the matter by washing his hands in front of the crowd. However, the Book of Acts attributes the responsibility of Jesus' death to Pilate. He bears the responsibility along with the Romans, King Herod, and the Jewish religious rulers.

Therefore, the New Testament, as well as the creeds of the Christian Church, all recognize that Jesus Christ was crucified by a decree of Pontius Pilate. The New Testament says nothing about Pilate's life after Jesus' death.

In 1961, an inscription was found in Israel in the city of Caesarea that had Pilate's name on it. This was the first archaeological evidence that Pilate existed. His existence as an historical figure is now beyond all doubt.

Interestingly, the Roman historian Tacitus gave Pilate the incorrect title of "Procurator" instead of "Prefect." While the duties were the same, their official title changed in the year A.D. 44. The New Testament makes no such error in describing this Roman governor.

In sum, Pilate will always be remembered for sentencing the innocent Jesus to His death on the cross. He ignored his opportunity to do the right thing. His legacy is there for all to see.

QUESTION 6

Who Were The Herods?

The family of Herod ruled over the Holy Land, or parts of it, before and after the time of Jesus Christ. Indeed, there are a number of members of the family of Herod that figure prominently in the life and ministry of Jesus Christ, as well as in the events of the early church.

Since they play such an important role in what took place, it is helpful if we know something about them. We can make the following observations about these Herod's which the New Testament mentions.

1. HEROD THE GREAT

The first Herod we meet in the New Testament is known as Herod the Great (73 B.C. to 4 B.C.). He was not a Jew. His father an Idumean and his mother was an Arabian. The Idumeans were descended from Abraham through Isaac and Esau, rather than through Isaac and Jacob. Hence, he was an Edomite. In other words, they were not part of the "chosen people."

While the Idumeans looked at themselves as participants in the covenant, or agreement, which the Lord had made with Abraham, their ancestors had not gone to Egypt with the descendants of Jacob.

Though not racially a Jew, Herod's Father, Herod Antipater, practiced certain principles of the Jewish religion. His family did not eat pork—neither did they allow any images on the coins which they issued. Yet they also followed certain Roman practices including things which were offensive to the Jews.

It was the Roman senate, not the people of Judea, which had made Herod the Great king of Judea in 40 B.C.

Herod was a great builder. Although his building accomplishments included the enlargement of the Temple Mount and the rebuilding of the Temple of Solomon, he eventually lost favor with the Jewish people. His mixed lineage with his Edomite blood would have made him unacceptable to them. Indeed, the Old Testament said of Edom.

> If Edom says, "We are shattered but we will rebuild the ruins," the Lord of hosts says, "They may build, but I will tear down, and they will be called 'the wicked country,' and 'the people with whom the Lord is angry forever" (Malachi 1:4 ESV).

Edom was seen as a place of wickedness. Therefore, Herod would have never gained complete favor with the people.

THE VISIT OF MAGI TO JERUSALEM ENCOUNTERS HEROD

It was during the reign of Herod the Great that the Magi, the wise men, visited Jerusalem. Matthew records the following.

> In the time of King Herod, after Jesus was born in Bethlehem of Judea, wise men from the East came to Jerusalem, asking, "Where is the child who has been born king of the Jews? For we observed his star at its rising, and have come to pay him homage." When King Herod heard this, he was frightened, and all Jerusalem with him" (Matthew 2:1-3 NRSV).

Herod was greatly bothered by the idea that a new king was born. Indeed, he wanted nothing to interfere with his rule.

HE ORDERED THE SLAUGHTER OF THE INNOCENTS

We also find that it was King Herod who ordered the slaughter of the innocents at the city of Bethlehem. Matthew writes.

QUESTION 6

> When Herod saw that he had been tricked by the wise men, he was infuriated, and he sent and killed all the children in and around Bethlehem who were two years old or under, according to the time that he had learned from the wise men (Matthew 2:16 NRSV).

This behavior was certainly consistent with what we know of Herod.

History tells us that Herod became increasing cruel toward the end of his reign. Thinking that his own family was about to overthrow him, he murdered one of his wives (Mariamne), her mother, two of her sons, and his own eldest son. This led the Roman Emperor Augustus to comment that it would be safer to be Herod's pig (*hus* in Greek) than his son (*huios* in Greek).

HEROD WAS BURIED NEAR BETHLEHEM

The irony is that Herod died a few weeks after the slaughter of the innocents and was buried in Herodium, near Bethlehem! It seems that someone may have been making a statement about the Messiah in the choice of Herod's burial place.

As a footnote, the tomb of Herod in Herodium was finally discovered in the year 2007—after years of searching for it.

2. ARCHELAUS

When Herod the Great died, Archelaus, his eldest son, was placed over Judea, Samaria, and Idumea. He did not rule over the Galilee. When Herod died, Joseph, Mary and the Child Jesus returned to the Holy Land. Matthew writes about Joseph hearing that Archelaus was ruling instead of his father Herod.

> But when he heard that Archelaus was ruling over Judea in place of his father Herod, he was afraid to go there. And being warned in a dream, he withdrew to the region of Galilee (Matthew 2:22 HCSB).

Joseph went to the one region where Archelaus did not rule, Galilee. The fear of Archelaus was justified. Caesar Augustus withheld the confirmation of his kingship until Archelaus proved himself. The confirmation never occurred because Archelaus began his reign by slaughtering 3,000 prominent citizens.

The Emperor removed him two years later. The Emperor then took away of the rule of Judea from the Herod family.

3. HEROD ANTIPAS

Though another son of Herod ruled over the Galilee, Herod Antipas, he was a more tolerant ruler. Galilee became known in his day as a place for revolutionary sentiments. This is something which his father never would have tolerated.

4. HEROD PHILIP

Herod Antipas ruled Galilee when Jesus began His public ministry. Yet he was not the only Herod ruling at the time. Herod Philip was also ruling. He was the son of Herod the Great and the brother of Herod Antipas. We read of both Herod's as Luke describes for us who was ruling at the time John the Baptist appeared.

> Now in the fifteenth year of the reign of Tiberius Caesar, Pontius Pilate being governor of Judea, Herod being tetrarch of Galilee, his brother Philip tetrarch of Iturea and the region of Trachonitis, and Lysanias tetrarch of Abilene (Luke 3:1 NKJV).

Herod Philip ruled over Iturea and the region of Trachonitis. Herod Antipas ruled over Galilee and Perea. Each is called a tetrarch which means the ruler over a fourth part.

We will find that Herod Philip will indirectly play a part in the death of John the Baptist. However, it was Herod Antipas who had the main role in John's murder.

QUESTION 6

HEROD ANTIPAS AND JOHN THE BAPTIST

John the Baptist spoke out against sin. Among other things, John denounced Herod Antipas because he had taken Herodias, the wife of his brother Philip, for himself. Herod did not appreciate John saying these things—so he had the Baptist arrested. Matthew writes.

> For Herod had arrested John, bound him, and put him in prison on account of Herodias, his brother Philip's wife, because John had repeatedly told him, "It is not lawful for you to have her" (Matthew 14:3-4 NET).

However, Herod did not kill John because the crowds considered him to be a prophet. Therefore, Herod did not harm him.

THE DAUGHTER OF HERODIAS DANCES FOR HEROD

Another family member of Herod enters the picture—the daughter of Herodias. On Herod's birthday, Salome, the daughter of Herodias, danced before Herod. This dancing pleased Herod so he told her she could have whatever she wished. Guided by her mother, she asked for the head of John the Baptist.

Herod Antipas though sad because of the rash promise that he made, gave her what she asked for. Mark explains what happened.

> The king immediately sent for an executioner and commanded him to bring John's head. So he went and beheaded him in prison (Mark 6:27 HCSB).

Therefore, in the death of John the Baptist, there were three members of the Herod family involved directly—Herod Antipas, Herodias, and Salome, the daughter of Herodias.

HEROD ANTIPAS THOUGHT JESUS WAS JOHN RISEN FROM THE DEAD

When Herod heard about Jesus, this ruler thought Jesus was John the Baptist raised from the dead. Matthew writes about what happened.

> At that time Herod the tetrarch heard the reports about Jesus, and he said to his attendants, "This is John the Baptist; he has risen from the dead! That is why miraculous powers are at work in him" (Matthew 14:1,2 NIV).

This gives us some insight into the beliefs of this man Herod Antipas. He thought someone could come back to life as another person.

HEROD WANTED TO KILL JESUS

We also find that King Herod wanted to kill Jesus—like he did John the Baptist. We read in Luke's gospel.

> At that time, some Pharisees came up and said to Jesus, "Get away from here, because Herod wants to kill you." But he said to them, "Go and tell that fox, 'Look, I am casting out demons and performing healings today and tomorrow, and on the third day I will complete my work' (Luke 13:31,32 NET).

Jesus was unconcerned about what Herod wanted to do. Indeed, the Lord called Herod, "that fox." This was not a flattering description of the king!!

JESUS WAS BROUGHT BEFORE HEROD FOR TRIAL

The New Testament tells us that one of the trials of Jesus was before Herod. Luke records what occurred.

> "Oh, is he a Galilean?" Pilate asked. When they answered that he was, Pilate sent him to Herod Antipas, because Galilee was under Herod's jurisdiction, and Herod happened to be in Jerusalem at the time. Herod was delighted at the opportunity to see Jesus, because he had heard about him and had been hoping for a long time to see him perform a miracle. He asked Jesus question after question, but Jesus refused to answer. Meanwhile, the leading priests and the

teachers of religious law stood there shouting their accusations. Now Herod and his soldiers began mocking and ridiculing Jesus. Then they put a royal robe on him and sent him back to Pilate. Herod and Pilate, who had been enemies before, became friends that day (Luke 23:6-12 NLT).

Herod was disappointed that Jesus did not perform any miracle or answer any of his questions. Consequently, he sent Jesus back to Pilate.

HEROD WAS EVENTUALLY EXILED

From secular history, we learn that Herod Antipas was eventually exiled from the land and was sent to what is modern-day France. He died in exile there. The year of his death is uncertain.

Thus, ended the inglorious careers of the Herod's who figured in the life and ministry of Jesus Christ.

5. HEROD AGRIPPA I

Another Herod became prominent with respect to the early Christians. Herod Agrippa I was the grandson of Herod the Great. In A.D. 37, this man, who had been a prisoner in Rome under Tiberius Caesar, was actually put in charge of the area where Herod Antipas had formerly ruled. In A.D. 41 Judea and Samaria were added to his realm.

HEROD AGRIPPA I PUT THE APOSTLE JAMES TO DEATH

The New Testament records that it was this same King Herod Agrippa who ordered the death James, the brother of John. We read about this in the Book of Acts.

> About that time Herod the king laid violent hands on some who belonged to the church. He killed James the brother of John with the sword, and when he saw that it pleased the Jews, he proceeded to arrest Peter also. This was during the days of Unleavened Bread (Acts 12:1-3 ESV).

Herod Agrippa found that he could please the Jewish religious leaders in his persecution of the followers of Jesus.

HEROD AGRIPPA'S DEATH IS RECORDED

The Lord did not allow Herod to get away with his evil deed. He died an agonizing death. The Bible records it as follows.

> Now Herod was very angry with the people of Tyre and Sidon. So they sent a delegation to make peace with him because their cities were dependent upon Herod's country for their food. They made friends with Blastus, Herod's personal assistant, and an appointment with Herod was granted. When the day arrived, Herod put on his royal robes, sat on his throne, and made a speech to them. The people gave him a great ovation, shouting, "It is the voice of a god, not of a man!" Instantly, an angel of the Lord struck Herod with a sickness, because he accepted the people's worship instead of giving the glory to God. So he was consumed with worms and died. But God's Good News was spreading rapidly, and there were many new believers (Acts 12:20-24 NLT).

This man, who put James to death, was eventually judged by the Lord for not giving God the proper glory He deserved.

6. HEROD AGRIPPA II

There is one other Herod who figures into the New Testament story, Herod Agrippa II—the son of Herod Agrippa I, and the great-grandson of Herod the Great. He ruled over parts of the Holy Land beginning in A.D. 53 until his death in the 90's of the first century. He lived a scandalous life by having his sister Bernice living with him as his wife.

It was this Herod, along with Bernice, whom the Apostle Paul appeared before as recorded in Acts 25 and 26.

Interestingly, it was Herod Agrippa II that used the word "Christian" in describing the Apostle Paul. We read of this in the Book of Acts.

> For the king knows about these matters. It is to him I am actually speaking boldly. For I'm not convinced that any of these things escapes his notice, since this was not done in a corner! King Agrippa, do you believe the prophets? I know you believe." Then Agrippa said to Paul, "Are you going to persuade me to become a Christian so easily?" "I wish before God," replied Paul, "that whether easily or with difficulty, not only you but all who listen to me today might become as I am—except for these chains" (Acts 26:27-29 HCSB).

Unfortunately, there is no record of Agrippa II ever becoming a believer in Jesus as the Christ.

This briefly sums up the lives of these Herod's which are mentioned in the four gospels, as well as in the Book of Acts. As can be readily seen, none of them lived a life which was glorifying to God.

SUMMARY TO QUESTION 6
WHO WERE THE HERODS?

There are a number of members of Herod's family figure prominently in the life and ministry of Jesus, as well as in the history of the early church. From secular history, as well as from the New Testament, we can make the following observations about these Herods.

Herod the Great was the king of Judea when Jesus was born. Though he ruled over the people from Jerusalem, Herod was not Jewish but rather an Idumean—a descendant of Esau, not Jacob.

Herod was installed as king by the Romans. He is known for the great amount of building which went on during his reign. Among other things, he doubled the size of the Temple Mount.

It was this Herod to whom the message came from the Magi that the Christ had been born. In fact, he is the one who ordered the slaughter of the innocents. This took place when the Magi did not return to him after they found the Christ Child.

When he died, Herod Archelaus ruled in his place. When Joseph, Mary and the child Jesus returned from Egypt after the death of Herod the Great, they settled in Galilee. This was the one area in which Archelaus did not rule over. He is only mentioned in the New Testament in connection of the Holy Family going to live in Nazareth after their return from Egypt.

It was Herod Antipas who ruled Galilee during the time of Jesus' public ministry. His brother Herod Philip also ruled at this time—though nothing is specifically said about him or his rule.

Herod Antipas was the one who had John the Baptist executed at the instigation of his wife Herodias. John had spoken out against the Herod because he had taken Herodias, the wife of his brother Philip, for himself.

On Herod's birthday, the daughter of Herodias danced before Herod. When he promised to give her anything she wished, the young girl asked for the head of John the Baptist. Herod sadly agreed. Thus, Herod Antipas, Herodias, and her daughter were directly responsible for the death of John the Baptist—the forerunner of the Messiah.

The superstitious Herod Antipas thought that Jesus was actually John the Baptist raised from the dead. Herod wanted to kill Jesus as he had done John. The New Testament says that Herod only saw Jesus during His trial but was disappointed that Jesus performed no miracle in his presence. Therefore, he sent Jesus back to Pontius Pilate.

We meet another Herod, Agrippa I, in the Book of Acts. We are told that this particular Herod had James, the brother of John, put to death. After this murderous act, the Lord struck Herod Agrippa I down with a painful illness, and he soon died.

Herod Agrippa II, the son of Agrippa I, eventually came to rule in Jerusalem. He was the king whom the Apostle Paul appeared before. In one instance, Agrippa used the word "Christian" in describing Paul. Though Paul attempted to convert Herod Agrippa II, there is no indication that this Herod ever believed in Jesus.

Hence, the family of Herod figures prominently into the New Testament story. Indeed, it mentions Herod the Great, Herod Archelaus, Herod Antipas, Herod Philip, Herodias, her daughter, Herod Agrippa I, Herod Agrippa II, and his sister Bernice.

The reason these particular Herod's and their family members are mentioned in the New Testament is in reference to the ministry of Jesus Christ—as well as the spread of the good news about Him to the various parts of the world. Otherwise, Scripture has no interest in them whatsoever.

Though they were important rulers in their day, as far as the Bible is concerned, they are only mentioned in connection with the work of God which was taking place at that time.

QUESTION 7

What Was The Sanhedrin?

The word "Sanhedrin" is a combination of two Greek words meaning, "seated together." They were a ruling body of seventy-one members with the High Priest as the chief officer. They were in existence as the time of Christ and figure prominently into His life. There are a number of observations that we can make about this group.

1. THEY MAY HAVE BEEN PATTERNED AFTER MOSES

The number was probably patterned after the seventy elders of Israel that the Lord established under Moses.

> The Lord said to Moses: Choose seventy of Israel's respected leaders and go with them to the sacred tent (Numbers 11:16 CEV).

The Lord commanded Moses to choose these elders. The Sanhedrin seems to have patterned themselves after this command.

2. THEY ARE CALLED THE ASSEMBLY OF THE ELDERS

They are called the "assembly of the elders" or "the nation's leaders" in the four gospels. Luke writes the following in his gospel.

> When day came, the assembly of the elders of the people gathered together, both chief priests and scribes. And they led him away to their council (Luke 22:66 ESV).

They are called "the nation's leaders" by the Contemporary English Translation.

> At daybreak the nation's leaders, the chief priests, and the teachers of the Law of Moses got together and brought Jesus before their council (Luke 22:66 CEV).

This title, variously translated as "the council of the elders," "the assembly of the elders or "the nation's leaders," shows that they were the leaders of the people.

3. THEY WERE UNDER ROMAN AUTHORITY

Since Israel was subject to the Romans in Jesus' day, the Sanhedrin ruled under the Romans in civil and religious matters. Among other things, they were not allowed to officially put anyone to death. Therefore, they sent Jesus to Pontius Pilate to have Him executed. Matthew records this in his account of Jesus' life. He wrote.

> When morning came, all the chief priests and elders of the people plotted against Jesus to put Him to death. And when they had bound Him, they led Him away and delivered Him to Pontius Pilate the governor (Matthew 27:1,2 NKJV).

Pilate alone had the authority to order Jesus' execution.

4. THEY HAD NO RIGHT TO EXECUTE JESUS

The council acknowledged to Pontius Pilate that they had no authority to execute Jesus. We read the following in John's gospel.

> Pilate came out and asked, "What charges are you bringing against this man?" They answered, "He is a criminal! That's why we brought him to you." Pilate told them, "Take him and judge him by your own laws." The crowd replied, "We are not allowed to put anyone to death." And so what Jesus said about his death would soon come true (John 18:29-32 CEV).

Jesus' prediction, of the way in which He was to die, was being fulfilled. He would be handed over to the Gentiles by the religious rulers of His own people, the Jews.

5. THE SANHEDRIN WAS ABOLISHED AFTER JERUSALEM WAS DESTROYED

The Sanhedrin was abolished after the city of Jerusalem and the temple were destroyed in A.D. 70. The control over the city of Jerusalem was no longer theirs. To this day, they cease to exist.

However, in recent years there has been an attempt to reinstitute this ancient council. This is not surprising in light of what the Scripture has to say about the "last days." For more information on "things to come" see our books, *The Jews, Jerusalem, And The Coming Temple*, and *The Final Antichrist*.

SUMMARY TO QUESTION 7
WHAT WAS THE SANHEDRIN?

One particular group who figures prominently in the account of Jesus' trial and execution was the Sanhedrin. The Sanhedrin was a Jewish council of seventy-one members. They seem to be patterned after the seventy elders that God established through the prophet Moses.

In the four gospels they are called such things as, "the council of the elders," or "the nation's leaders."

One of Jesus' trials was before this body of elders. However, in Judea, they were under Roman authority, and thus could not carry out capital punishment. Yet they wanted Jesus to die for His words and deeds. This is why we find them sending Jesus to Pontius Pilate after they had condemned Him to death. They acknowledged to Pilate that they did not have the authority to officially execute anyone.

Therefore, for Jesus to be executed, Rome had to give the order. As we know, the order was given by Pontius Pilate and Jesus was led away for crucifixion.

When Jerusalem was destroyed in A.D. 70, the Sanhedrin ceased to exist. They have never banded together again. Yet there is a movement today in Israel to re-institute this ancient council.

QUESTION 8

Who Were The High Priest's Annas And Caiaphas?

Two High Priests are mentioned during Jesus public ministry—Annas and Caiaphas. Since they figure prominently into the events of His death, it is important that we know something about them.

1. ANNAS HAD BEEN THE HIGH PRIEST

Annas had been high priest from A.D. 6 to 15. The Romans had removed him from office—yet he still wielded considerable power behind the scenes. Five of his sons succeeded him as high priest. He was the father-in-law of Caiaphas—the high priest who was in office at the time of Jesus ministry. Luke wrote.

> Now in the fifteenth year of the reign of Tiberius Caesar, Pontius Pilate being governor of Judea, Herod being tetrarch of Galilee, his brother Philip tetrarch of Iturea and the region of Trachonitis, and Lysanias tetrarch of Abilene, while Annas and Caiaphas were high priests, the word of God came to John the son of Zacharias in the wilderness (Luke 3:1,2 NKJV).

Annas is still called "high priest" even though he was not serving in that capacity at the time. This indicates that much of the power was still in his hands.

2. JESUS WAS BROUGHT TO ANNAS FIRST

His power was obvious. Indeed, when Jesus was arrested He was brought to Annas first, rather than Caiaphas. John wrote.

> First they took him to Annas, the father-in-law of Caiaphas, the high priest that year. Caiaphas was the one who had told the other Jewish leaders, "Better that one should die for all" (John 18:13,14 NLT).

Annas was the first to examine Jesus. The fact that Jesus was eventually sent on to others shows the power that this man had.

The examination before Annas was unproductive. The Bible gives the following account of what occurred when Jesus went before Annas. —

> While this was happening, the high priest questioned Jesus about his disciples and about his teaching. Jesus replied, "I have spoken publicly to the world. I always taught in the synagogues and in the temple courts, where all the Jewish people assemble together. I have said nothing in secret. Why do you ask me? Ask those who heard what I said. They know what I said." When Jesus had said this, one of the high priest's officers who stood nearby struck him on the face and said, "Is that the way you answer the high priest?" Jesus replied, "If I have said something wrong, confirm what is wrong. But if I spoke correctly, why strike me?" (John 18:19-23 NET).

Since the meeting did not achieve its desired result, Annas then sent Jesus away to Caiaphas, the current high priest.

John also records this. He put it in this manner.

> Then Annas sent him bound to Caiaphas the high priest (John 18:24 NRSV).

Caiaphas, the ruling high priest, then conducted the next phase of Jesus' trial.

3. CAIAPHAS WAS THE RULING HIGH PRIEST

As we just mentioned, Joseph Ben Caiaphas was the ruling high priest at the time of Jesus' ministry—as well as beyond (A.D. 18-36). He was the son-in-law of Annas. It was Caiaphas who predicted the necessity of the death of Jesus. We read about this in the gospel of John. It says.

> And one of them, Caiaphas, who was high priest that year, said, "How can you be so stupid? Why should the whole nation be destroyed? Let this one man die for the people." This prophecy that Jesus should die for the entire nation came from Caiaphas in his position as high priest. He didn't think of it himself; he was inspired to say it. It was a prediction that Jesus' death would be not for Israel only, but for the gathering together of all the children of God scattered around the world. So from that time on the Jewish leaders began to plot Jesus' death (John 11:49-53 NLT).

Caiaphas said it was necessary for Jesus to die for the survival of the nation. These words set in motion the plot on Jesus' life.

We find the same thing taught in Matthew's gospel. Caiaphas is the one who plotted to kill Jesus. Matthew records the following.

> Then the chief priests and the leaders of the people gathered in the palace of the chief priest Caiaphas. They made plans to arrest Jesus in an underhanded way and to kill him (Matthew 26:3,4 God's Word).

It was by trickery that Caiaphas planned to arrest Jesus.

4. CAIAPHAS CHARGED JESUS WITH BLASPHEMY

We also find that Caiaphas is the one who charged Jesus with blasphemy. At Jesus' trial the following exchange took place.

> But Jesus remained silent. And the high priest said to him, "I adjure you by the living God, tell us if you are the Christ, the Son of God." Jesus said to him, "You have said so. But I tell you, from now on you will see the Son of Man seated at the right hand of Power and coming on the clouds of heaven." Then the high priest tore his robes and said, "He has uttered blasphemy. What further witnesses do we need? You have now heard his blasphemy. What is your judgment?" They answered, "He deserves death" (Matthew 26:63-66 ESV).

The Jewish leaders wanted Jesus dead! They did not merely want Him judged according to Jewish law.

5. CAIAPHAS SENT JESUS TO PILATE

It was Caiaphas who sent Jesus to Pontius Pilate to have the death sentence carried out. The Gospel of John records the following.

> Early in the morning, Jesus was taken from Caiaphas' house to the governor's palace. The Jews wouldn't go into the palace. They didn't want to become unclean, since they wanted to eat the Passover. So Pilate came out to them and asked, "What accusation are you making against this man?" The Jews answered Pilate, "If he weren't a criminal, we wouldn't have handed him over to you." Pilate told the Jews, "Take him, and try him by your law." The Jews answered him, "We're not allowed to execute anyone." In this way what Jesus had predicted about how he would die came true (John 18:28-32 God's Word).

From all reports, it is obvious that Caiaphas wanted Jesus dead. Indeed, he was the man behind the plot to kill Him.

6. THE CHIEF PRIESTS COMPLAINED ABOUT THE TITLE

Not content with merely having Jesus put to death, these religious leaders watched the crucifixion. In addition, they complained to Pilate about the title he placed above the cross. John records the following.

So the chief priests went to Pilate and said, "Why did you write that he is King of the Jews? You should have written, 'He claimed to be King of the Jews'" (John 19:21 CEV).

They objected to the title that was placed over Jesus' cross—"King of the Jews." Pilate did not listen to their request and kept the title to be read by all.

7. THEY PERSECUTED JESUS' FOLLOWERS

After the death, resurrection, and ascension of Jesus, we find Annas and Caiaphas interrogating Peter and John about a miracle they performed. We read of this in the Book of Acts.

> The high priest Annas was there, as well as Caiaphas, John, Alexander, and other members of the high priest's family. They brought in Peter and John and made them stand in the middle while they questioned them. They asked, "By what power and in whose name have you done this?" (Acts 4:6,7 CEV).

We note that these two were still prominent in their attempting to silence the ministry of Jesus. Try as they might, they could not stop it! Indeed, nobody can.

Jesus made this clear. We read His prediction in the Gospel of Matthew.

> I will build My church, and the forces of Hades will not overpower it (Matthew 16:18 HCSB).

The English Standard Version puts it this way.

> I will build my church, and the gates of hell shall not prevail against it (Matthew 16:18 ESV).

In other words, nothing will stop this work of God. Nothing!

8. THE BONES OF CAIAPHAS HAVE SEEMINGLY BEEN FOUND

There was an exciting archaeological discovery in November 1990. Workers constructing a water park south of the Old City of Jerusalem accidentally uncovered a burial cave. In the cave were a dozen limestone chests that contained bones. These types of chests, known as ossuaries, were primarily used in the first century A.D.

One of the chests had the word "Joseph, son of Caiaphas" carved on it. The bones were that of a man that had died at approximately the age of sixty. Because of the lavish decoration on the burial chest there is a high probability that these were the bones of Caiaphas the high priest—the one who charged Jesus with blasphemy. If so, then this would be the first physical remains ever discovered of a person mentioned in the Bible.

This is ironic. The man whom Caiaphas unjustly put to death, Jesus, has no burial box where His bones reside—He has risen from the dead! Yet Caiaphas' bones have been discovered. Death visited him. Such is the awesome reminder of what each of us face.

SUMMARY TO QUESTION 8
WHO WERE THE HIGH PRIEST'S ANNAS AND CAIAPHAS?

The Bible speaks of two high priests that were prominent in the events in the life of Jesus Christ—Annas and Caiaphas. Scripture records that Caiaphas was the high priest during the ministry of Jesus. He was also the son-in-law to Annas—who had previously been the high priest.

Each of these men had important roles to play in the death of Jesus.

Annas, though not the ruling high priest, was seemingly the power behind the office. Indeed, it was to Annas that Jesus was first brought after His arrest in the Garden of Gethsemane. After interrogating Jesus, Annas sent Him to his son-in-law, Caiaphas.

Caiaphas figures more prominently in the events which led up to Jesus' death. To begin with, He is the one who prophesied that it was necessary for Jesus to die for the nation. In other words, he was the main instigator behind the plot to kill Jesus.

In front of the Jewish council, Caiaphas charged Jesus with blasphemy. He then sent Jesus away to Pontius Pilate for execution. This man was determined to have Jesus killed.

After Jesus' death and resurrection, we find that both Annas and Caiaphas persecuted Jesus' disciples. While they attempted to stop the movement by killing Jesus and then threatening His disciples, their attempts ended in failure. As Jesus had predicted, He was going to build His church and not even the gates of hell could stop it!

In an historical irony, the bones of Caiaphas have seemingly been found in Jerusalem in November of 1990. If so, then this is the first physical remains ever discovered of a person who is mentioned in Scripture. The man who sentenced Jesus to death has his bones still intact. Yet the One whom He sentenced to death does not have any bones rotting away in some burial box. Jesus Christ is risen indeed!

QUESTION 9

Who Were The Scribes?
(The Teachers Of The Law)

The Greek word *grammateus* translated "scribe," in some older English translations, means "writer." The scribes were the teachers of the Law—the ones who drew up legal documents. They also copied the Old Testament Scripture. The scribes also devoted themselves to the study of the law, and the determination of its applications on daily life. These men also studied the Scripture with respect to doctrinal and historical matters. Noted scribes, or teachers of the Law, had their own disciples. Many of them were members of the Jewish council—the Sanhedrin.

From the New Testament we learn the following about these teachers of the Law and their interaction with Jesus.

1. SOME OF THEM BELIEVED IN JESUS

Some of the teachers of the Law, the scribes, responded favorably toward Jesus and His message. Mark records this exchange between Jesus and one of them.

> One of the scribes came near and heard them disputing with one another, and seeing that he answered them well, he asked him, "Which commandment is the first of all?" Jesus answered, "The first is, 'Hear, O Israel: the Lord our God, the Lord is one; you shall love the Lord your God with all your heart, and with all your soul, and with all your mind,

and with all your strength.' The second is this, 'You shall love your neighbor as yourself.' There is no other commandment greater than these." Then the scribe said to him, "You are right, Teacher; you have truly said that 'he is one, and besides him there is no other' (Mark 12:28-32 NRSV).

In this instance, we find one of these teachers of the Law in agreement with Jesus. This shows that not all of them were unresponsive to the message of Christ.

2. ONE OFFERED TO FOLLOW JESUS

On another occasion, a teacher of the law came to Jesus and offered to follow Him as a disciple. The Bible says.

> Then one of the teachers of religious law said to him, "Teacher, I will follow you no matter where you go!" (Matthew 8:19 NLT).

Consequently, there was not a total rejection of Jesus by these teachers of the Law. Indeed, some actually became His disciples.

3. MOST OF THEM OPPOSED JESUS

While there were some of the teachers of the law who believed in Jesus, the New Testament makes it clear that most of them were opposed to Him. In fact, these scribes were, in a large part, responsible for Jesus' death. We read the following in Matthew.

> From that time on, Jesus began to show his disciples that he must go to Jerusalem and undergo great suffering at the hands of the elders and chief priests and scribes, and be killed, and on the third day be raised (Matthew 16:21 NRSV).

They were part of the group who wanted to kill Jesus.

4. THEY WERE STRONGLY DENOUNCED BY JESUS

These teachers of religious law, along with the Pharisees, were strongly denounced by Christ. Matthew records Jesus saying some very harsh things about them, and their behavior.

> The teachers of religious law and the Pharisees are the official interpreters of the Scriptures. So practice and obey whatever they say to you, but don't follow their example. For they don't practice what they teach (Matthew 23:2-3 NLT).

These religious leaders would say one thing—yet, they would do something else. Their hypocrisy was evident to everyone.

5. THEY CONTINUED THE PERSECUTION OF JESUS' DISCIPLES

These religious teachers were also associated with the later persecutions of Peter and John. We read about this in the Book of Acts.

> The next morning the leaders, the elders, and the teachers of the Law of Moses met in Jerusalem. The high priest Annas was there, as well as Caiaphas, John, Alexander, and other members of the high priest's family. They brought in Peter and John and made them stand in the middle while they questioned them. They asked, "By what power and in whose name have you done this?" (Acts 4:5-7 CEV).

The persecution of Jesus and His message did not stop with His death. Those who followed Him were also persecuted. Among the persecutors were these scribes—the teachers of the religious law. They wanted to stop this movement which Jesus started.

6. THEY WERE INVOLVED IN THE MARTYRDOM OF STEPHEN

These scholars of the law were involved in the martyrdom of the righteous man Stephen. In the Book of Acts, we read about his death. It says.

And they stirred up the people, the elders, and the scribes; and they came upon *him*, seized him, and brought *him* to the council (Acts 6:12 NKJV).

Again, they are concerned with stopping the movement that began with Jesus. Yet, they could not. Indeed, nothing could stop it!

Therefore, when we look at the overall picture of these religious rulers we find that, for the most part, they were not receptive toward Jesus or to His message. In fact, they were among His greatest enemies.

SUMMARY TO QUESTION 9
WHO WERE THE SCRIBES? (THE TEACHERS OF THE LAW)

The scribes were scholars of the Old Testament Law. They were not mere copyists of the Scripture—as the name sometimes implies. Indeed, these men figured prominently in the ministry of Jesus. The New Testament has the following to say about them.

To begin with, they were not all unbelievers of Jesus. The Scripture records that certain of them actually became Jesus' followers. However, this was certainly the minority. Indeed, while there was a few of them who believed in Jesus, for the most part they persecuted Him.

In fact, we find that they were responsible for bringing Him to trial. When Jesus predicted His upcoming death, He specifically mentioned these teachers of the Law as instigators. The Scriptures then tell us that they were involved in the plot to kill Him.

Their struggle against Jesus did not stop when He completed His earthly ministry. The Book of Acts records the fact that the persecution of Christians continued after the ascension of Jesus into heaven. Indeed, we find the scribes persecuting Peter and John, as well as being directly involved in the death of Stephen. Yet, their attempt to stop the ministry of Jesus failed—as have all attempts.

QUESTION 9

In sum, the New Testament picture of the scribes, or teachers of religious law, is not that of a group who was seeking the truth of God. Otherwise they would have believed in Jesus.

QUESTION 10

Who Were The Pharisees?

The group which probably had most confrontations with Jesus during His earthly ministry was the Pharisees. Since they are prominent in the New Testament, it is important that we know something about them.

The word Pharisee is derived from an Aramaic word meaning, "separated." From the New Testament we learn the following about them.

1. THEY BELIEVED IN A FUTURE LIFE

The Pharisees were a group that held to the immortality of the soul, the resurrection of the dead, and punishment in a future life. These people believed that punishment was based upon how one behaved in this life. The souls of the wicked would be in prison forever under the earth. Those who were righteous would live again.

In the Book of Acts, some of the differences between the Pharisees and Sadducees are explained to us. It says.

> The Sadducees do not believe in angels or spirits or that the dead will rise to life. But the Pharisees believe in all of these, and so there was a lot of shouting. Some of the teachers of the Law of Moses were Pharisees. Finally, they became angry and said, "We don't find anything wrong with this man. Maybe a spirit or an angel really did speak to him" (Acts 23:8,9 CEV).

They had a hope in a future resurrection.

2. THEY ADDED TRADITION TO SCRIPTURE

In Jesus' day, the Pharisees practiced righteousness externally. In other words, they were more concerned with the outward appearance than the inward feeling. For example, in obeying the commandments of God, the Pharisees added an enormous amount of traditional material that was passed down from one generation to the next. They considered this tradition as authoritative as Scripture. They asked Jesus.

> "Why do your disciples disobey our age-old traditions?" they demanded. "They ignore our tradition of ceremonial hand washing before they eat." Jesus replied, "And why do you, by your traditions, violate the direct commandments of God? For instance, God says, 'Honor your father and mother,' and 'Anyone who speaks evil of father or mother must be put to death.' But you say, 'You don't need to honor your parents by caring for their needs if you give the money to God instead.' And so, by your own tradition, you nullify the direct commandment of God (Matthew 15:2-6 NLT).

Note that Jesus strongly denounced their traditions. Indeed, He said that they were opposed to the truths of God's Word. In fact, we find that these people were the worst persecutors of Jesus and the objects of His strongest criticism.

3. THEY APPEARED AT JOHN'S BAPTISM

Earlier, we find them at the baptism of John the Baptist where they were met with stern words from John. The Bible records the following.

> But when he saw many Pharisees and Sadducees coming for baptism, he said to them, "You brood of vipers! Who warned you to flee from the wrath to come?" (Matthew 3:7 NRSV).

John recognized their hypocrisy and was not afraid to point it out.

4. THE PHARISEES ACCUSED JESUS OF DEMONIC PRACTICE

When these religious rulers saw the miracles of Jesus, they could not deny them. Instead of attributing these miracles to God, the Pharisees actually accused Jesus of demonic practices. We read their response in Matthew.

> But the Pharisees said, "He can cast out demons because he is empowered by the prince of demons" (Matthew 9:34 NLT).

They did not acknowledge where His power truly came from. Instead they claimed His power was from a demonic source.

5. THE PHARISEES INTIMIDATED PEOPLE WHO BELIEVED IN JESUS

The New Testament says that the Pharisees would personally intimidate anyone who believed in Jesus. John wrote.

> Nevertheless, many, even of the authorities, believed in him. But because of the Pharisees they did not confess it, for fear that they would be put out of the synagogue (John 12:42 NRSV).

These religious leaders could not tolerate anyone who put their faith in Jesus. Therefore, they would make certain those who followed the Lord were put out of the synagogue. To the Jews of that time, this was a horrible punishment!

6. THE PHARISEES PLOTTED JESUS' DEATH

The Pharisees are the ones who plotted the death of Jesus over His breaking of the Sabbath. Matthew wrote about their decision to kill Jesus after He broke their human-made rules. He explained it this way.

> The Pharisees left and started making plans to kill Jesus (Matthew 12:14 CEV).

Their plans would eventually come to pass. However, Jesus' death would be in God's timing, not theirs.

We also read about how they plotted to catch Him saying something that could lead to His arrest. Matthew again writes.

> Then the Pharisees went out and planned together to entrap him with his own words (Matthew 22:15 NET).

They were set on silencing Jesus. Yet they could not.

7. JESUS CONDEMNED THE PHARISEES IN THE STRONGEST OF TERMS

Not surprisingly, Jesus' strongest words of condemnation were aimed at these hypocritical Pharisees. He said the following to His disciples about these religious hypocrites.

> How horrible it will be for you, scribes and Pharisees! You hypocrites! You lock people out of the kingdom of heaven. You don't enter it yourselves, and you don't permit others to enter when they try (Matthew 23:13 God's Word).

Their behavior clearly demonstrated what happens when people are only outwardly righteous, but inwardly hypocritical. They have an outward form of godliness but are lifeless on the inside. Jesus had very harsh words of punishment directed toward them.

8. THEY PERSECUTED JESUS' FOLLOWERS AFTER HIS DEATH

They continued the persecution of Jesus' followers. We discover that Jesus' disciples continued to preach His message against the direct order of the Sanhedrin (which included the Pharisees). The Sanhedrin wanted Peter and John put to death. We read in the Book of Acts.

> When the council members heard this, they became so angry that they wanted to kill the apostles (Acts 5:33 CEV).

They were not satisfied with simply killing Jesus—they wanted everyone dead who was associated with Him.

In sum, the Pharisees, the ones who were supposed to be the guardians of the truth of God, were actually the ones stopping people from believing in Him! They had this outward form of godly living but inside they were spiritually dead. Therefore, it is not surprising that Jesus had His harshest words of punishment aimed at them.

SUMMARY TO QUESTION 10
WHO WERE THE PHARISEES?

The main opposition to Jesus Christ and His ministry came from a group of people known as the Pharisees. They were the religious conservatives. This group believed in an afterlife and a final judgment. They were at odds with other groups such as Sadducees, and the Herodians.

However, they all joined together against their common enemy—Jesus. From the four gospels, we find that these Pharisees were Jesus' chief persecutors. They rejected His claims to be the Messiah and were the ones who plotted to have Him killed. In fact, the Jewish leaders who believed in Jesus were afraid to come forward because of the intimidation of the Pharisees.

We find that Jesus' strongest words of condemnation were aimed at these religious hypocrites. He actually called them "children of the devil."

The Book of Acts tells us that the Pharisees continued to persecute Jesus' disciples after His death, resurrection, and ascension. However, like every other group, they miserably failed in their attempt to stop the message of Jesus, or silence those who proclaimed it. Indeed, nothing can stop His Word from going forth.

QUESTION 11

Who Were The Sadducees?

One of the main opponents of Jesus Christ during the time of His public ministry was a group known as the Sadducees. There are a number of important things that we need to know about them. We can sum them up as follows.

1. THEY WERE A JEWISH POLITICAL PARTY

The Sadducees were a Jewish political party. They were members of the priesthood who made up part of the Jewish council—the Sanhedrin. The High Priest was taken from the Sadducees. Although they were few in number, they were educated and usually wealthy. We read a description of them in the Book of Acts.

> For the Sadducees say that there is no resurrection, nor angel, nor spirit; but the Pharisees acknowledge them all (Acts 23:8 RSV).

They had a different perspective on these matters from the Pharisees.

2. THEY WERE OPPOSED TO THE PHARISEES

From a reading of the New Testament, we discover that the Sadducees were opposed to the Pharisees. The Apostle Paul used their theological differences to cause a division between them. The Book of Acts records what took place.

> But when Paul perceived that one part were Sadducees and the other Pharisees, he cried out in the council, "Men and brethren, I am a Pharisee, the son of a Pharisee; concerning the hope and resurrection of the dead I am being judged!" And when he had said this, a dissension arose between the Pharisees and the Sadducees; and the assembly was divided (Acts 23:6,7 NKJV).

Paul used this division between these two groups for his own advantage.

3. THEY CAME TO TRAP JESUS

During the public ministry of Jesus, we find that the Sadducees sent some of their people to question Jesus about the subject of the resurrection of the dead. Matthew's gospel records for the following.

> The same day Sadducees came to him, who say that there is no resurrection, and they asked him a question (Matthew 22:23 ESV).

They had different views on the nature of the resurrection. Consequently, they thought they could trap Jesus with their question on this subject.

4. THEY WERE IGNORANT OF TWO BASIC TRUTHS

In reply, Jesus said the Sadducees were ignorant of two basic things. We read about this in Matthew's gospel.

> Jesus answered them, "You are wrong, because you know neither the scriptures nor the power of God" (Matthew 22:29 NRSV).

These people did not know the Scriptures—neither did they know the power of God. Unfortunately, this type of ignorance is still with us today in many people. They do not really know what the Bible teaches, neither do they know the power of the God of the Bible.

5. THEY JOINED WITH THE PHARISEES AGAINST JESUS

Although they were usually opposed to the Pharisees, we find them uniting together in their mutual hatred of Jesus. The Bible explains it in this manner.

> The Pharisees and Sadducees came, and to test Jesus they asked him to show them a sign from heaven (Matthew 16:1 NRSV).

Former enemies became friends in an attempt to stop Jesus. As much as they despised each other, they despised Jesus all the more.

6. THEY CONTINUED THE PERSECUTION OF JESUS' FOLLOWERS

After the death, resurrection, and ascension of Jesus, the Book of Acts says that the Sadducees, like the Pharisees, continued with the persecution of Jesus' disciples. We read the following.

> While Peter and John were speaking to the people, the leading priests, the captain of the Temple guard, and some of the Sadducees came over to them. They were very disturbed that Peter and John were claiming, on the authority of Jesus, that there is a resurrection of the dead. They arrested them and, since it was already evening, jailed them until morning (Acts 4:1-3 NLT).

They, like the Pharisees, could not allow the message of Jesus to continue. Therefore, they tried vainly to stop it. Yet, the message of Jesus Christ will never be stopped. Indeed, it cannot be.

7. THEY DISAPPEARED AFTER A.D. 70

With the destruction of the city of Jerusalem in A.D. 70, the Sadducees disappeared from history. We hear no more from them after this time. Jesus Christ, as well as His message, lives on—the Sadducees do not.

In sum, the Sadducees, like the Pharisees, were opponents of the ministry of Jesus Christ. While they were instrumental in putting Him to death, they could not stop His message from going out to the ends of the earth.

SUMMARY TO QUESTION 11
WHO WERE THE SADDUCEES?

The Sadducees were a Jewish political party which consisted largely of wealthy landowners. The High Priest of Israel was taken from the Sadducees. The Sadducees were opponents of the religious Pharisees. However, they joined the Pharisees in their opposition and persecution of Jesus. As much as they had nothing to do with each other, the mutual hatred of Jesus caused these opposing groups to unite.

There is an incident recorded for us in the gospels where the Sadducees approached Jesus with a question concerning the resurrection of the dead. Jesus told them that their question showed ignorance of two basic things—they knew neither the Scriptures nor the power of the God of the Bible. Unfortunately, this type of ignorance is still with us today. People truly do not know what the Bible has to say, nor do they understand the power of the God of Scripture.

While these wealthy landowners along with the religious Pharisees were successful in having Jesus wrongfully put to death, this did not stop Him or His message. Jesus came back from the dead three days after His death. The message of Jesus and His resurrection from the dead continued to be told. From the Book of Acts, we find that the Sadducees attempted to stop Jesus' disciples from proclaiming His truth. Yet, in all their attempts, the Sadducees failed completely.

While they continued to persecute Jesus' followers after His death and resurrection, this persecution soon stopped. With the destruction of the city of Jerusalem, as well as the temple, in the year A.D. 70, the Sadducees ceased to exist.

Today the message of Jesus Christ is embraced by untold millions while these opponents are a distant memory. This further points out the truth of Jesus' prediction that He will build His church, His group of people, and no power on earth can stop it. Certainly the Sadducees were not able to accomplish the halting of the gospel message. Neither can anyone else.

QUESTION 12

Who Were The Herodians?

There was a group of people, known as the Herodians, that receives slight mention in the New Testament. While they were not highlighted by the gospel writers, we should understand something about them.

The Herodians derived their name as followers of King Herod. They were a political party that wanted to restore a Herod to the throne in Judea—as well as other areas ruled by Herod the Great. They were political foes of the Pharisees, who wished to restore the kingdom with a relative of King David—rather than a Herod.

1. THEY ARE MENTIONED IN CONNECTION WITH THE PHARISEES

We only find them being mentioned three times in the gospels and always in conjunction with the Pharisees. Although they were politically opposed to the Pharisees, the Herodians participated with them in the persecution of Jesus.

After Jesus did not observe their particular interpretation of the Sabbath, they, along with the Pharisees, plotted to kill Him.

> Then the Pharisees went out and immediately plotted with the Herodians against Him, how they might destroy Him (Mark 3:6 NKJV).

Like the relationship between the Pharisees and the Sadducees, these enemies became united in their goal of destroying Jesus.

The Herodians also attempted to trap Jesus into saying something that could be used to arrest Him. Matthew wrote about this. He said.

> They sent some of their followers and some of Herod's followers to say to him, "Teacher, we know that you are honest. You teach the truth about what God wants people to do. And you treat everyone with the same respect, no matter who they are" (Matthew 22:16 CEV).

Their hypocrisy was as obvious as that of the Pharisees and the Sadducees. They did not want to know the truth. Instead they wanted to get rid of Jesus.

2. JESUS WARNED OF THE LEAVEN, OR YEAST, OF HEROD

On one occasion, we find that Jesus spoke of the leaven, or yeast, of Herod. He said the following to His disciples.

> Jesus warned them, "Be careful! Watch out for the yeast of the Pharisees and the yeast of Herod!" (Mark 8:15 God's Word).

This may refer to Herod Antipas—the Herod who was ruling at that time—or it may be a reference to the party—the Herodians. In this context, it refers to something evil. The people were warned of both Herod and the Herodians. They were not doing God's work.

3. THE HERODIANS SOON CEASED TO EXIST

Like the Pharisees and Sadducees, the Herodians soon ceased to exist. The dynasty of Herod, with all its evil rulers, finally came to an end.

Consequently, we again have the lesson. Those who oppose Jesus, such as the family of Herod, will never ultimately prosper. While they may prosper for a short time, their rule is limited to the will of the God of the Bible—the God whom they rejected. Since these evil rulers rejected Him, He also rejected them.

SUMMARY TO QUESTION 12
WHO WERE THE HERODIANS?

We find a group opposed to Jesus Christ and His ministry known as the Herodians. While not prominent in the New Testament, we should know something about them, as well as what they stood for.

Simply state, the Herodians were a political party who wanted to restore a Herod to the throne in Judea. They were opposed to the Pharisees who wanted a descendant of David on the throne. Hence, there was a difference of opinion as to who should rule the people.

While they were enemies of the Pharisees, the New Testament tells us that they joined with them in attempting to silence Jesus. As so often happens, these enemies of God's truth put aside their differences to fight what is right.

Jesus warned the people of their evil. This includes the evil of the political party, as well as the evil of the Herod who was still ruling in Galilee.

As is true with all opponents of Jesus and His message, the Herodians quickly became a footnote in history. No descendant of Herod has ever ruled again in the Holy Land. On the other hand, the message of Jesus, which they attempted to destroy, continues to resound throughout the world!

QUESTION 13

Who Were The Samaritans?

During the earthly ministry of God the Son, Jesus Christ, He had contact with a group of people known as the Samaritans. The Samaritans were half-Jew, half-Gentile. The race came about after the Assyrian captivity of the northern kingdom of Israel in 721 B.C.

There were certain people from the nation of Israel who stayed behind. These people intermarried with the Assyrians—producing the Samaritans. We can make a number of observations about these people.

1. THEY HAD NO DEALINGS WITH THE JEWS

The Bible says that the Jews had no dealings with the Samaritans. In a conversation that Jesus had with a Samaritan woman, we are told that she said the following.

> The Samaritan woman said to him, "How is it that you, a Jew, ask for a drink from me, a woman of Samaria?" (For Jews have no dealings with Samaritans) (John 4:9 ESV).

They would not have any dealings with one another.

2. THEY HAD THEIR OWN TEMPLE AND RELIGIOUS SYSTEM

We also discover that the Samaritans had their own temple, their own copy of the Torah—the first five books of the Old Testament—as well as their own religious system.

There was also a burning issue among the Jews and Samaritans as to where was the proper place of worship. The following exchange took place between Jesus and the Samaritan woman which highlighted these differences.

> "Sir," the woman said, "I can see that you are a prophet. Our fathers worshiped on this mountain, but you Jews claim that the place where we must worship is in Jerusalem." Jesus declared, "Believe me, woman, a time is coming when you will worship the Father neither on this mountain nor in Jerusalem. You Samaritans worship what you do not know; we worship what we do know, for salvation is from the Jews. Yet a time is coming and has now come when the true worshipers will worship the Father in spirit and truth, for they are the kind of worshipers the Father seeks" (John 4:19-23 NIV).

Jesus responded to the woman's accusations about the proper place to worship. He made it clear that the Samaritans were wrong. God had established the city of Jerusalem, with its temple, as the place the people were to worship and offer sacrifices.

3. MANY SAMARITANS BELIEVED IN JESUS

From this episode we find that a number of the people of that Samaritan town came to faith in Jesus as the Messiah. John records what took place.

> Many Samaritans from that town believed in him because of the woman's testimony, "He told me all that I ever did." So when the Samaritans came to him, they asked him to stay with them, and he stayed there two days. And many more believed because of his word. They said to the woman, "It is no longer because of what you said that we believe, for we have heard for ourselves, and we know that this is indeed the Savior of the world" (John 4:39-42 HCSB).

While they had a different system of worship than the Jews, these Samaritans were still able to receive the message of Jesus—the genuine Messiah.

4. ONE SAMARITAN VILLAGE REJECTED JESUS WHEN HE PASSED THROUGH THEIR REGION

The gospels tell us that when Jesus was on His way to Jerusalem to die for the sins of the world, He passed through the area of Samaria. The Samaritans did not receive Him—because He was on His way to Jerusalem. Luke records it as follows.

> When the days drew near for him to be taken up, he set his face to go to Jerusalem. And he sent messengers ahead of him, who went and entered a village of the Samaritans, to make preparations for him. But the people did not receive him, because his face was set toward Jerusalem (Luke 9:51-53 NKJV).

Jesus was on His way to die for the sins of the world—including the sins of the Samaritans. Though this particular village would not receive Him, He would receive any of them who turned to Him in faith.

SUMMARY TO QUESTION 13
WHO WERE THE SAMARITANS?

The Samaritans were a group of people who lived in Samaria, an area north of Jerusalem. They were half-Jews and half-Gentiles. When Assyria captured the northern kingdom of Israel in 721 B.C. some were taken in captivity while others left behind. The ones left behind intermarried with the Assyrians. Thus, these people were neither fully Hebrews, nor fully Gentiles.

The Samaritans had their own unique copy of the first five books of Scripture, the Law of Moses, as well as their own unique system of worship.

At the time of Jesus, the Jews and the Samaritans did not have dealings with one another. Jesus, however, ministered to the people of Samaria preaching the good news to them. He brought them a message of hope. Consequently, we find that a number of people from Samaria did believe in Jesus as the Promised Messiah. Though they had a different system of worship, a different temple, and a different copy of the Torah, they recognized the genuine Messiah when He arrived.

Luke tells us that later in Jesus' ministry one particular Samaritan village did not receive Jesus because He was on His way to Jerusalem to die for the sins of the world.

In sum, we find certain of the Samaritans believing in Jesus as the long-awaited Messiah—even though they had a running dispute with the Jews of their day as to the proper place of worship. This illustrates how God's truth can certainly break down all barriers which people put up.

QUESTION 14

Who Were The Essenes?

During the time of Jesus Christ, there was a shadowy group of people who lived alongside the Dead Sea known as the Essenes. We know about their existence from the first-century Jewish writers Flavius Josephus, and Philo of Alexandria. Since they do play a role in our knowledge of the Scriptures we should find out certain things about them.

THEY LEFT BEHIND THE DEAD SEA SCROLLS

The Dead Sea Scrolls were discovered in 1947. They contained some 800 ancient manuscripts which were written around the time of Christ. Among the documents were copies of every Old Testament book except Esther. These manuscripts were found in caves not far from the Dead Sea. Discovery was also made of buildings next to the Dead Sea. It has been argued that the buildings were where the Essenes lived and the scrolls found in the caves, the Dead Sea Scrolls, were placed there by the Essenes. This continues to be the general consensus of scholars—although there have been alternative theories.

Since these people lived alongside the Dead Sea at the time of Christ, is there anything in the New Testament about them?

We can make the following observations about the Essenes and the New Testament.

THEY ARE NOT DIRECTLY MENTIONED IN THE NEW TESTAMENT

While the New Testament does not mention the Essenes directly, there are a couple of passages that may refer to them. This includes the man carrying the jug that the disciples were to find, and the priests who became believers as recorded in the Book of Acts. The evidence is as follows.

THE MAN CARRYING THE JAR OF WATER MAY HAVE BEEN AN ESSENE

There is some evidence that the Jesus had contact with the Essenes. In His last visit to the city of Jerusalem, Jesus told His disciples to find a man carrying a jar of water. Luke records this incident as follows.

> Jesus told them, "As you go into the city, you will meet a man carrying a jar of water. Follow him into the house and say to the owner, 'Our teacher wants to know where he can eat the Passover meal with his disciples.' The owner will take you upstairs and show you a large room ready for you to use. Prepare the meal there" (Luke 22:10-12 CEV).

We know that in Jesus' day, only women carried water. Even if male slaves carried water they did not use pots or jars like the women did. Instead they would carry the water in skins. Furthermore, the man Jesus told His disciples to follow is not identified as a slave.

It is argued that these facts point to a community of people that did not have either women or slaves. We know that a group of celibate Essenes lived in Jerusalem during the time of Christ.

Consequently, some argue that the man carrying the jar was an Essene. While we cannot be certain of this, it is an interesting possibility.

THE PRIESTS WHO BECAME BELIEVERS MAY HAVE BEEN ESSENES

There is a passage in the Book of Acts that may refer to the Essenes. It speaks of priests who were converted to faith in Christ. We read.

> God's message was preached in ever-widening circles. The
> number of believers greatly increased in Jerusalem, and many
> of the Jewish priests were converted, too (Acts 6:7 NLT).

Some have identified these priests with the Essenes. There were very few priests among the Pharisees and the Sadducees who accepted the message of Jesus. The only other priestly community that resided in Jerusalem was the Essenes. Consequently, it has been argued that this reference is to them.

Again, while we cannot be confident of this, it is certainly possible.

To sum up, the Essenes, though not directly mentioned in the New Testament, may be indirectly referred to in a couple of instances.

SUMMARY TO QUESTION 14
WHO WERE THE ESSENES?

The Essenes were a group that we know little about. The first-century Jewish writers Josephus and Philo mention them. They lived somewhere alongside the Dead Sea. The general consensus of scholars is that the ancient manuscripts found alongside the Dead Sea in the late 1940's, the Dead Sea Scrolls, were copied by the Essenes.

The New Testament does not have anything to say about them directly but there may be a couple of passages that allude to them.

This would include the incident of the man carrying the jug of water that Jesus told His disciples to follow in preparation for the Passover. It seems that he was a member of a community that did not include slaves or women. If this is the case, then it is possible that he was a member of the Essenes. We know that a community of celibate Essenes lived in Jerusalem at the time of Christ. Of course, we cannot be certain of this but it does raise some interesting possibilities.

There is also a reference in the Book of Acts to a number of priests that believed in Jesus as the Messiah. Some have interpreted this to refer to the Essenes. Since there were few among the Sadducees and Pharisees which believed in Jesus as the Christ, it is possible that this is a reference to them.

However, because of the lack of specific information we cannot be certain.

QUESTION 15

Who Was John The Baptist?

One of the most important characters in the New Testament is John the Baptist, the forerunner of Jesus. His life and ministry were extremely important in preparing the way for the coming of Christ.

Consequently, we should know what we can about him and his ministry. The New Testament gives the following details about his life and ministry.

1. HE HAD A MIRACULOUS CONCEPTION

To begin with, we find that John the Baptist was conceived in a miraculous way. His parents, Zechariah and Elizabeth, were beyond the childbearing years when John was conceived. His conception was miraculous as Luke records in his gospel account.

> All at once an angel from the Lord appeared to Zechariah at the right side of the altar. Zechariah was confused and afraid when he saw the angel. But the angel told him: Don't be afraid, Zechariah! God has heard your prayers. Your wife Elizabeth will have a son, and you must name him John. His birth will make you very happy, and many people will be glad. Your son will be a great servant of the Lord. He must never drink wine or beer, and the power of the Holy Spirit will be with him from the time he is born. John will lead many people in Israel to turn back to the Lord their God.

THE LIFE AND MINISTRY OF JESUS CHRIST

> He will go ahead of the Lord with the same power and spirit that Elijah had. And because of John, parents will be more thoughtful of their children. And people who now disobey God will begin to think as they ought to. That is how John will get people ready for the Lord (Luke 1:11-17 CEV).

This is an extremely significant event. The appearance of the angel Gabriel to Zechariah broke the four hundred years of God's silence. The New Testament era begins with this announcement of the coming birth of the forerunner of the Messiah. It also reminds us of the miraculous birth of Isaac to Abraham and Sarah—for they too were beyond the childbearing years when Isaac was born.

2. HE LIVED IN THE DESERT UNTIL THE TIME OF HIS PUBLIC MINISTRY

John was born as the angel had predicted. Scripture says that when John grew up, he lived in the desert—away from the city of Jerusalem. There he waited until it was his time to tell the nation about the coming Messiah. Luke writes.

> The child grew and became strong in spirit, and he was in the wilderness until the day he appeared publicly to Israel (Luke 1:80 NRSV).

John prepared for his ministry by being away from the crowds. Exactly where he was during this time, and who he associated with, is not told to us.

3. JOHN WAS THE FORERUNNER OF JESUS THE CHRIST

When the proper time had come, John the Baptist began his public ministry. He prepared the way for the King and His coming Kingdom. His ministry was predicted in the Old Testament. Isaiah wrote.

> A voice of one crying out: Prepare the way of the LORD in the wilderness; make a straight highway for our God in the

desert. Every valley will be lifted up, and every mountain and hill will be leveled; the uneven ground will become smooth, and the rough places a plain. And the glory of the LORD will appear, and all humanity will see [it] together, for the mouth of the LORD has spoken (Isaiah 40:3-5 HCSB).

The prophet Malachi also wrote of his coming.

"See, I am going to send My messenger, and he will clear the way before Me. Then the Lord you seek will suddenly come to His temple, the Messenger of the covenant you desire—see, He is coming," says the LORD of Hosts (Malachi 3:1 HCSB).

Thus, John the Baptist was the last of the Old Testament prophets. He baptized the people in anticipation of the coming Messiah. Matthew records John beginning his ministry.

In those days John the Baptist came, preaching in the Wilderness of Judea and saying, "Repent, because the kingdom of heaven has come near!" (Matthew 3:1,2 HCSB).

John the Baptist prepared the way for the nation of Israel to receive their Messiah—Jesus of Nazareth.

4. JOHN PREACHED A MESSAGE OF REPENTANCE

We are told that John preached a message of repentance. Instead of trying to reform the religious system of his day, John told people to repent of their sin—to make way for the coming of the Christ. We read.

But when he saw many of the Pharisees and Sadducees coming for baptism, he said to them, "You brood of vipers! Who warned you to flee from the wrath to come? Bear fruit in keeping with repentance. And do not presume to say to yourselves, 'We have Abraham as our father,' for I tell you, God is able from these stones to raise up children for Abraham. Even now the axe is laid to the root of the trees. Every tree therefore that does not bear good fruit is cut down and thrown into the fire (Matthew 3:7-10 ESV).

John did not mince his words. Indeed, he warned the people that they should not trust in their heritage as children of Abraham to save them. They had to personally repent of their sins. This included everyone from the soldiers, tax collectors, as well as the religious rulers and the king.

Interestingly, John did this as an outsider. While he was the son of the priest Zacharias, John did not preach the necessity of the system being revived. Instead of attempting to make changes in the corrupt religious system which was in place, John called the people to come out from it. Something new was taking place. The age of the Messiah had arrived!

The message was immediately received by the people. Indeed, Scripture says that they came from Jerusalem and all Judea and as far away as Syria to hear John's message and to be baptized by him.

Yet, the intensity of the response faded. Jesus would later make this comment.

> John was a burning and shining lamp, and for a time you were willing to enjoy his light (John 5:35 HCSB).

Note that Jesus said that "for a time" they were willing to enjoy the light of John.

5. JOHN ADMITTED THAT HE WAS NOT THE MESSIAH

When questioned by the religious rulers, John the Baptist admitted that he was not the Messiah. We read the following exchange between John and these leaders.

> Now this is the testimony of John, when the Jews sent priests and Levites from Jerusalem to ask him, "Who are

> you?" He confessed, and did not deny, but confessed, "I am not the Christ." And they asked him, "What then? Are you Elijah?" He said, "I am not." "Are you the Prophet?" And he answered, "No." Then they said to him, "Who are you, that we may give an answer to those who sent us? What do you say about yourself?" He said: "I am 'The voice of one crying in the wilderness: "Make straight the way of the LORD,"' as the prophet Isaiah said (John 1:19-23 NKJV).

John's ministry was to prepare the people for the coming of the Messiah. He was not the One whom they had been waiting for.

In fact, in contrast to the Messiah, John did not perform any miracles. His ministry was preparatory for the One who would have the proper credentials.

6. THE RELIGIOUS LEADERS REJECTED JOHN'S MESSAGE

As they would eventually do with the Person John was speaking about— Jesus—the religious rulers rejected John as the forerunner to the Messiah. His message was something which they did not choose to hear. Indeed, John spoke of Jesus the Messiah being the "Lamb of God." The Gospel of John states the following.

> The next day John saw Jesus coming toward him and said, "Here is the Lamb of God, who takes away the sin of the world! Again the next day, John was standing with two of his disciples. When he saw Jesus passing by, he said, "Look! The Lamb of God!" (John 1:29,35-36 HCSB).

This was not the type of Messiah they were looking for. Instead, the people were expecting someone who would come to the land and overthrow the Roman rule.

Jesus explained their rejection of John in this manner.

> And when all the people, including the tax collectors, heard this, they acknowledged God's way of righteousness, because they had been baptized with John's baptism. But since the Pharisees and experts in the law had not been baptized by him, they rejected the plan of God for themselves (Luke 7:29-30 HCSB).

The religious leaders did not submit to John's baptism—thus rejecting the plan of God.

7. JOHN WAS IMPRISONED BY HEROD

On one occasion, we find that John the Baptist was publicly saying that Herod Antipas should not have taken his brother's wife. This caused John's imprisonment. We read of this in Luke's gospel.

> But Herod the tetrarch, who had been reproved by him for Herodias, his brother's wife, and for all the evil things that Herod had done, added this to them all, that he locked up John in prison (Luke 3:19,20 ESV).

King Herod put John the Baptist in prison for his condemnation of his behavior. Herod, however, realized John was a prophet so he did not kill him.

8. JOHN EVENTUALLY QUESTIONED JESUS ABOUT HIS ROLE AS MESSIAH

While in prison, John sent messengers to question Jesus about His Messiahship. Matthew records what John wanted to know.

> When John heard in prison what the Messiah was doing, he sent word by his disciples and said to him, "Are you the one who is to come, or are we to wait for another?" (Matthew 11:2,3 NRSV).

John wanted to be certain that Jesus was the long-awaited Messiah. Therefore, the Baptist sent two of his disciples to Jesus to receive His answer.

Jesus made it clear to John that He was indeed the promised Messiah. Matthew tells us how Jesus responded to John's questions.

> Jesus answered John's disciples, "Go back, and tell John what you hear and see: Blind people see again, lame people are walking, those with skin diseases are made clean, deaf people hear again, dead people are brought back to life, and poor people hear the Good News. Whoever doesn't lose his faith in me is indeed blessed" (Matthew 11:4-6 God's Word).

John's question was answered in a manner which he would clearly understand. At that moment, Jesus healed the people of a number of ailments. These were signs that the Messiah would demonstrate when He arrived. Thus, by performing these miracles, Jesus made it clear to John that He was the One whom the Lord had promised.

9. JOHN WAS EXECUTED BY HEROD

The gospels record that John the Baptist was executed after Herod made a careless promise at his birthday party. Mark records that Herod sent a man to have John beheaded.

> So he sent an executioner to the prison to cut off John's head and bring it to him. The soldier beheaded John in the prison (Mark 6:27 NLT).

While Herod did not want to kill John, he felt it necessary to keep his promise. Therefore, he gave the command to have John beheaded.

10. ACCORDING TO JESUS THERE WAS NO ONE GREATER THAN JOHN

Jesus made it clear what He thought of John the Baptist. Indeed, the Lord said that "no one born of woman was greater than John." Matthew records Him saying.

> This is the one about whom it is written, 'See, I am sending my messenger ahead of you, who will prepare your way before

you.' Truly I tell you, among those born of women no one has arisen greater than John the Baptist; yet the least in the kingdom of heaven is greater than he (Matthew 11:10,11 NRSV).

Jesus had the highest praise for John.

11. THE MINISTRY OF JOHN AND JESUS PROVES THAT UNBELIEF IS NEVER SATISFIED

We find that John the Baptist, as well as Jesus, were both rejected by the religious establishment of that day. Jesus listed the reasons as to why this was so. He said.

> For John the Baptist did not come eating bread or drinking wine, and you say, 'He has a demon!' The Son of Man has come eating and drinking, and you say, 'Look, a glutton and a drunkard, a friend of tax collectors and sinners! Yet wisdom is vindicated by all her children' (Luke 7:33-35 HCSB).

We learn from this illustration of Jesus' that unbelief is never really satisfied. John came living the life as an ascetic, one who gave up the human comforts, and he was rejected as one having a demon.

Jesus, on the other hand, feasted with the people. He enjoyed life. Yet He too was rejected. In His case, it was for being a drunkard and a glutton! In other words, no matter how they acted, they were not going to be accepted by the religious establishment of that day. Unbelief is never satisfied!

This sums up some of the things we know about John the Baptist from the Scripture. Truly, he was a remarkable man with a remarkable ministry.

SUMMARY TO QUESTION 15
WHO WAS JOHN THE BAPTIST?

One of the key characters in the New Testament is John the Baptist—the forerunner of Jesus Christ. It is essential that we understand who he was, as well as his God-given mission. The Bible has the following to say about his life and ministry.

To begin with, John was conceived in a miraculous way. His parents, Zechariah and Elizabeth were beyond the childbearing years when he was conceived.

Furthermore, when the angel of the Lord appeared to his father and spoke about this miraculous birth which was about to take place, this broke the four hundred years of silence between the Old and New Testament. Therefore, the announcement of the coming birth of the forerunner of the Messiah was indeed a momentous event!

Scripture says that John lived in the desert until the time of his public ministry. This ministry was something that had been predicted by the Old Testament prophets Isaiah and Malachi. Indeed, a forerunner would arrive on the scene heralding the coming of the Messiah.

When he began his public ministry, John preached a baptism of repentance which looked forward to the coming of the Messiah. John did not spare anyone with his harsh words of condemnation of sin. Everyone had to repent! This included the religious rulers as well as the King Herod himself.

When asked, John the Baptist told the religious leaders that he was not the Messiah but was one who had arrived to proclaim the Messiah's coming. However, they rejected his message—as they later would with the message of Jesus.

King Herod eventually imprisoned John for speaking out against the king's unlawful marriage to his brother's wife. However, Herod did not want to harm John because he was afraid of him. He knew John was God's prophet.

While in prison, John the Baptist sent two of his disciples to question Jesus if He were indeed the Messiah. Jesus assured John that He was the promised Messiah. He demonstrated this by performing a number of miracles in front of the messengers which John had sent. Consequently, John would realize that these were signs which would prove the credentials of the Messiah were found in Jesus of Nazareth.

After making a rash vow, Herod was forced to execute John while the Baptist was in prison. The ministry of this man of God, the forerunner of the Christ, ended in his unlawful death. After John's death, Jesus testified that no one born of woman was greater than John.

As we all know, the same unlawful end came to the Messiah Himself. Indeed, Jesus, the Lamb of God, was also illegally put to death. Although it was acknowledged that Jesus had not committed any crime, the forces of darkness were not satisfied until He too was dead.

Many lessons can be learned from the life and ministry of John the Baptist. One important lesson was taught to us by Jesus. Jesus said that John was rejected because he lived a life of self-denial. On the other hand, Jesus Himself was rejected for living a life of eating and drinking! In other words, unbelief is never satisfied. Therefore, with respect to the message of Jesus' forerunner John the Baptist, it is not that the people could *not* believe what he said, rather it is that they *would* not believe what he preached. The same thing occurred in Jesus' earthly ministry. They chose not to believe in Him.

In sum, John the Baptist was God's appointed man to make way for the coming of the Christ. He did the job which God called him to do.

QUESTION 16

What Do We Know About The Twelve Disciples?

The New Testament says that Jesus personally handpicked twelve men to be His inner core of disciples—the "Twelve Disciples," or the "Twelve Apostles." Some of them have become famous while others of them are little-known. From the Scripture we can make the following observations about these particular men which Jesus chose.

SIMON PETER

Simon Peter is probably the most well-known of Jesus' disciples. Simon is a Greek name, but in the New Testament, it is probably a contraction of the Hebrew "Simeon." From Scripture, we can learn much about this man.

1. HIS NAME IS FIRST ON EVERY LIST OF DISCIPLES

To begin with, Peter is first in every list of the apostles (first among equals) and plays a prominent role in the gospels. His father's name was Jonah, or John. He was a native of Bethsaida—a town on the Sea of Galilee. We read of this in John's gospel. It says.

> Now Philip was from Bethsaida, the city of Andrew and Peter (John 1:44 NKJV).

Here Peter is mentioned in connection with his brother Andrew, as well as another disciple of Jesus, Philip.

Jesus would later condemn Bethsaida for their unbelief in Him. Matthew records the Lord saying the following against this city.

> Woe to you, Chorazin! Woe to you, Bethsaida! For if the deeds of power done in you had been done in Tyre and Sidon, they would have repented long ago in sackcloth and ashes (Matthew 11:21 NRSV).

This town, which was exposed to the miracles of Jesus, rejected His testimony. Consequently, they received greater condemnation.

Interestingly, the reference of Peter being first among the apostles is not found in Mark. Since Mark wrote his gospel from Peter's perspective, likely recording Peter's very words, it is understandable why this reference would be omitted.

2. HE WAS A FISHERMAN BY TRADE

The gospels tell us that Peter and his brother Andrew were fisherman who worked on the Sea of Galilee. They were disciples of John the Baptist before becoming disciples of Jesus. John wrote of this.

> The next day John again was standing with two of his disciples. . . One of the two who heard John speak and followed him was Andrew, Simon Peter's brother (John 1:35,40 NRSV).

Thus, Peter and Andrew were John's disciples before they followed Jesus.

3. JESUS GAVE SIMON THE NAME PETER

Jesus gave to Simon, when he first approached Him, the surname *Cephas* which in Aramaic signified a *rock* or a *stone*. Again, we read about this in the Gospel of John.

> Andrew brought Simon to Jesus. Jesus looked at Simon and said, "You are Simon, son of John. Your name will be Cephas" (which means "Peter") (John 1:42 God's Word).

This was translated into Greek as *Petros*, which also means "rock." The Latin form is *Petrus*, and in English it is Peter.

The Aramaic form of his name, Cephas, is always used by the Apostle Paul in describing him. It is found nowhere else in the New Testament except John 1:42.

4. PETER IS THE FIRST WHO CONFESSED JESUS AS THE CHRIST

Peter is the first of Jesus' disciples who confessed Him as the Christ, the Messiah. Matthew records the event as follows.

> Then Jesus asked them, "But who do you say I am?" Simon Peter spoke up, "You are the Messiah, the Son of the living God" (Matthew 16:15,16 CEV).

Peter vocalized what the rest of the disciples were thinking about Jesus. Indeed, they came to believe that He was truly the Christ, God the Son.

5. PETER WROTE TWO NEW TESTAMENT BOOKS

Peter wrote two New Testament books (First and Second Peter) as well as being the source for the Gospel of Mark. In fact, it is possible, even likely, that the Gospel of Mark was taken down word-for-word from Peter's speeches given in Rome.

Therefore, three of the twenty-seven writings which became our "New Testament" have Peter's authority behind them. Peter was indeed an important figure in the spread of the Christian gospel.

ANDREW

Andrew was the brother of Simon Peter. His name is Greek and it has the meaning of "manly." The facts concerning his parentage, residence, occupation and early discipleship are all mentioned in connection with Peter.

His life, however, has a great lesson for believers. Andrew was the one who brought his brother Simon to Jesus. John records the incident as follows.

> One of the two who heard John *speak*, and followed Him, was Andrew, Simon Peter's brother. He first found his own brother Simon, and said to him, "We have found the Messiah" (which is translated, the Christ). And he brought him to Jesus. Now when Jesus looked at him, He said, "You are Simon the son of Jonah. You shall be called Cephas" (which is translated, A Stone)" (John 1:40-42 NKJV).

Thus, the usefulness of Simon Peter is, in one sense, due to the brother who told him of Jesus. Therefore, we learn an important lesson here. We should never underestimate what it can mean to bring someone to the knowledge of the Savior.

While the life and ministry of Andrew may not have been as remarkable as the life of Simon Peter, yet, if it were not for Andrew, Peter would have never met Jesus.

JACOB (JAMES) THE SON OF ZEBEDEE

James (Jacob) was the brother of John. He was probably the elder since he is usually mentioned first. While John is sometimes placed first (Luke 9:28; Acts 12:2) it is probably because he was the more prominent of the two.

Jacob (James) was the first martyr among the Twelve Apostles. This is recorded for us in the Acts of the Apostles. It says of Herod Agrippa I.

> He had the apostle James (John's brother) killed with a sword (Acts 12:2 NLT).

James is originally the same name as Jacob being written in Greek *Iacobos*, and transliterated into Latin, as *Iacobos*.

JOHN THE SON OF ZEBEDEE

John, the brother of James, the son of Zebedee, was the author of the fourth gospel. He describes himself as follows in that gospel. He said.

> This is that disciple who saw these events and recorded them here. And we all know that his account of these things is accurate (John 21:24 NLT).

John saw the events in the life of Jesus. Therefore, his testimony is that of an eyewitness.

James and John, with Peter made up a kind of inner circle of the disciples. They both appeared together with Peter in the Transfiguration. Matthew records what took place.

> Six days later, Jesus took with him Peter and James and his brother John and led them up a high mountain, by themselves (Matthew 17:1 NRSV).

It was only these disciples to whom Jesus showed His glory. Why Jesus chose only these three is not revealed to us.

James and John also appear in connection with their mother's special request. Mathew records the following.

> Then the mother of the sons of Zebedee came up to him with her sons, and kneeling before him she asked him for something. (Matthew 20:20 ESV).

The favor she asked Jesus was for her sons to sit in the places of power, or authority, in Jesus' kingdom. The request made the other disciples unhappy.

John the son of Zebedee wrote five books that make up the New Testament. They include the Gospel of John, 1,2,3 John, and Revelation. Obviously he was a very important figure in the spreading of the message of Jesus Christ.

WERE JAMES AND JOHN JESUS' COUSINS?

One more thing, it is highly likely that James and John, the sons of Zebedee, were actually Jesus' cousins! We can come to this conclusion by examining the following evidence.

THE THREE WOMEN AT THE CROSS ARE NAMED

Matthew lists three women who were standing near the cross of Jesus.

> Many women were there, watching from a distance. They had followed Jesus from Galilee to care for his needs. Among them were Mary Magdalene, Mary the mother of James and Joseph, and the mother of Zebedee's sons (Matthew 27:55-56 NIV).

Mark lists the women as follows.

> Some women were watching from a distance. Among them were Mary Magdalene, Mary the mother of James the younger and of Joseph, and Salome (Mark 19:40 NIV).

John explains who was there in this manner.

> Near the cross of Jesus stood his mother, his mother's sister, Mary the wife of Clopas, and Mary Magdalene (John 19:25 NIV).

When we put these three accounts together we find something fascinating.

According to Matthew, there was Mary Magdalene, Mary the mother of James and Joseph, and mother of the sons of Zebedee.

In the Gospel of Mark, Mary Magdalene is also mentioned, as is Mary the mother of James and Joseph. The mother of the sons of Zebedee is now named for us—Salome.

Finally, John also mentions Mary Magdalene. In addition, he tells us that the "other Mary," who is the mother of James and Joseph, is also the wife of Clopas.

However, John alone tells us that Mary the Mother of Jesus was also there at the cross. We are then told she was standing with "her sister." Therefore, the other woman at the cross, according to the gospel writers was "the mother of the sons of Zebedee" (Matthew) her name was "Salome" (Mark) and she was "the sister of Mary, the mother of Jesus (John). This would make James and John, the sons of Zebedee, cousins of Jesus—seeing that their mothers were sisters.

If this is the correct way of looking at this, then it would shed light on a number of things recorded in the New Testament. Indeed, it would explain why the Gospel of John, traditionally believed to have been written by John the son of Zebedee, does not mention himself by name in the entire work. Instead, he calls himself "the disciple whom Jesus loved." This would make complete sense if they were cousins—for they grew up together.

Furthermore, it would add to the intrigue when we read the first chapter of the Book of Revelation. There was John, the last of the living disciples of Jesus, banished to the isle of Patmos. While he was there, he had an encounter with the risen Jesus. The person who John grew up with, his cousin, was now the resurrected glorified Christ. One can only imagine the feelings that he experienced when Christ appeared!

PHILIP

This name Philip in Greek means "lover of horses." He must be distinguished from Philip the evangelist, of whom, we read about in the Book of Acts.

1. THE CALL OF PHILIP

The Scripture tells us Philip immediately answered Jesus' call to follow Him. In John's gospel, we read of that call.

> The next day Jesus wanted to go to Galilee. He found Philip and told him, "Follow me!" (John 1:43 God's Word).

Philip followed Jesus when the Lord called. This is certainly a good example for us to imitate.

2. PHILIP AND THE FEEDING OF THE FIVE THOUSAND

When Jesus fed the five thousand He asked Philip what He should do. We read about this in the Gospel of John.

> When Jesus saw the large crowd coming toward him, he asked Philip, "Where will we get enough food to feed all these people?" He said this to test Philip, since he already knew what he was going to do (John 6:5,6 CEV).

Notice that Jesus was not asking Philip for advice. Indeed, Jesus already knew what He was about to do.

3. PHILIP WISHES TO SEE GOD THE FATHER

We also find Philip asking Jesus a question on the night of His betrayal. John records the dialogue between the two.

> Philip said, "Lord, show us the Father, and we will be content." Jesus replied, "Have I been with you for so long, and you have not known me, Philip? The person who has seen me has seen the Father! How can you say, 'Show us the Father'?" (John 14:8-9 NET).

Philip wanted Jesus to show them God the Father. Jesus replied by saying "the one who has seen Him has seen the Father."

This is all that is said about Philip. We hear no more from him in Scripture.

QUESTION 16

NATHANIEL

Nathaniel is probably the same person mentioned in Matthew's gospel as Bartholomew. Bartholomew is not a name. He is actually *Bar Talmai* (the son of Talmai). The only account we have of Nathaniel is found in John's gospel. It reads as follows.

> Philip found Nathanael and told him, "We have found the man whom Moses wrote about in his teachings and whom the prophets wrote about. He is Jesus, son of Joseph, from the city of Nazareth." Nathanael said to Philip, "Can anything good come from Nazareth?" Philip told him, "Come and see!" Jesus saw Nathanael coming toward him and remarked, "Here is a true Israelite who is sincere." Nathanael asked Jesus, "How do you know anything about me?" Jesus answered him, "I saw you under the fig tree before Philip called you." Nathanael said to Jesus, "Rabbi, you are the Son of God! You are the king of Israel!" Jesus replied, "You believe because I told you that I saw you under the fig tree. You will see greater things than that." Jesus said to Nathanael, "I can guarantee this truth: You will see the sky open and God's angels going up and coming down to the Son of Man" (John 1:45-51 God's Word).

We learn a number of interesting things from this encounter.

First, Nazareth was not the place where the people were looking for the Messiah to come out of. Indeed, Nathaniel's statement may reflect jealousy between the various cities—or it may reflect the view that Nazareth was a place where nothing good could come from. In other words, it was a hopeless place.

We also find that Jesus knew certain things about Nathaniel which caused him to confess that Jesus was the Messiah, the Son of God. Many people have speculated as to what Nathaniel was doing under the fig tree. He may have thinking about the Messiah, or studying about Him. Possibly he was in the act of teaching others about Him. We just do not know. Since we are not told, any speculation is fruitless. What we do know is that whatever he was doing, Jesus had some insight into what was occurring.

Nathaniel is not mentioned elsewhere.

THOMAS

Thomas is the well-known "doubter." The name Thomas means "twin," as does the Greek *Didymus*. The Gospel of John describes him responding in the following manner when Jesus told the disciples they must go back to Judea.

> Thomas, who was called the Twin, said to his fellow disciples, "Let us also go, that we may die with him" (John 11:16 NRSV).

Thomas obviously knew of the impending danger.

1. THOMAS ASKS JESUS A QUESTION

We also find Thomas asking Jesus a particular question which caused the Lord to give one of His most memorable statements.

> Thomas said, "Lord, we don't know where you are going. How can we know the way?" Jesus replied, "I am the way, and the truth, and the life. No one comes to the Father except through me. If you have known me, you will know my Father too. And from now on you do know him and have seen him" (John 14:5-7 NET).

Jesus told Thomas, as well as the others, that *He* was the way, truth, and the life. Apart from Him, nobody could come to God the Father.

2. DOUBTING THOMAS

Thomas is famous for doubting the disciple's testimony of seeing the risen Christ. John wrote about the famous episode of Thomas wanting

QUESTION 16

to touch the body of the risen Christ before believing in Him. John writes.

> Now Thomas, called the Twin, one of the twelve, was not with them when Jesus came. The other disciples therefore said to him, "We have seen the Lord." So he said to them, "Unless I see in His hands the print of the nails, and put my finger into the print of the nails, and put my hand into His side, I will not believe" (John 20:24,25 NKJV).

Thomas had to see for himself. When Thomas saw that Christ had indeed risen, he testified that he too believed.

> Thomas responded to Him, "My Lord and my God!" (John 20:28 HCSB).

Thomas confessed that Jesus was both Lord and God. He recognized that Jesus had truly risen from the dead.

This is the last of the details which we read of Thomas. He is not mentioned again in Scripture.

MATTHEW

Matthew was author of the first gospel. He is known as the tax collector, or a customs official. The gospels tell us that Jesus called Matthew and he immediately followed. We read about his conversion in the gospel that he wrote.

> As Jesus was leaving, he saw a tax collector named Matthew sitting at the place for paying taxes. Jesus said to him, "Come with me." Matthew got up and went with him (Matthew 9:9 CEV).

Matthew immediately followed Jesus when the Lord had invited him. Matthew then, in turn, invited Jesus and others to his house for a meal. This caused a problem with the religious leaders. Matthew explains what took place.

> While He was reclining at the table in the house, many tax collectors and sinners came as guests to eat with Jesus and His disciples. When the Pharisees saw this, they asked His disciples, "Why does your Teacher eat with tax collectors and sinners?" But when He heard this, He said, "Those who are well don't need a doctor, but the sick do. Go and learn what this means: I desire mercy and not sacrifice. For I didn't come to call the righteous, but sinners" (Matthew 9:10-13 HCSB).

The religious leaders did not think that a Teacher such as Jesus should mingle with "sinners." This provided Jesus with the occasion of explaining why He came into our world.

Nothing more is said of Matthew after this event.

JAMES THE SON OF ALPHAEUS

The "son of Alphaeus" distinguishes him from the other James—the brother of John. He may have been the brother of Matthew who was also a son of Alphaeus. Yet this is nowhere stated as a fact.

Basically, we know nothing of him other than he was one of the Twelve. He is never singled out for us in the gospels—or in the remainder of the New Testament. Indeed, he is one of those among the Twelve who is only known from his name on the list.

THADDAEUS (JUDAS, PERHAPS LEBBAEUS)

The disciple is known by a number of different names. This includes Thaddaeus; Judas the son of James; Judas, not Iscariot; and possibly Lebbaeus.

First, the name Thaddaeus is only mentioned in two of the gospels, Matthew and Mark. Matthew listed the disciples as follows.

> Philip and Bartholomew; Thomas and Matthew the tax collector; James the son of Alphaeus, and Thaddaeus (Matthew 10:3 NET).

In this list, he is mentioned with James the son of Alphaeus.

He is probably to be equated with Judas, the son of James, who is mentioned in Luke and the Book of Acts. Luke lists the Twelve in this manner.

> And when day came, he called his disciples and chose from them twelve, whom he named apostles . . . Judas the son of James, and Judas Iscariot, who became a traitor (Luke 6:13,16 ESV).

In this instance, a distinction is made between him and Judas Iscariot. The name Judas may have been superseded by a new one—Thaddaeus—in order for there to be one Judas among the Twelve.

This name is also used of him in the Book of Acts. We read.

> When they had entered Jerusalem, they went to the upstairs room where they were staying. Peter and John, and James, and Andrew, Philip and Thomas, Bartholomew and Matthew, James son of Alphaeus and Simon the Zealot, and Judas son of James were there (Acts 1:13 NET).

It is also possible that after the betrayal of Jesus by Judas Iscariot he did not want the stigma that would be attached with the name Judas.

Indeed, in John's gospel, we find him asking Jesus a question about making Himself known to the world.

> Judas (not Iscariot) said to him, "Lord, how is it that you will manifest yourself to us, and not to the world?" Jesus answered him, "If anyone loves me, he will keep my word, and my Father will love him, and we will come to him and make our home with him. Whoever does not love me does not keep my words. And the word that you hear is not mine but the Father's who sent me" (John 14:22-24 ESV).

Notice that John also makes the distinction between this Judas and Judas Iscariot. He did not want his readers to be confused.

LEBBAEUS

In Matthew 10:4, some manuscripts add the name Lebbaeus to Thaddaeus.

> Philip and Bartholomew; Thomas and Matthew the tax collector; James the *son* of Alphaeus, and Lebbaeus, whose surname was Thaddaeus (Matthew 10:3 NKJV).

Most modern translations do not have this name in the text. They believe that it was a later addition, and thus, not one of the names of Thaddaeus.

SIMON THE CANANEAN

Some believe that the word "Cananean" is derived from Canaan or Cana. However others contend that it comes from the Aramaic word *qanan* meaning "zealot" or "enthusiast." The name is thus equivalent to the label "zealot" given to Simon in the lists of Luke and Acts and may refer to his intense nationalism and hatred of Rome.

If this is correct, then Simon was working with others to see the Roman rule overthrown. The zealots would use force, if necessary, to achieve their goal. Jesus would have taught Simon that there is indeed something worse than the bondage of Rome—it was the bondage of sin. By following Jesus, Simon was set free from this real bondage.

JUDAS ISCARIOT

Judas is mentioned more often than any of the other disciples—except for Peter. The name "Iscariot" is the Greek equivalent of the transliterated *Iscarioth* (man from Kerioth). Kerioth is located in southern Judea, twelve miles south of Hebron.

1. JUDAS THE THIEF

John describes Judas as a thief. When Mary of Bethany anointed Jesus with perfume in anticipation of His impending death, we find that Judas objected. John explains why.

> But Judas Iscariot, one of his disciples (the one who was going to betray him) said, "Why wasn't this oil sold for three hundred silver coins and the money given to the poor?" (Now Judas said this not because he was concerned about the poor, but because he was a thief. As keeper of the money box, he used to steal what was put into it.) (John 12:4-6 NET).

The motives of Judas were not pure.

2. JUDAS THE DEVIL

Jesus actually called Judas "the devil."

> Jesus replied, "Didn't I choose you, the twelve, and yet one of you is the devil?" (Now he said this about Judas son of Simon Iscariot, for Judas, one of the twelve, was going to betray him.) (John 6:70,71 NET).

It is hard to imagine anything worse than to be called "the devil" by Jesus!

3. JUDAS THE BETRAYER

Later, we are told that the devil entered Judas.

> The Festival of Unleavened Bread, which is called Passover, was drawing near. The chief priests and the scribes were looking for a way to put Him to death, because they were afraid of the people. Then Satan entered Judas, called Iscariot, who was numbered among the Twelve. He went away and discussed with the chief priests and temple police how he could

hand Him over to them. They were glad and agreed to give him silver. So he accepted [the offer] and started looking for a good opportunity to betray Him to them when the crowd was not present (Luke 22:1-6 HCSB).

Judas eventually brought the authorities to Jesus in the Garden of Gethsemane.

4. THE BETRAYER HANGS HIMSELF

After he betrayed Jesus, Judas then hanged himself in remorse. The Bible explains it in this manner.

> Judas threw the money into the temple and then went out and hanged himself (Matthew 27:5 CEV).

Such was the end of his pathetic life.

5. MATTHIAS REPLACED JUDAS

Judas was replaced by Matthias. We read of this in the first chapter of the Book of Acts, Peter stood up and said the following to the other ten disciples.

> From among the men who have accompanied us during the whole time the Lord Jesus went in and out among us—beginning from the baptism of John until the day He was taken up from us—from among these, it is necessary that one become a witness with us of His resurrection. So they proposed two: Joseph, called Barsabbas, who was also known as Justus, and Matthias. Then they prayed, "You, Lord, know the hearts of all; show which of these two You have chosen to take the place in this apostolic service that Judas left to go to his own place." Then they cast lots for them, and the lot fell to Matthias. So he was numbered with the 11 apostles (Acts 1:21-26 HCSB).

Matthias was the twelfth disciple—the one who replaced Judas. However, we hear nothing whatsoever of him after this episode.

THE DISCIPLES OF JESUS WERE A DIVERSE GROUP

Notice the diverse character of the twelve. They include: fishermen, a former tax collector, a zealot, and a traitor. The twelve represent the core of the new movement that will reveal the new activity of God. They were not taken from the elite of society—neither from the lowest levels.

There were two sets of brothers, Peter and Andrew and James and John. There was possibly a third set with Matthew and James the son of Alphaeus.

This sums up what we know for certain about these twelve men which Jesus chose to be His disciples.

SUMMARY TO QUESTION 16
WHAT DO WE KNOW ABOUT THE TWELVE DISCIPLES?

While here on earth Jesus chose twelve disciples to be His intimate pupils. However, not all of them were prominent. In fact, we know almost nothing about a few of them. This includes Simon the Cananean, Thaddaeus, Nathaniel, and James the son of Alphaeus. The New Testament gives us more information about the other eight. We can highlight them as follows.

Peter is the one most prominently mentioned in Scripture. Indeed, he is placed first in every list of disciples. It was Peter who first publicly confessed Jesus as the Messiah, the Christ, when the Lord asked the group who they believed that He was. Peter went on to write two books that became part of our New Testament—as well as being the person behind the Gospel of Mark.

Andrew was the brother of Peter. His is only mentioned in connection with Peter. However, Andrew is the one who brought Peter to

Jesus. Therefore, his contribution to the spread of the gospel cannot be overestimated.

James and John were also brothers. They were called the "sons of Zebedee." James was the first martyr of the Christian church. He was murdered by the evil King Herod Agrippa I.

John seemingly lived to a ripe old age. In fact, seems to be the only one of the Twelve who was not martyred. John is the writer of the fourth gospel. He testified that he was an eyewitness to the life and ministry of Jesus. John also wrote the three letters which bear his name, 1,2,3 John, as well as the Book of Revelation. He was indeed an important New Testament character.

In addition, we also discovered that James and John were actually Jesus' cousins—their mothers were sisters. This would explain why John's name is not found in the gospel that bears his name—the Gospel of John. Instead, he is always called, "the disciple whom Jesus loved."

Philip is specifically mentioned on three occasions. First, his calling by Jesus is recorded. He then tells Nathaniel that they have found the Messiah—Jesus of Nazareth.

Next, we find Jesus asking Philip as to how they could feed five thousand people with a few loaves and fish.

Finally, on the night of Jesus' betrayal, Philip asks Jesus to show God the Father to them.

Nathaniel is probably the same person known as Bartholomew. The only thing known about him is when he first met Jesus. When Jesus said that he saw Nathaniel under a fig tree, this caused Nathaniel to confess Jesus as the Messiah.

Matthew was a customs official who collected taxes for Rome. This position was hated by the Jews. Matthew's conversion is recorded for us in his own gospel. After this, he arranged a great feast for Jesus and many others. Nothing else is known of Matthew apart from these two episodes.

Thomas is the famous doubter. He is specifically mentioned on three occasions in the New Testament. First, he warned the disciples if they went to Judea with Jesus they would probably die with Him. Thomas also asked Jesus to show them where He was going when Christ spoke of going away.

Finally, we have the episode of Thomas demanding to see the scars on the body of the risen Christ.

Almost nothing is known of James the son of Alphaeus except for his listing among the Twelve.

Thaddaeus is also called Judas (and perhaps Lebbaeus). He is distinguished from Judas Iscariot. The only thing known of him is a question he asked Jesus on the night of His betrayal.

Simon the Cananean is Simon the Zealot. This means that he belonged to the political party that was attempting to overthrow Rome. We know absolutely nothing about him apart from the fact that he is listed as one of the twelve.

Apart from Peter, Judas Iscariot is the disciple whom the most is said about. We know that he held the money bag for the Twelve. John tells us that he was a thief. Jesus also called him "the devil."

Of course, he will always be known as the one who betrayed Jesus for thirty pieces of silver. Judas then went out and hanged himself when he realized he had betrayed an innocent man.

After Jesus' ascension into heaven, Judas was replaced by Matthias. Nothing else is known of Matthias.

This basically sums up what we know about these men from the New Testament. While there are sources outside of the Bible which tell us other things about them, the only information that we can be certain about is that which we find in the New Testament.

QUESTION 17

Who Was Mary Magdalene?

Mary Magdalene is certainly an important character in the life and ministry of Jesus Christ. Indeed, while many godly men and women in the Scripture remain nameless, this particular woman is mentioned by name in all four gospels with fourteen specific mentions in all.

Since she receives much attention by the gospel writers, as well being the object of so many wild speculative theories, it is crucial that we know exactly what the authoritative sources, the four gospels, have to say about her.

WHY WAS SHE CALLED MARY MAGDALENE?

The name "Mary Magdalene" represents the town from which she came. In the same way Jesus was called as a Nazarene, as one who came from city of Nazareth, Mary Magdalene is a description of Mary who came from the town of Magdala.

The town of Magdala was located two miles north of Tiberius along the lakeshore of the Sea of Galilee. While it is only briefly mentioned in the gospels, the first century Jewish writer Flavius Josephus tells us that at the time of the Jewish revolt, A.D. 66-70, Magdala had a population of around 40,000. In other words, it was not a small town.

THERE ARE FIVE MARY'S MENTIONED IN THE FOUR GOSPELS

To discover what the New Testament says about Mary can become a bit complicated. Indeed, it is easy to become confused when reading of "Mary" in the four gospels—since there are actually five different women with the name Mary that are mentioned in the life and ministry of Jesus. They include: Jesus' mother Mary, Mary Magdalene, Mary the wife of Cleopas, Mary of Bethany, and Mary the mother of James and Joseph—who is also called "the other Mary."

MISIDENTIFICATIONS OF MARY MAGDALENE

The fact that there are a number of women named "Mary" in the New Testament has led to a several misidentifications of Mary Magdalene. Indeed, over the course of church history, there have been three major misidentifications of this woman. Each of these has made its way to the general public. They can be listed as follows.

MISIDENTIFICATION 1: SHE IS NOT THE UNNAMED PROSTITUTE WHO WASHED JESUS FEET (LUKE 7:37-50)

This is one of the common mistakes about Mary. Many people believe that Mary Magdalene was a prostitute. However, there is no evidence of this whatsoever. The mistake is made when she is identified with the woman who washed Jesus' feet at the home of Simon the Pharisee. This unnamed woman is not only misidentified as Mary Magdalene, she is also misidentified as Mary of Bethany. She was neither of these women.

MISIDENTIFICATION 2: SHE WAS NOT MARY OF BETHANY, LAZARUS' SISTER (MARK 14:3-9, JOHN 11:2)

This leads us to our second misidentification—Mary of Bethany. She was the woman who anointed Jesus' in anticipation of His coming death and burial. Mary of Bethany is an entirely different person than Mary Magdalene. The problem comes when people attempt to equate Mary Magdalene with the anointing mentioned in Luke's gospel, Luke 7:37-50, and then assume that the accounts given in Mark and John are speaking of the same event. They are not.

QUESTION 17

MISIDENTIFICATION 3: SHE WAS NOT THE WOMAN CAUGHT IN ADULTERY (JOHN 7:53-8:11)

There has also been the popular idea that Mary Magdalene was actually the woman whom Jesus forgave for her adultery after she had been brought to Him by the religious rulers. Again, there is no historical basis for this whatsoever. However, this has not stopped people from making this connection.

MARY MAGDALENE WAS AMONG THE INNER CIRCLE OF JESUS DISCIPLES

If Mary Magdalene was none of these women, then who was she? What do we know of her?

For one thing, we know that she was in the inner circle of Jesus' disciples. Luke tells us that she, along with several other women, were helping to support the ministry of Jesus. He explained it in this manner.

> After this, Jesus traveled about from one town and village to another, proclaiming the good news of the kingdom of God. The Twelve were with him, and also some women who had been cured of evil spirits and diseases: Mary (called Magdalene) from whom seven demons had come out; Joanna the wife of Chuza, the manager of Herod's household; Susanna; and many others. These women were helping to support them out of their own means. (Luke 8:1-3 NIV).

We learn from this that Mary had been demon-possessed at one time. However, Jesus had cast seven demons out of her. The grateful Mary then followed with Him in His ministry. Mary eventually became one of the inner circle of Jesus' followers.

There is a passage in Mark's gospel which also speaks of Mary as one who had been demon-possessed. It reads.

> Early on the first day of the week, after He had risen, He appeared first to Mary Magdalene, out of whom He had

driven seven demons. She went and reported to those who had been with Him, as they were mourning and weeping. Yet, when they heard that He was alive and had been seen by her, they did not believe it (Mark 16:9-11 HCSB).

The problem is that this passage is in a contested section of the Gospel of Mark. While the authenticity of this passage is questioned, there is no question about the authenticity of the passage in Luke's gospel which also tells us that Mary had been demon-possessed.

MARY MAGDALENE WAS AT THE CROSS

We also find Mary Magdalene at Jesus' cross when He was crucified. Matthew records who was present at that time.

> Many women who had followed Jesus from Galilee and given him support were also there, watching from a distance. Among them were Mary Magdalene, Mary the mother of James and Joseph, and the mother of the sons of Zebedee (Matthew 27:55-56 NET).

When the other disciples of Jesus had fled, Mary and some other women who had given Him support, continued to support Him until the end.

SHE WAS THE FIRST WITNESS OF JESUS' RESURRECTION

Mary Magdalene had the honor of being the first person to whom the resurrected Christ appeared. It started when she and some other women went to Jesus' tomb on Easter Sunday morning. John records what happened.

> Early on the first day of the week, while it was still dark, Mary Magdalene went to the tomb and saw that the stone had been removed from the entrance (John 20:1 NIV).

Thinking that the body of her Lord had been taken away by someone, Mary hurried to find Jesus' disciples. She convinced Peter and John to come to the empty tomb and view things for themselves.

MARY SEES THE RISEN CHRIST

Finding the tomb of Jesus empty, these two disciples returned to their homes. Yet Mary remained weeping outside the tomb. She was still unwilling to abandon her Lord—the One who had done so much for her. Such faithfulness on her part was soon rewarded.

Suddenly two angels appeared wearing white garments. With them was another man who Mary mistook for a gardener. John explains what took place.

> And she saw two angels in white, sitting where the body of Jesus had lain, one at the head and one at the feet. They said to her, "Woman, why are you weeping?" She said to them, "They have taken away my Lord, and I do not know where they have laid him." Having said this, she turned around and saw Jesus standing, but she did not know that it was Jesus. Jesus said to her, "Woman, why are you weeping? Whom are you seeking?" Supposing him to be the gardener, she said to him, "Sir, if you have carried him away, tell me where you have laid him, and I will take him away." Jesus said to her, "Mary." She turned and said to him in Aramaic "Rabboni!" (which means Teacher) (John 12:12-16 ESV).

Her response to recognizing the Lord was immediate as well as telling. She said, "*Rabboni!*" The word means, "Teacher." This made clear the nature of their relationship—Jesus was the Teacher while Mary was the pupil. They certainly were *not* husband and wife!

JESUS TELLS MARY TO SPREAD THE WORD

Jesus then gave a commandment to Mary Magdalene—tell others the good news that He has risen from the dead.

> Jesus said to her, "Do not cling to me, for I have not yet ascended to the Father; but go to my brothers and say to them, 'I am ascending to my Father and your Father, to my God and your God.'" Mary Magdalene went and announced to the disciples, "I have seen the Lord"--and that he had said these things to her (John 20:17,18 ESV).

She was obedient to the command of the Lord. Mary told the disciples that she had indeed "seen the Lord."

This is the last we read of Mary Magdalene from Scripture. It becomes clear that she was an important person in the life and ministry of Jesus Christ.

Indeed, when others abandoned Him, she remained faithful. She not only followed Him during His public ministry but she was there when He was crucified, as well as the first person to whom He appeared after His resurrection from the dead. We can certainly learn many positive lessons from her behavior.

ONE FINAL ISSUE: THERE IS NO EVIDENCE THAT SHE WAS MARRIED TO JESUS

There is one other issue which must be dealt with concerning Mary Magdalene and her relationship with Jesus. We cannot say this strongly enough: there is no evidence whatsoever that Jesus and Mary were married, or even romantically involved! None!

Apart from the fact that we do not have the slightest hint of any relationship between the two, we can also mention some things which we do know.

SHE CALLED JESUS MY LORD AND MY TEACHER

There is the fact that Mary referred to Jesus as "my Lord" when looking for His body at the Garden tomb. She never said "my husband."

When the resurrected Christ appeared to her, Mary addressed Him as the "Teacher." There was no endearing term we would expect a wife to give to her beloved husband.

Therefore, we should not give any credence to theories which attempt to say Jesus and her were romantically involved, that they married, or that they had children. None of this is true.

SUMMARY TO QUESTION 17
WHO WAS MARY MAGDALENE?

Mary Magdalene, along with Mary the mother of Jesus, are the two most important women in the gospel story. Therefore, we should know certain things about her.

The gospels tell us that Mary Magdalene was a woman whom Jesus cast out seven demons. She became His follower. She, along with several other women, helped finance Jesus' public ministry.

Mary Magdalene eventually became one of the inner circle of the followers of Jesus. Indeed, she was a witness to his crucifixion, and the first witness to His resurrection.

Unfortunately, too often Mary has been misidentified. Indeed, she has been identified with the prostitute who anointed Jesus' feet, with Mary of Bethany who anointed Jesus body for burial, and with the woman Jesus forgave who had been caught in the act of adultery. Yet Mary was none of these people.

Neither was she romantically involved with Jesus, married to Him, or bore Him any children.

Mary called the crucified and risen Jesus her "Lord" and "Teacher." This was her relationship to Him—as should it be with the rest of us.

QUESTION 18

What Was Golgotha? (Mount Calvary)

One of the most important places with respect to the life and ministry of Jesus Christ was Golgotha—the place where He was crucified. There are a number of observations we need to make about this place.

1. JESUS WAS CRUCIFIED AT GOLGOTHA (SKULL HILL)

Golgotha is an Aramaic word meaning, "the place of the skull." All four gospels testify that it was the site of Jesus' crucifixion. We read in Matthew.

> Then they went out to a place called Golgotha (which means Skull Hill). The soldiers gave him wine mixed with bitter gall, but when he had tasted it, he refused to drink it (Matthew 27:33 NLT).

Matthew tells us the meaning of the word Golgotha.

Mark describes it this way. We read.

> The soldiers took Jesus to Golgotha, which means "Place of a Skull" (Mark 15:22 CEV).

He too defines the meaning of the word for his readers.

Luke, on the other hand, does not use the word Golgotha. Rather he calls it "the place called The Skull."

> When they arrived at the place called The Skull, they crucified Him there, along with the criminals, one on the right and one on the left Luke 23:33 HCSB).

John like Matthew and Mark, uses the term Golgotha. He also explains its meaning.

> Carrying His own cross, He went out to what is called Skull Place, which in Hebrew is called *Golgotha* (John 19:17 HCSB).

Consequently, all four gospels agree that Jesus was crucified at a place which was called Golgotha, or "the Skull"

2. CALVARY IS LATIN FOR SKULL

The Latin word for "skull" is *Calvaria*. This is where the term "Mount Calvary" was derived. When the New Testament was translated into Latin, the word *Calvaria* was used for Golgotha. The *King James* translators used the familiar word "Calvary" in their translation rather than using the term Golgotha.

3. THE NAME SKULL HILL HAS AN UNKNOWN ORIGIN

The exact reason why it is called "Skull hill" is unknown. A number of possible explanations have been put forward. They include the following.

IT WAS THE PLACE OF EXECUTION

It has been suggested that this was the place of public execution and skulls were left lying around after people had been executed. This does not seem very likely because of the Jewish practice of the burial of their dead.

THE HILL WAS SHAPED LIKE A SKULL

It has also been argued that the name "Skull hill" was actually derived from the physical shape of the hill in which Jesus was crucified—it looked like a human skull. The fact that executions took place on this hill was merely coincidental.

THE EXACT SITE IS DEBATED

There is something else which must be noted. The exact site of Christ's crucifixion is a matter of debate. The two most prominent candidates are the church of the Holy Sepulcher and Gordon's Calvary. Gordon's Calvary is on a hill that looks like a skull.

While most Bible scholars believe the site was the church of the Holy Sepulcher, no one can be certain as to the exact location of Jesus' death.

4. THE SITE WAS OUTSIDE OF THE CITY

We do know that Jesus was taken outside the city of Jerusalem to be executed. We read of this in the Book of Hebrews. It says.

> Therefore Jesus also suffered outside the city gate in order to sanctify the people by his own blood (Hebrews 13:12 NRSV).

Therefore, the exact site had to be outside the city at that time.

5. THE SITE WAS NEAR A ROAD

The site of the crucifixion was also near a public road.

> And the people passing by shouted abuse, shaking their heads in mockery (Matthew 27:39 NLT).

People were able to view the horrible sight of crucifixion as they passed by.

6. THE SITE WAS NEAR THE CITY

We also know that the site was near the city. John wrote.

Many of the Jews read this inscription, because the place where Jesus was crucified was near the city; and it was written in Hebrew, in Latin, and in Greek (John 19:20 NRSV).

The site was also near to the city of Jerusalem.

Consequently, from all the descriptions given in the gospels, we find that the actual site was on a public road, outside of the city, but near to it.

Whether the exact site of Jesus' crucifixion is ever determined, the fact remained that Jesus Christ was indeed crucified for the sins of the world. However, that certainly was not the end of the story. Three days later, Jesus came back from the dead!

SUMMARY TO QUESTION 18
WHAT WAS GOLGOTHA? (MOUNT CALVARY)

According to all four gospels Jesus Christ was crucified at a place called Golgotha. This is an Aramaic word for skull. The Latin term is *Calvaria*—where the name Calvary comes from.

The reason why it was called "Skull hill" is unknown. Possibly it was so named because it was the site of executions. It is also possible that the hill was shaped like a human skull.

The exact location is also unknown. We do know that Jesus was crucified outside of the city walls on a public road. The site was near the city of Jerusalem. Beyond that we cannot be certain.

There are two places which claim to be the site of Jesus' crucifixion—Gordon's Calvary and the church of the Holy Sepulcher. Yet nobody can be certain as to the exact site. However, we can be certain that Jesus has died for the sins of the world, as well as having risen from the dead.

PART TWO
The Life And Ministry Of Jesus

This section examines some of the key elements of the public ministry of Jesus. Although His public life was for a period of a few short years, He has influenced the course of this world as none other.

In this first section we will find out why He came to this world, His relationship to the Law of Moses, His miraculous deeds, and His relationship to Bible prophecy.

QUESTION 19

Why Did God The Son, Jesus Christ, Become A Human Being? (The Incarnation)

The great truth revealed in the New Testament is that the eternal God became one of us—He became a human being. John wrote.

> And the Word became flesh and lived among us, and we have seen his glory, the glory as of a father's only son, full of grace and truth (John 1:14 NRSV).

This is one of the most important verses in the entire New Testament—if now "the" most important.

The Apostle Paul echoes John's thoughts. He wrote the following to the Church at Philippi about God the Son coming to our earth.

> Though he was God, he did not demand and cling to his rights as God. He made himself nothing; he took the humble position of a slave and appeared in human form (Philippians 2:6,7 NLT).

Jesus Christ, while being Almighty God for all eternity, became a human being at a certain point in time in our history.

THE INCARNATION OF JESUS CHRIST

This is the main message of the New Testament—God became a human in Jesus Christ. It is known as the "incarnation." Incarnation is from the Latin meaning "in flesh." Although it is not a biblical word, it presents a biblical truth. Jesus is the eternal God who became flesh and blood—God the Son became a man some two thousand years ago.

It is important that we realize that He did so without giving up His oneness with God. God the Son became a human being without a sin nature. "In flesh" means more than Jesus had a physical body. Indeed, He was a complete human personality.

GOD THE SON TOOK ON A NEW NATURE

By the incarnation, we do not mean that God was turned into a human being, or that He ceased to be God while He was a human. The incarnation means that while remaining God, He took upon Himself a new nature—a human nature. The incarnation was the uniting of the divine and the human into one being, one Person—Jesus Christ. Therefore, God the Son, Jesus Christ, was fully God, as well as fully human.

WHY DID GOD COME TO OUR EARTH?

In becoming a human being, God the Son laid aside His heavenly glory to live among us. The question is, "Why did He do it?"

The Scriptures give us at least ten reasons as to why God came to earth in the Person of Jesus Christ. They are as follows.

REASON 1: HE WANTED TO FURTHER REVEAL GOD TO HUMANITY

The first and foremost reason was to give a further revelation of the living God to humanity. If you wish to know what God is like, then you need go no further than to look at Jesus Christ. The Bible puts it this way.

> No one has ever seen God. The One and Only Son the One who is at the Father's side—He has revealed Him (John 1:18 HCSB).

This verse teaches that Jesus Christ explained God to humanity. We need no longer wonder what God is like. Indeed, God the Son, Jesus, shows us.

In fact, Jesus Himself said this. We read the following in the Gospel of John after one of His disciples, Philip, asked Jesus to show them, "God the Father."

> Jesus replied, "Philip, don't you even yet know who I am, even after all the time I have been with you? Anyone who has seen me has seen the Father! So why are you asking to see him" (John 14:9 NLT).

Jesus Christ perfectly revealed God the Father in a number of important ways.

JESUS DID THIS BY BOTH WORDS AND DEEDS—GUIDED BY GOD THE FATHER

Jesus claimed that God the Father guided both His words and deeds. We read in John's gospel about this claim.

> Jesus said to them, "Very truly, I tell you, the Son can do nothing on his own, but only what he sees the Father doing; for whatever the Father does, the Son does likewise. The Father loves the Son and shows him all that he himself is doing; and he will show him greater works than these, so that you will be astonished" (John 5:19,20 NRSV).

Note well that Jesus said He only does what He sees the Father doing. In other words, He perfectly revealed the Father.

Jesus also emphasized that He was doing the work of the Father. We read Him saying the following words.

> But if I do his work, believe in what I have done, even if you don't believe me. Then you will realize that the Father is in me, and I am in the Father (John 10:38 NLT).

Jesus pointed to the deeds which He accomplished to demonstrate that He was God the Son. Indeed, only God Himself could do the sort of deeds which Jesus did.

THE OLD TESTAMENT REVELATION IS INCOMPLETE

While the God of the Bible revealed Himself to humankind in the Old Testament era, the revelation was incomplete. There were a number of things that waited till God Himself came to earth in the Person of Jesus Christ. Hence, when Jesus came to our earth, He revealed God to humanity in a personal way—a way which had never before taken place.

REASON 2: JESUS CAME TO FULFILL GOD'S PROMISES TO CERTAIN PEOPLE

The God of the Bible makes promises and He keeps His promises. From a study of the Scripture, we find that God made a number of promises to people like Adam and Eve, Abraham, and King David. They are as follows.

ADAM AND EVE

To Adam and Eve, the first two humans, Jesus was the promised Messiah—the seed of the woman that would crush the head of the serpent. In fact, the Lord gave the serpent the following warning.

> From now on, you and the woman will be enemies, and your offspring and her offspring will be enemies. He will crush your head, and you will strike his heel (Genesis 3:15 NLT).

The Lord promised Adam and Eve that the "seed of the woman" would strike at the head of the serpent—He would crush it. Jesus fulfilled this. Indeed, He defeated Satan at the cross. Eventually, Satan will be thrown into the lake of fire where He will be punished forever.

ABRAHAM

To Abraham, Jesus was his one descendant who would bless the world. God promised Abraham the following.

> I will bless those who bless you, and whoever curses you I will curse; and all peoples on earth will be blessed through you (Genesis 12:3 NIV).

Abraham was promised that one of his descendants would bless all humanity. God the Son, Jesus Christ, was that descendant.

DAVID

To David, the king over Israel, Jesus was the promised King that would come from His family. He is the One whom the Lord said would rule forever. We read of this promise to David in the Book of Second Samuel.

> When your days are over and you rest with your fathers, I will raise up your offspring to succeed you, who will come from your own body, and I will establish his kingdom (2 Samuel 7:12 NIV).

The coming of Jesus Christ fulfilled this promise that was made to King David. The angel Gabriel said to the following to Mary.

> You will become pregnant and have a son, and you are to name him Jesus. He will be very great and will be called the Son of the Most High. And the Lord God will give him the throne of his ancestor David. And he will reign over Israel forever; his Kingdom will never end! (Luke 1:31-33 NLT).

Jesus Christ fulfilled the promises that the Lord had made to King David. He was a descendant of the David and the rightful heir to the throne.

JESUS CAME TO BRING SALVATION TO ALL HUMANITY

The covenants, or agreements, the Lord made with these people promised salvation for both Israel and the Gentiles. With the coming of Jesus to the world, these promises were fulfilled. Paul wrote the following to the believers in the city of Rome.

> For I tell you that Christ has become a servant of the circumcised on behalf of the truth of God in order that he might confirm the promises given to the patriarchs, and in order that the Gentiles might glorify God for his mercy. As it is written, "Therefore I will confess you among the Gentiles, and sing praises to your name" (Romans 15:8,9 NRSV).

Jesus, therefore, came to earth to fulfill God's promises that were made to a number of people. One of these promises was salvation for the Gentiles.

REASON 3: JESUS CAME TO FULFILL THE LAW OF MOSES

God the Son, Jesus, also came to fulfill the Law that God had given through Moses. Jesus Himself testified that His coming was to fulfill the Law—not to abolish it. Matthew records the Lord saying the following about the Law.

> Don't misunderstand why I have come. I did not come to abolish the law of Moses or the writings of the prophets. No, I came to fulfill them. I assure you, until heaven and earth disappear, even the smallest detail of God's law will remain until its purpose is achieved (Matthew 5:17,18 NLT).

By living a perfect life here upon the earth, a sinless life, Jesus fulfilled the requirements of the Law in every respect.

Furthermore, in doing so, He was able to become the perfect sacrifice for our sins.

REASON 4: JESUS CAME TO DIE FOR THE SINS OF THE WORLD

This brings us to our next point. When sin first entered the world, God instituted the concept of substitutionary sacrifice—where He required the sacrifice to die. However, the sacrifices of animals could not take away sin. Neither would the death of an ordinary human being be satisfactory to take away sin. What was needed was the perfect sacrifice—someone who was not a sinner.

This was accomplished with God the Son becoming a human being. Christ's coming was for the purpose to die on the cross for the sins of the world. Indeed, when Christ came, He sacrificed Himself on Calvary's cross. Jesus testified to this important truth. He said.

> Just as the Son of Man came not to be served but to serve, and to give his life a ransom for many (Matthew 20:28 NRSV).

His death on the cross has paid the penalty for ours sins. He died in our place so that we do not have to suffer eternally for our misdeeds.

The Apostle Paul explained this truth further in his second letter to the Corinthians. He put it in this manner.

> Now everything is from God, who reconciled us to Himself through Christ and gave us the ministry of reconciliation: that is, in Christ, And all of this is a gift from God, who brought us back to himself through Christ. And God has given us this task of reconciling people to him. For God was in Christ, reconciling the world to himself, no longer counting people's sins against them. And he gave us this wonderful message of reconciliation. So we are Christ's ambassadors; God is making his appeal through us. We speak for Christ when we plead, "Come back to God!" For God made Christ, who never sinned, to be the offering for our sin, so that we could be made right with God through Christ (2 Corinthians 5:18-21 NLT).

Jesus Christ came into the world to become humanity's Savior—He was the "offering for our sin." Indeed, without His coming, humanity would not have a Savior. Again, we stress that He was able to accomplish this by living a sinless life.

REASON 5: JESUS CAME TO BRING IN A NEW COVENANT

Jesus not only fulfilled the promises of the old covenant, His coming brought a new covenant into existence. On the night of His betrayal Jesus instituted the new covenant. Matthew recorded what happens as follows.

> As they were eating, Jesus took bread, blessed and broke it, gave it to the disciples, and said, "Take and eat it; this is My body." Then He took a cup, and after giving thanks, He gave it to them and said, "Drink from it, all of you. For this is My blood [that establishes] the covenant; it is shed for many for the forgiveness of sins" (Matthew 26:26-28 HCSB).

God now deals with humanity exclusively through the new covenant. In fact, Scripture emphasizes that the only way in which a person can have a relationship with the true God is through Jesus—God the Son. John wrote.

> Anyone who denies the Son doesn't have the Father, either. But anyone who acknowledges the Son has the Father also (1 John 2:23 NLT)

Therefore, the new covenant which God has made with humanity means that it is exclusively through Jesus Christ. In other words, you cannot have God the Father without believing in God the Son.

REASON 6: JESUS CAME TO DESTROY THE WORKS OF THE DEVIL

The coming of God the Son, Jesus Christ, into the world was also to destroy the works of the devil—and the hold he has had over humanity. John wrote about this.

> But when people keep on sinning, it shows they belong to the Devil, who has been sinning since the beginning. But the Son of God came to destroy these works of the Devil (1 John 3:8 NLT).

Jesus' death on the cross frees us from the power of sin. The devil no longer has any right to control us because Jesus Christ has given us the freedom to choose not to sin.

REASON 7: JESUS CAME TO JUDGE THE WORLD RIGHTEOUSLY

Jesus came to be the righteous judge of humanity. Scripture says that it is He who will ultimately judge the world. Jesus said.

> And the Father leaves all judgment to his Son (John 5:22 NLT).

The Son will be the Judge.

Jesus repeated this statement again.

> And he has given him authority to judge all mankind because he is the Son of Man (John 5:27 NLT).

God the Son is qualified to judge humanity because He became a human being. Since He has lived as a human being, His judgment will always be righteous and fair.

REASON 8: JESUS CAME TO SYMPATHIZE WITH BELIEVERS AS THE GREAT HIGH PRIEST

Because Jesus, the God-man, lived here upon the earth and experienced the limitations of being a human being, He is able to sympathize with the problems and concerns that human beings face. The Bible says the following.

> Since, then, we have a great high priest who has passed through the heavens, Jesus, the Son of God, let us hold fast to our confession. For we do not have a high priest who is unable to sympathize with our weaknesses, but we have one who in every respect has been tested as we are, yet without sin. Let us therefore approach the throne of grace with

boldness, so that we may receive mercy and find grace to help in time of need (Hebrews 4:14-16 NRSV).

When we ask Him for help, He is able to give it to us because He understands our struggles. This is truly comforting to know.

REASON 9: JESUS CAME TO BE AN EXAMPLE FOR BELIEVERS

God the Son also came to provide an example for the believer on how to live one's life. When a person puts their faith in Jesus Christ, they have an example to follow. Indeed, Jesus lived the perfect life as the perfect man with faith in His Father. Hence we are told, "to walk just as He walked."

> The one who says he remains in Him should walk just as He walked (1 John 2:6 HCSB).

He is our example.

Peter, when writing about the following about the sufferings of Christ, also emphasized that we are to follow in His steps.

> This suffering is all part of what God has called you to. Christ, who suffered for you, is your example. Follow in his steps (1 Peter 2:21 NLT).

Jesus Christ provides the pattern concerning how believers should live.

REASON 10: JESUS CAME TO PREPARE HUMANITY FOR A HEAVENLY DESTINY

Finally, God the Son came to earth to prepare humanity for their heavenly destiny. The Son of God became a human so that human beings could eventually be fitted with a new nature—a perfect one. One day we shall be like Him. John wrote.

> Beloved, we are God's children now; what we will be has not yet been revealed. What we do know is this: when he

is revealed, we will be like him, for we will see him as he is (1 John 3:2 NRSV).

This is a wonderful promise for the believers.

We shall have a body like His—a glorified body. The Apostle Paul emphasized this when he wrote the following to the Philippians.

> But we are citizens of heaven, where the Lord Jesus Christ lives. And we are eagerly waiting for him to return as our Savior. He will take these weak mortal bodies of ours and change them into glorious bodies like his own, using the same mighty power that he will use to conquer everything, everywhere (Philippians 3:20,21 NLT).

The bodies of believers in Jesus Christ will be changed into a body like His.

Believers in Christ, who have borne the image of the earthly man Adam, will also bear the image of the heavenly man, Jesus. Paul wrote about this to the Corinthians about this promise.

> Adam, the first man, was made from the dust of the earth, while Christ, the second man, came from heaven. Every human being has an earthly body just like Adam's, but our heavenly bodies will be just like Christ's (1 Corinthians 15:47,48 NLT).

The thing that hindered this from happening was sin. Jesus has taken care of the sin problem by dying on the cross for the sins of the world.

In sum, God the Son became a human being for a number of reasons. It is important that we have a clear understanding of why He did indeed come to the earth.

SUMMARY TO QUESTION 19
WHY DID GOD THE SON, JESUS CHRIST, BECOME A HUMAN BEING? (THE INCARNATION)

The great truth revealed in the New Testament is that God the Son came to our earth in human form in the Person of Jesus Christ. This is also known as the "incarnation." When the Bible speaks about God the Son coming in the flesh, or as a human being, it means that He was fully human, a complete being, but with a sinless human nature.

This is what God did. The question before us is "why" did He do it? Why did God the Son become a human being? We can list ten reasons.

First, Jesus Christ tells us what God is like, as well as what He expects from us. Indeed, if we want to know the character, or nature, of the God of the Bible, then we merely have to look at Jesus. The revelation of God in the Old Testament, though true, was incomplete. Additional truth from God was necessary. Jesus came to bring that revelation.

This brings us to our second reason. The Old Testament was incomplete in the sense that certain promises had been made to individuals which had not been fulfilled. This included Adam and Eve, Abraham, and David. The coming of Christ fulfilled these promises.

Jesus also came to fulfill the Law of Moses—He perfectly kept the commandments of the Law. What the nation of Israel failed to do, Jesus Christ accomplished.

Since Jesus perfectly kept the Mosaic Law, living a sinless life, He could be the sacrifice for the sins of the world. This is another purpose of His coming—to die for our sins. This allows us to receive His offer of salvation for our sins.

The coming of Jesus Christ not only fulfilled the old covenant which the Lord had established, it also brought a new covenant, a new agreement, into effect. This new covenant, or agreement, states that it is only through Jesus Christ that a person can have a relationship with God the Father. Simply put, you cannot know God the Father without believing in God the Son.

In addition, His coming was to destroy the works of the devil. The sinful state of our world is a result of the devil's work. Jesus' coming was for the purpose of destroying this evil work. Eventually, there will be no more sin—evil will no longer exist.

Jesus' first coming to earth also allows Him to righteously judge the world in the future—at His Second Coming. Indeed, He is in a position to be the "righteous Judge" of the human race.

Moreover, Christ is now able to identify with humanity as our Great High Priest. Since God the Son became a human being and suffered the limitations which we endure, He understands our situations. In other words, Jesus can sympathize with us because He fully understands us.

Jesus Christ also came to this earth to become an example for believers as to how we should live. His perfect life sets the standard. Jesus is our pattern, our example.

Finally, Jesus' coming has prepared the way for believers to receive their new body—one without sin. When He comes again this will become a reality. However, it was His first coming which allowed this to take place.

These are ten of the reasons as to why God the Son came to our earth. It is obvious that He has done this because of His great love for us.

QUESTION 20

Why Did Jesus Come At That Particular Time In History?

The question often comes up as to why Jesus came to earth at the specific time that He did. Why didn't He come at another time that perhaps could have been better suited to spread the message?

This is summed up in the 1973 rock opera, "Jesus Christ Superstar," where Judas sings the following.

> Every time I look at you
> I don't understand
> Why you let the things you did
> Get so out of hand
> You'd have managed better
> If you'd had it planned
> Now why'd you choose such a backward time
> And such a strange land?
> If you'd come today
> You could have reached a whole nation
> Israel in 4 BC
> Had no mass communication

Could Jesus have picked a better time to arrive in history? Was there any special reason He came when He did?

The Bible tells us the following.

HE CAME IN THE FULLNESS OF TIME

The Bible is clear that Jesus came at the prescribed time. Paul told the Galatians that Christ came in the "fullness of time" or at the "appropriate time." He said.

> But when the appropriate time had come, God sent out his Son, born of a woman, born under the law to redeem those who were under the law, so that we may be adopted as sons with full rights (Galatians 4:4,5 NET).

Jesus Christ came to earth at the perfect time.

HIS COMING HAD BEEN PREDICTED

His coming had been predicted in the Old Testament. Indeed, Jesus denounced the people for not knowing the time of His coming. In the Gospel of Luke, we read the following account of Jesus weeping over the city of Jerusalem for their rejection of Him.

> When Jesus came closer and could see Jerusalem, he cried and said: It is too bad that today your people don't know what will bring them peace! Now it is hidden from them. Jerusalem, the time will come when your enemies will build walls around you to attack you. Armies will surround you and close in on you from every side. They will level you to the ground and kill your people. Not one stone in your buildings will be left on top of another. This will happen because you did not see that God had come to save you (Luke 19:41-44 CEV).

All the signs had been given, the prophecies fulfilled regarding His coming, yet the people still rejected Him. They were held responsible for their unbelief.

THERE IS NOTHING EXPLICITLY STATED AS TO WHY HE CAME AT THAT TIME

Though everything indicates that Jesus came according to God's schedule, nothing is said in Scripture about why He chose that particular time in history. God is silent on that matter except to say it was at the "perfect time." To assume things would be different, if instead He had chosen to come in the twenty-first century, is untrue.

Twenty-first century humanity has sufficient reason to believe in Jesus. The fact that He chose to come some two thousand years ago does not change the fact that He came and fulfilled that which the Bible had predicted.

The evidence is clear: God the Son has come to our earth in the Person of Jesus Christ. We who are living today are also held responsible to respond to His claims. Indeed, we have no excuse.

SUMMARY TO QUESTION 20
WHY DID JESUS COME AT THAT PARTICULAR TIME IN HISTORY?

There is nothing in Scripture which specifically tells us as to why God the Son came at that particular time in history. We can, however, make a few observations about the time of His coming.

The Bible says that Jesus came into our world "in the fullness of time" in God's program. In other words, it was the perfect time, as far as God the Father was concerned, to send His Son into our world.

His coming had been clearly predicted in the Old Testament. Since these specific prophecies were recorded in their Holy Scriptures, the people should have been waiting for One who would come along and fulfill these predictions.

Jesus had all of the credentials of the Messiah. Though He presented Himself to the people as the Promised One, they still rejected Him. Jesus, in turn, rebuked them for not being ready for His appearing.

Other than that the Bible is silent on the matter. For reasons known only to God, He picked that time in history to send His Son. The fact that He came some two thousand years ago does not give modern day humanity an excuse for not accepting Him. Like those in Jesus' time, the evidence of who He is, as well as what He did, is clear for all to see. We today, like those in His day, have no excuse.

QUESTION 21

If Jesus Was Without Sin, Then Why Was He Baptized?

Before Jesus began His public ministry He came to John the Baptist for baptism. Matthew records this event as follows.

> Then Jesus came from Galilee to John at the Jordan to be baptized by him (Matthew 3:13 NKJV).

The problem that this causes is that John's baptism was one of "repentance." John told the multitudes the purpose of his baptism.

> I baptize you with water for repentance, but one who is more powerful than I is coming after me; I am not worthy to carry his sandals. He will baptize you with the Holy Spirit and fire (Matthew 3:11 NRSV)

If sinless, why did Jesus submit Himself to a water baptism that had to do with repentance?

There are a couple of things that should be noted in answering this question. They are as follows.

1. HE FULFILLED ALL RIGHTEOUSNESS AT HIS BAPTISM

First, we find that John the Baptist did not want to baptize Him. However, Jesus explained why He was baptized. It was to "fulfill all righteousness." Matthew records the account as follows.

> Then Jesus came from Galilee to John to be baptized by him in the Jordan River. But John tried to prevent him, saying, "I need to be baptized by you, and yet you come to me?" So Jesus replied to him, "Let it happen now, for it is right for us to fulfill all righteousness." Then John yielded to him. (Matthew 3:13-15 NET).

Jesus' life was to serve as a pattern, an example, to all believers. Those who trust Jesus Christ as their Savior are to follow Him in His behavior. Therefore, Jesus submitted to water baptism to establish a pattern for believers. John wrote.

> He who says he abides in Him ought himself also to walk just as He walked (1 John 2:6 NKJV).

Therefore, Jesus' baptism set an example for those who were to follow—it was not to repent of any sins which He had committed.

2. JESUS CAME OUT OF THE WATER IMMEDIATELY

The Bible also emphasizes that Jesus came "immediately" out of the water after He was baptized. Matthew also wrote.

> And when Jesus was baptized, immediately he went up from the water, and behold, the heavens were opened to him, and he saw the Spirit of God descending like a dove and coming to rest on him; and behold, a voice from heaven said, "This is my beloved Son, with whom I am well pleased" (Matthew 3:16 ESV).

People stayed in the water to confess their sins. The fact that He came immediately out of the water is another indication that He had no sin. This is another indication the Jesus' baptism was an example for us to follow—not a confession, or admission of sin.

3. JESUS HAD NO SIN

Scripture is clear that Jesus Christ was without sin. Paul would later write to the Corinthians declaring this truth.

> God made the one who did not know sin to be sin for us, so that in him we would become the righteousness of God (2 Corinthians 5:21 NET).

Among other reasons, this is why Jesus came out of the water immediately.

4. IT WAS UNLIKE ANY OTHER BAPTISM

Therefore, the baptism of Jesus Christ was unlike the baptism of anyone else. Jesus, the sinless Lamb of God, had nothing to confess yet He submitted to John's baptism. In doing so, it was a fulfillment of the righteous requirements of the Law of God.

SUMMARY TO QUESTION 21
IF JESUS WAS WITHOUT SIN, THEN WHY WAS HE BAPTIZED?

John the Baptist, the forerunner of the Messiah, preached a baptism of repentance. People who came to him were to confess their sins in anticipation of the coming Messiah and His kingdom. Jesus, the One whom John spoke about, also came to John to be baptized by him.

However, John attempted to stop Him because John knew Jesus was without sin. Jesus explained the necessity of Him being baptized—it was to fulfill all righteousness. In other words, it was not to confess His sins but rather for another reason.

Consequently, Jesus submitted to John's baptism to set a pattern for believers to follow. The Bible says that those who believe in Jesus Christ are to walk as He walked. We are to pattern our Christian experience after His life. Therefore, in obedience to Him, we should also be baptized in water to make a public profession of our faith.

In addition, there is something else which we must note. The gospels tell us that Jesus came up immediately from the water. This is another indication that He had nothing to confess. His baptism was to set the pattern for us.

Therefore, the fact that Jesus Christ submitted to the baptism of John the Baptist, a baptism of repentance, had nothing to do with Him confessing sin.

QUESTION 22

Did Jesus Fulfill The Prophecies About The Messiah?

Jesus made it clear that the Old Testament predicted His coming. He said to the religious leaders of His day.

> You search the Scriptures because you believe they give you eternal life. But the Scriptures point to me! (John 5:39 NLT).

Jesus said that the Old Testament was all about "Him." This being the case, we should take a look at the various prophecies which He fulfilled at His First Coming. Some of the Old Testament prophecies that Jesus fulfilled include the following.

THE FAMILY LINE OF THE MESSIAH WAS PREDICTED

God the Son, Jesus Christ, fulfilled a number of predictions that have to do with the Messiah's genealogy, or family line. As we study the Scripture, we find that God narrowed down the family line of the Messiah in such a way that eliminated most people who have ever been born. The evidence can be seen in this manner.

PREDICTION: HE WILL COME FROM THE FAMILY OF SHEM

First of all, the Messiah was to come from the family line of Noah's son Shem. We read of this in the Book of Genesis.

> He also said, "Blessed be the LORD, the God of Shem! May Canaan be the slave of Shem. May God extend the territory of Japheth; may Japheth live in the tents of Shem, and may Canaan be his slave" (Genesis 9:26,27 NIV).

Noah had three sons, Shem, Ham and Japheth. God eliminated one third of humanity when He said the Messiah would come through the line of Shem. The line of Japheth and Canaan were not given the same blessings as the line of Shem. While there is no specific reference to the Messiah in these verses, it sets the stage for what will follow.

THE FULFILLMENT RECORDED

Luke records the fulfillment that Jesus was a descendant of Shem.

> Shelah was the son of Cainan. Cainan was the son of Arphaxad. Arphaxad was the son of Shem. Shem was the son of Noah. Noah was the son of Lamech (Luke 3:36 NLT).

Luke lists the genealogy of Jesus. It records Jesus was a descendant of Shem.

PREDICTION: THE CHRIST, OR MESSIAH, WILL BE A DESCENDANT OF ABRAHAM

While Shem had many descendants, the Lord made it plain that the Messiah would come through the line of Abraham. We read of this promise in the Book of Genesis. It says.

> Then the LORD told Abram, 'Leave your country, your relatives, and your father's house, and go to the land that I will show you. I will cause you to become the father of a great nation. I will bless you and make you famous, and I will make you a blessing to others. I will bless those who bless you and curse those who curse you. All the families of the earth will be blessed through you" (Genesis 12:1-3 NLT).

Now God eliminates all the families of the earth but one—the family of Abraham. Whoever claims to be the Messiah has to be a descendant of Abraham—for God told Abraham that one of his descendants will bless all the earth. This prediction is clear.

THE FULFILLMENT RECORDED

The fulfillment is recorded in Matthew. He writes.

> The book of the genealogy of Jesus Christ, the Son of David, the Son of Abraham (Matthew 1:1 NKJV).

The Apostle Paul, in the New Testament, emphasized that God specified that someone from Abraham's line would be the Christ.

> God gave the promise to Abraham and his child. And notice that it doesn't say the promise was to his children, as if it meant many descendants. But the promise was to his child—and that, of course, means Christ (Galatians 3:16 NLT).

The Apostle Paul says that God uses the "singular" rather than the "plural" to emphasize that it will be one particular descendant of Abraham who will bless the world. That descendant would be Jesus.

PREDICTION: HE WILL BE A DESCENDANT OF ISAAC

Abraham had two sons, Isaac and Ishmael. God promised Isaac that the Messiah would be through his family line.

> Stay in this land for a while, and I will be with you and will bless you. For to you and your descendants I will give all these lands and will confirm the oath I swore to your father Abraham. I will make your descendants as numerous as the stars in the sky and will give them all these lands, and through your offspring all nations on earth will be blessed (Genesis 26:3,4 NIV).

Isaac was the son of promise. The Messiah would come through his descendants—not through the descendants of Ishmael as some claim.

THE FULFILLMENT RECORDED

The New Testament records the fulfillment of this prophecy. We read about this in the following in the Gospel of Matthew.

> An account of the genealogy of Jesus the Messiah, the son of David, the son of Abraham. Abraham was the father of Isaac, and Isaac the father of Jacob, and Jacob the father of Judah and his brothers (Matthew 1:1,2 NRSV).

Jesus was from Isaac's line. Again, the predictions were fulfilled.

PREDICTION: THE MESSIAH WILL COME FROM THE FAMILY OF JACOB

The Messiah was also to be a descendant of the younger of Isaac's two sons, Jacob. In the Book of Genesis, it records God saying the following to Jacob.

> And God said to him, "I am God Almighty; be fruitful and increase in number. A nation and a community of nations will come from you, and kings will come from your body. The land I gave to Abraham and Isaac I also give to you, and I will give this land to your descendants after you" (Genesis 35:11,12 NIV).

Isaac had two sons, Jacob and Esau. Scripture says that the chosen line was through Jacob. This continues to narrow the possible candidates for the Messiah.

THE FULFILLMENT RECORDED

Matthew records how this was fulfilled. He writes.

> The book of the genealogy of Jesus Christ, the Son of David, the Son of Abraham: Abraham begot Isaac, Isaac begot Jacob (Matthew 1:1,2 NKJV).

Jesus was also from the line of Jacob.

PREDICTION: HE WILL COME FROM TRIBE OF JUDAH

Jacob had twelve sons. God eliminated 11/12 of the line of Jacob by saying the Messiah would come from the tribe of Judah. The prediction reads as follows.

> The scepter shall not depart from Judah, nor the ruler's staff from between his feet, until tribute comes to him; and to him shall be the obedience of the peoples. (Genesis 49:10 ESV).

Only a descendant of Judah could claim the right to be the Messiah. The ruler's staff belongs to one of his descendants.

THE FULFILLMENT RECORDED

Jesus Christ descended from the line of Judah. In the first chapter of Matthew we read of this. It says.

> An account of the genealogy of Jesus the Messiah, the son of David, the son of Abraham. Abraham was the father of Isaac, and Isaac the father of Jacob, and Jacob the father of Judah and his brothers (Matthew 1:1-3 NRSV).

Again, Jesus fulfilled the prediction.

PREDICTION: THE MESSIAH WILL BE FROM FAMILY LINE OF JESSE

There were many family lines in the tribe of Judah, but only through the family line of Jesse could the Messiah come. He is the "Branch that will bear fruit." We read of this in the Book of Isaiah. It says.

A shoot will come up from the stump of Jesse; from his roots a Branch will bear fruit (Isaiah 11:1 NIV).

The Branch is a title for the Messiah. He would have to be a descendant of Jesse.

THE FULFILLMENT RECORDED

Matthew records how this was fulfilled. He writes.

> This is a record of the ancestors of Jesus the Messiah, a descendant of King David and of Abraham . . . Salmon was the father of Boaz (his mother was Rahab). Boaz was the father of Obed (his mother was Ruth). Obed was the father of Jesse (Matthew 1:1,5 NLT).

Jesus descended from Jesse.

PREDICTION: HE WILL DESCEND FROM THE HOUSE OF DAVID

God told King David that the Messiah would be from His line. The promise is given by the Lord as follows.

> When your days are fulfilled and you lie down with your ancestors, I will raise up your offspring after you, who shall come forth from your body, and I will establish his kingdom (2 Samuel 7:12 NRSV).

Jesse had at least eight sons. God eliminated 7/8 of the sons of Jesse when He said the Messiah would be through the line of David. Again, the list of potential candidates gets narrower and narrower.

THE FULFILLMENT RECORDED

The very first verse of the New Testament records the fulfillment of this prophecy. Matthew writes.

QUESTION 22

> Jesus Christ came from the family of King David and also from the family of Abraham. And this is a list of his ancestors (Matthew 1:1 CEV).

Jesus descended from David.

When the angel Gabriel appeared to Mary, announcing Jesus' birth, he confirmed that Mary's child would be a descendant of David. Luke writes.

> And behold, you will conceive in your womb and bring forth a Son, and shall call His name JESUS. He will be great, and will be called the Son of the Highest; and the Lord God will give Him the throne of His father David (Luke 1:31,32 NKJV).

Jesus was David's descendant.

ALL OF THESE PROPHECIES WERE FULFILLED BY JESUS

Consequently, whoever the promised Messiah would be, He would have to be a male physical descendant of David the king. No other individuals would qualify. Therefore, from the predictions with respect to the genealogy of the Messiah, the great majority of the people who have ever been born are eliminated from contention. Jesus, however, fulfilled the Old Testament prophecies about the family line of the Messiah by being a descendant of David.

THE PLACE OF HIS COMING WAS PREDICTED

Not only is the family line of the Messiah predicted, In addition, the exact place of His birth was predicted in the Old Testament.

PREDICTION: HE WILL BORN IN BETHLEHEM

God predicted, through the prophet Micah, the exact city where the Messiah would be born—it would be the tiny town of Bethlehem. He wrote.

> But you, Bethlehem Ephrathah, though you are small among the clans of Judah, out of you will come for me one who will be ruler over Israel, whose origins are from of old, from ancient times. (Micah 5:2 NIV).

Every city in the world was eliminated but one, Bethlehem. Thus, even if someone was a male descendant of King David, yet was born in any other city than Bethlehem, he would not qualify as the promised Messiah. The descendant of David had to be born in this particular city to qualify.

THE FULFILLMENT RECORDED

Matthew records this fulfillment of this prediction. Jesus was born in Bethlehem.

> When Jesus was born in the village of Bethlehem in Judea, Herod was king. During this time some wise men from the east came to Jerusalem (Matthew 2:1 CEV).

Jesus was not only born from the predicted family—He was also born at the predicted place.

THE TIME OF HIS COMING WAS PREDICTED

Finally, we have the prediction with respect to the time in history of the Messiah's coming. These predictions are as follows.

PREDICTION: HE WILL BE KILLED BEFORE THE TEMPLE AND THE CITY OF JERUSALEM ARE DESTROYED

The Scripture predicted the death of the Messiah. We find this in the writings of Daniel the prophet. Scripture says.

> After this period of sixty-two sets of seven, the Anointed One will be killed, appearing to have accomplished nothing, and a ruler will arise whose armies will destroy the city

and the Temple. The end will come with a flood, and war and its miseries are decreed from that time to the very end (Daniel 9:26 NLT).

We learn three things from this verse.

1. The Messiah will come on the scene of history.

2. He will be killed.

3. After His death, the city of Jerusalem and the temple will be destroyed.

These three predictions are specific.

THE FULFILLMENT RECORDED

When Jesus Christ came to the earth, the city of Jerusalem and the temple were still standing. Teaching at the temple courts was an important part of Jesus' ministry. The temple, as well as the city, was destroyed in the year A.D. 70. This was about forty years after His death and resurrection.

Therefore, Jesus fulfilled certain prophecies about the coming Messiah.

1. He was born in the right family line—David's.

2. He was born at the right place—the city of Bethlehem.

3. He was born at the right time in history—before the city of Jerusalem and the temple were destroyed.

TWO IMPORTANT POINTS NEED TO BE NOTED

These three areas of prophecy that we have looked at reveal two startling things—literal fulfillment and no human manipulation. The evidence is as follows.

THE PROPHECIES WERE FULFILLED LITERALLY BY JESUS

First, the prophecies were fulfilled literally. In other words, exactly as they were written. Jesus was literally a descendant of King David, He was literally born in the city of Bethlehem, and He literally came upon the scene of history and was killed before the city of Jerusalem and the temple were destroyed. He fulfilled the predictions exactly as they were written.

JESUS' BIRTH FULFILLED THESE PROPHECIES

Second, these three lines of prophecy were all fulfilled without any human manipulation. There is no way Jesus could have deliberately fulfilled them—seeing they were all fulfilled by His birth.

Before He gave any sermons, before He did anything miraculous, Jesus supernaturally fulfilled these prophecies. He was born in the right family, at the right place, and at the right time in history. Humanly speaking, there is no way Jesus could control these factors. However, Jesus was more than a human being. Indeed, He is God Almighty.

Therefore, we conclude that Jesus of Nazareth did indeed fulfill the Old Testament predictions about the coming of the Messiah. Many of these were, humanly speaking, impossible to arrange. Indeed, only God Himself could arrange Jesus being born in the right family, at the right place, and at the right time.

SUMMARY TO QUESTION 22
DID JESUS FULFILL THE PROPHECIES ABOUT THE MESSIAH?

Jesus Christ told the religious leaders of His day to search the Scriptures. If they would do this, they would discover that they spoke about Him. Indeed, He claimed to have fulfilled the predictions of the coming Messiah. The evidence says that He did indeed do this.

From the Old Testament we find that the coming Messiah was to be born in one particular family. This would be through Shem, Abraham,

Isaac, Jacob, Judah, and David. The New Testament is clear that Jesus was a descendant of David. This means that Jesus was born in the proper family to have the credentials of the predicted Messiah.

Next, we discover that the Old Testament prophet Micah predicted the Messiah would be born in the small town of Bethlehem. Matthew tells us that Jesus was born in Bethlehem. Again, Jesus fulfilled that which was prophesied.

Add to this, Daniel the prophet said the Messiah would be killed before the city of Jerusalem and the temple were destroyed. This assumes that the Messiah would come, and then after that, that the city and temple would again be destroyed.

Daniel was correct. Jesus Christ came upon the scene of history before the destruction of Jerusalem and the temple. He was crucified about forty years before they were both destroyed.

We note that the prophecies that Jesus fulfilled were fulfilled literally. He was a literal descendant of David, literally born in Bethlehem, and He literally died before the city and temple were destroyed.

Furthermore, these three lines of prophecy were all fulfilled by Jesus' birth. There is no way, humanly speaking, that He could have deliberately fulfilled them. Yet Jesus fulfilled them as they were written.

In sum, the coming of the Messiah was predicted in the Old Testament. Jesus fulfilled these prophecies and, in doing so, has the right to claim to be the promised Messiah.

QUESTION 23

Did Jesus Come To Bring Peace On Earth?

The Gospel according to Luke records that when the angel announced the birth of the baby Jesus, the host of heaven appeared with him and praised God in these familiar words.

> Glory to God in the highest, and on earth peace, good will toward men (Luke 2:14 KJV).

Jesus is also called the "Prince of Peace." The prophet Isaiah wrote about the child that would be born would be given the title the "Prince of Peace."

> For to us a child is born, to us a son is given, and the government will be on his shoulders. And he will be called Wonderful Counselor, Mighty God, Everlasting Father, Prince of Peace (Isaiah 9:6 NIV)

The question then arises: Did Jesus come to earth to bring peace? If so, then He failed in His mission because the world has not known peace since His coming. However, there are a number of things that need to be said.

1. THERE IS A DIFFERENT READING OF THE TEXT

First, it should be noted that the text in Luke reads a little differently in modern versions. The New Living Translation puts it this way.

> Glory to God in the highest heaven, and peace on earth to all whom God favors (Luke 2:14 NLT).

The peace that was promised is not to every person but rather to those whom God favors. In other words, Jesus did not come to bring peace to everyone.

Why is there the difference between the reading in the King James Version and the reading in almost every other version? The difference is due to a variation in the Greek text.

The King James translators accepted as original a reading that had Christ bringing peace to all humanity. However, based on other Greek manuscripts, most modern translations follow the reading that says Christ came to bring peace upon people "in whom God was well-pleased." This is why we find the difference in these translations.

2. HE CAME TO BRING PEACE TO BELIEVERS ONLY

Jesus has promised peace to believers. He made this clear to His disciples on the night of His betrayal. He said.

> Peace I leave with you. My peace I give to you. I do not give to you as the world gives. Your heart must not be troubled or fearful (John 14:27 HCSB).

The peace of Jesus is not the same as we find in this world system. It is a supernatural peace.

THE APOSTLE PAUL WROTE OF GOD'S PEACE.

If you do this, you will experience God's peace, which is far more wonderful than the human mind can understand. His peace will guard your hearts and minds as you live in Christ Jesus (Philippians 4:7 NLT).

God's peace only comes to God's people.

3. THERE WILL NOT BE PEACE FOR EVERYONE

The idea of Jesus coming to earth for the purpose of bringing a lasting peace is contrary to His words. Although one of the designations of Jesus is the "Prince of Peace," His first coming was not for the purpose of bringing peace on earth.

In fact, He was never called by this title during His earthly ministry. Indeed, Jesus made it clear that He did not come to bring peace to the earth. He said.

> Don't assume that I came to bring peace on the earth. I did not come to bring peace, but a sword. For I came to turn a man against his father, a daughter against her mother, a daughter-in-law against her mother-in-law; and a man's enemies will be the members of his household (Matthew 10:34-36 HCSB).

Jesus specifically said that He came to divide—not to unite.

According to His own words, Jesus' kingdom is not of this world-system. John records the following dialogue between Jesus and Pontius Pilate.

> Jesus replied, "My kingdom is not from this world. If my kingdom were from this world, my servants would be fighting to keep me from being handed over to the Jewish authorities. But as it is, my kingdom is not from here." Then Pilate said, "So you are a king!" Jesus replied, "You say that I am a king. For this reason I was born, and for this reason I came into the world—to testify to the truth. Everyone who belongs to the truth listens to my voice." Pilate asked, "What is truth?" (John 18:36-38 NET).

Jesus' kingdom is not of this world system. The Bible teaches that His kingdom will be brought in supernaturally when He returns to the earth.

4. PEOPLE MUST MAKE A CHOICE REGARDING JESUS

The nature of Jesus' message called for people to make a choice. Rather than uniting humanity, it divided friends and families. It still has that effect today. Those who believe in Jesus Christ are separated from those who do not believe. Thus, His mission was not that of bringing peace but rather bringing the truth of God. This message always divides.

5. THERE WILL BE UNIVERSAL PEACE SOMEDAY

One day Jesus Christ will return and establish an everlasting kingdom— a kingdom where peace will be the rule—rather than the exception to the rule. The prophet Isaiah wrote of the coming day.

> Of the increase of his government and peace there will be no end. He will reign on David's throne and over his kingdom, establishing and upholding it with justice and righteousness from that time on and forever. The zeal of the LORD Almighty will accomplish this (Isaiah 9:7 NIV).

At some time in the future, Jesus will rule on David's throne. Until that time, the message of Jesus divides those who love God's truth from those who do not.

Therefore, we can rightly conclude that Jesus' certainly did not come to bring peace to everyone in our world.

SUMMARY TO QUESTION 23
DID JESUS COME TO BRING PEACE ON EARTH?

When Jesus Christ came to earth, the angels announced that there would be peace. Jesus is called the, "Prince of Peace," yet there has been no peace for the world since He came. There are several reasons for this. The can be summed up in this manner.

First, there is a question as to what the angels actually said at the announcement of the birth of Jesus. The reading of the text in the King

James translation is not accepted by most modern scholars. Instead of Jesus coming to bring, "Peace, good will toward men" most Bible scholars believe the text should read, "Peace among men, or people, in whom He is well-pleased."

Consequently, the peace which the angels promised was to those who have trusted Him—it is not to everyone. Believers alone can enjoy the peace of God.

Second, Jesus Himself testified that His coming had the result of dividing people—not uniting them.

Indeed, the message of Jesus is a message which divides. As the One who brought the truth, His words will divide families. It always has, it always will.

In addition, we find that Jesus told Pontius Pilate that His kingdom was not of this world system. Although He will rule over a "kingdom of peace," it will be supernaturally brought in when He returns.

One day there will indeed be peace on the earth. However, Jesus did not come into our world to bring that peace to everyone at His first coming.

QUESTION 24

Did Jesus Get Involved In The Contemporary Politics In Israel?

Jesus was the promised Messiah, the Christ. He had the right to rule over the entire nation of Israel. However, when we look at the public ministry of Jesus, we find that He avoided any involvement in the current political issues of His day. From the New Testament, we can make the following observations about Jesus' political involvement.

1. JESUS DID NOT SPEAK OUT ON CURRENT POLITICAL ISSUES

There is nothing recorded in the New Testament about Jesus Christ speaking out against any of the political issues of His day. Nothing in His teachings gives even the slightest hint that He had any political involvement.

2. HE REFUSED HIMSELF TO BE MADE KING

In fact, we find that Jesus refused to lead any political movement. He resisted when the people wanted to make Him king. John records what took place.

> Jesus saw that they were ready to take him by force and make him king, so he went higher into the hills alone (John 6:15 NLT).

He did not want to be made King by these people. This was not the way in which His kingdom was going to be established.

3. HE TOLD HIS DISCIPLES NOT TO TELL OTHERS HE WAS MESSIAH

When Jesus first acknowledged that He was the Messiah, He did not allow His disciples to publicly tell others. Matthew records the following.

> Then he [Jesus] sternly ordered the disciples not to tell anyone that he was the Messiah (Matthew 16:20 NRSV).

Instead of openly telling anyone, Jesus ordered His disciples to keep silent as to His identity.

4. HE TOLD NO ONE TO TELL OF HIS TRANSFIGURATION

Jesus told the disciples that were with Him on the Mount of Transfiguration that they were to tell nobody about it. We read the following in the Gospel of Matthew.

> On their way down from the mountain, Jesus warned his disciples not to tell anyone what they had seen until after the Son of Man had been raised from death (Matthew 17:9 CEV).

This event was a clear demonstration that Jesus was the promised Messiah. Yet, He told His disciples to keep silent about it.

5. JESUS WITHDREW FROM CONFRONTATION

We find that Jesus also withdrew from confrontation with the religious rulers. We read the following in the Gospel of Matthew.

> But Jesus knew what they were planning. He left that area, and many people followed him. He healed all the sick among them, but he warned them not to say who he was (Matthew 12:15,16 NLT).

Again, His mission was not to confront these religious rulers.

6. JESUS DID NOT INCITE THE PEOPLE AGAINST ROME

Although Jesus did not incite the people against Rome, this was one of the charges brought before Pilate by the religious leaders.

> But they were urgent, saying, "He stirs up the people, teaching throughout all Judea, from Galilee even to this place" (Luke 23:5 ESV).

Yet there is no evidence that Jesus ever incited the people against Rome.

7. JESUS REFUSED TO GET ENTANGLED IN A POLITICAL DEBATE

Jesus refused to get into a debate with the religious leaders about paying taxes to Rome. Matthew records the episode as follows.

> Then the Pharisees went away and planned to trap Jesus into saying the wrong thing. They sent their disciples to him along with Herod's followers. They said to him, "Teacher, we know that you tell the truth and that you teach the truth about the way of God. You don't favor individuals because of who they are. So tell us what you think. Is it right to pay taxes to the emperor or not?" Jesus recognized their evil plan, so he asked, "Why do you test me, you hypocrites? Show me a coin used to pay taxes." They brought him a coin. He said to them, "Whose face and name is this?" They replied, "The emperor's." Then he said to them, "Very well, give the emperor what belongs to the emperor, and give God what belongs to God." They were surprised to hear this. Then they left him alone and went away (Matthew 22:15-22 God's Word).

Jesus would not let Himself be involved in this issue—He had a higher calling.

8. JESUS BEHAVIOR WAS IN CONTRAST TO FALSE MESSIAHS

Jesus' behavior was in contrast to some false Messiahs that preceded Him. Scripture records some of these failed attempts.

> For some time ago Theudas rose up, claiming to be somebody. A number of men, about four hundred, joined him. He was slain, and all who obeyed him were scattered and came to nothing. After this man, Judas of Galilee rose up in the days of the census, and drew away many people after him. He also perished, and all who obeyed him were dispersed. And now I say to you, keep away from these men and let them alone; for if this plan or this work is of men, it will come to nothing (Acts 5:36-38 NKJV).

While these "messiahs" attempted to cause a political and military overthrow, Jesus did not.

Luke also records of another attempt to lead a rebellion again the rule of Rome. In the Book of Acts, we read of a question asked the Apostle Paul.

> Aren't you the Egyptian who led a rebellion some time ago and took four thousand members of the Assassins out into the desert? (Acts 21:38 NLT).

This speaks of another attempt to rebel against the authority of Rome.

While these different leaders attempted to stage a revolt against Rome, Jesus did not.

9. HIS KINGDOM WAS NOT OF THIS WORLD SYSTEM

Jesus kingdom was not of this world system. Jesus made this plain when He appeared before Pontius Pilate. The Bible says.

> Jesus answered, "My kingdom doesn't belong to this world. If it did, my followers would have fought to keep me from being handed over to our leaders. No, my kingdom doesn't belong to this world." "So you are a king," Pilate replied. "You are saying that I am a king," Jesus told him. "I was

born into this world to tell about the truth. And everyone who belongs to the truth knows my voice." (John 18:36,37 CEV).

He is the King and His kingdom is coming. However, it is not from this world system.

In sum, we find that Jesus did not get involved in the contemporary politics in Israel. Instead, He was also concerned about a different calling which He had—a much higher calling.

SUMMARY TO QUESTION 24
DID JESUS GET INVOLVED IN THE CONTEMPORARY POLITICS IN ISRAEL?

Although Jesus was the promised Messiah, the one who could rightfully rule over Israel, He refused to become involved in any political issue of His day. We see this in a number of ways.

First, there is nothing whatsoever recorded about Jesus getting involved in contemporary politics.

Indeed, after He fed the multitudes, the people attempted to force Jesus to be made king. Knowing this, He withdrew from them. Jesus would not be made "King" in this manner.

When He first acknowledged that was the promised Messiah, He told His disciples not to tell others. There was a specific time where He would reveal this truth.

We also find that He also withdrew from confrontation with the religious rulers when they brought up political issues. This was not His fight.

Although He was accused before Pilate as inciting the people against Rome, He never did this. This was in contrast to a number of false Messiahs who attempted to revolt against the Roman occupation.

The reason Jesus acted this way has to do with the nature of His kingdom—it was not of this world system. This is why we find Jesus not getting involved in the political discussions of His day. Indeed, He had a much higher calling.

QUESTION 25

What Was Jesus' Relationship To The Law Of Moses?

The law that God gave to Moses for the people Israel was a central part of their existence. It was the perfect standard by which they were to conduct their lives. Though the law was perfect, it revealed how imperfect each individual was. The law gave people the knowledge of sin but not the solution. Paul wrote.

> Now we know that whatever the law says it speaks to those who are under the law, so that every mouth may be stopped, and the whole world may be held accountable to God. For by works of the law no human being will be justified in his sight, since through the law comes knowledge of sin (Romans 3:19,20 ESV).

Scripture says the following about the relationship of Jesus to the Old Testament law.

1. JESUS WAS BORN UNDER LAW

Jesus was born under, or subject to, the Law of Moses. The Apostle Paul wrote the following to the Galatians.

> But when the right time came, God sent his Son, born of a woman, subject to the law. God sent him to buy freedom for us who were slaves to the law, so that he could adopt us as his very own children (Galatians 4:4,5 NLT).

Jesus was subject to being obedient to the Law of Moses.

2. HE WAS SINLESS UNDER THE LAW

Jesus was also sinless under the law. In the Gospel of John, it records Him giving the following testimony of His own behavior.

> Which of you convicts me of sin? If I tell the truth, why do you not believe me? (John 8:46 NRSV).

With respect to the Law, Jesus was without sin.

3. JESUS FULFILLED THE LAW

Jesus, as the promised Messiah, came and fulfilled the Law of Moses. He testified to the purpose of His coming to the world.

> Don't suppose that I came to do away with the Law and the Prophets. I did not come to do away with them, but to give them their full meaning (Matthew 5:17 CEV).

He fulfilled the Law down to the smallest detail.

4. JESUS KEPT THE LAW

Jesus is the only person who has ever kept the law perfectly. He did everything the law required, never once breaking any of its commandments. Because He was sinless, Jesus was able to meet the requirements of the law to be the perfect sacrifice. His death redeemed humanity from the curse of the law. Paul wrote.

> Christ redeemed us from the curse of the law by becoming a curse for us—for it is written, "Cursed is everyone who is hanged on a tree" (Galatians 3:13 ESV).

Jesus perfectly kept the Law.

5. JESUS TAUGHT THE LAW

Jesus faithfully taught the law. He rejected the unbiblical traditions of the Scribes and Pharisees. On one occasion, an expert in the law stood up to test Jesus.

> An expert in the Law of Moses stood up and asked Jesus a question to see what he would say. "Teacher," he asked, "what must I do to have eternal life?" Jesus answered, "What is written in the Scriptures? How do you understand them?" The man replied, "The Scriptures say, 'Love the Lord your God with all your heart, soul, strength, and mind.' They also say, 'Love your neighbors as much as you love yourself'" (Luke 10:25-27 CEV).

Jesus was a faithful teacher of the Law of Moses.

6. THE CURSE OF THE LAW WAS REMOVED BY HIS DEATH

The curse that the law had over humanity was now removed. The death of Christ meant that those who were previously slaves under the law could become the children of God and heirs to His promises. The Bible says.

> But when the time was right, God sent his Son, and a woman gave birth to him. His Son obeyed the Law, so he could set us free from the Law, and we could become God's children. Now that we are his children, God has sent the Spirit of his Son into our hearts. And his Spirit tells us that God is our Father. You are no longer slaves. You are God's children, and you will be given what he has promised (Galatians 4:4-7 CEV).

Christ has taken away the bondage of the law for the believer and given freedom in the place of slavery.

7. THERE IS A NEW LAW OF CHRIST

Those who have become Christians are now under the law of Christ. Jesus told His disciples what they are now to do.

> I'm giving you a new commandment: Love each other in the same way that I have loved you. Everyone will know that you are my disciples because of your love for each other (John 13:34,35 God's Word).

The mark, or brand, of the Christian is the love believers will have one for another.

Paul also wrote about the Law of Christ. He said.

> Share each other's troubles and problems, and in this way obey the law of Christ (Galatians 6:2 NLT).

The law of Christ is to love others as Jesus has loved us.

In sum, the Law of Moses is no longer operating in the lives of believers. We now have a greater law to follow—the Law of Christ.

SUMMARY TO QUESTION 25
WHAT WAS JESUS' RELATIONSHIP WITH THE LAW OF MOSES?

When Jesus Christ, God the Son, came into our world the people of Israel were under the law of God—also known as the "Law of Moses. The Bible tells us of the relationship of Jesus Christ to the Law of Moses. We can summarize it as follows.

First, Jesus Christ was born under the Law. When He came into this world, the Law of Moses was in place.

While the Law was in place, Jesus Christ was sinless under the law. Indeed, He fulfilled the Law perfectly, keeping all its commandments.

In addition, we find that Jesus faithfully taught the Law to others. He was not a lawbreaker in any sense of the Word.

The New Testament emphasizes that His death on the cross removed the curse of the law from humanity. The responsibility of people now is not to obey the Law of Moses but rather believe in Jesus Christ. This is how a person gets into a right relationship with God.

Believers in Christ thus have a new law to follow. These are the commandments of the Lord Jesus Christ.

A sign, or mark, that people are believers in Jesus is the love which they will have one for another. This is how the world will know the identity of the true believers.

QUESTION 26

Why Was Jesus Called Lord?

The gospels record people addressing Jesus Christ as, "Lord." This is a translation of the Greek word, *kurios*. What does it mean when they used this title? Was it referring to Him as the God of the Old Testament or did it mean something else?

YAHWEH OR JEHOVAH IS TRANSLATED AS LORD IN NEW TESTAMENT

Whenever God's name, "Jehovah" or "Yahweh," is given in the New Testament, it is rendered by the Greek word "kurios." We read of this usage in Paul's letter to the Romans. He wrote of people confessing Jesus as Lord.

> Because if you confess with your lips that Jesus is Lord [kurios] and believe in your heart that God raised him from the dead, you will be saved. For one believes with the heart and so is justified, and one confesses with the mouth and so is saved (Romans 10:9,10 NRSV).

In this instance, Paul calls Jesus "LORD" or "Yahweh." This is a reference to His Deity. Jesus is Yahweh—the God of the Old Testament.

IT DOES NOT ALWAYS MEAN DEITY

While the Greek word kurios is used to translate the divine name of God, Jehovah or Yahweh, this is not always the case. The word can also mean a polite title like, "Sir."

For example, when a woman in Samaria addressed Jesus, she used the same word—kurios. However, in this context it is translated, "Sir." We read the following in John's gospel about the conversation between Jesus and this woman.

> The woman said to him, "Sir, [kurios] you don't have anything to use to get water, and the well is deep. So where are you going to get this living water? (John 4:11 God's Word).

In this instance, she was not recognizing His Deity. She was merely addressing Him with the polite title, "Sir."

THEY ARE NOT NECESSARILY RECOGNIZING HIS DEITY

Consequently, the fact that Jesus is addressed as kurios on some occasions, does not necessarily mean that people acknowledged His Deity. As we just noted, the Greek word for Lord, kurios, can indeed be used for God's name—Jehovah or Yahweh but kurios can also be merely a polite way of addressing someone.

For example, there are people apart from Jesus who are addressed as kurios in the New Testament.

> Some Greeks who had come to Jerusalem to attend the Passover paid a visit to Philip, who was from Bethsaida in Galilee. They said, "Sir, [kurios] we want to meet Jesus" (John 12:20,21 NLT).

Here we have Philip, the disciple of Jesus, being addressed with the Greek word kurios. Obviously this is not a reference to Deity!

Therefore, while Jesus is the Lord, Yahweh, not every instance where the English translation calls Him Lord refers to His deity. The context must be the determining factor.

SUMMARY TO QUESTION 26
WHY WAS JESUS CALLED LORD?

In a number of places in the New Testament Jesus is called "Lord." The word translated Lord is from the Greek word kurios. It is important to understand why He was called "Lord."

At times, it is a translation of the divine name for God—Yahweh or Jehovah. Therefore, on a number of occasions when Jesus is addressed as "Lord" it means that He is addressed with the divine name for God! No mere mortal could ever be spoken of in this manner. The fact that He was addressed in this way means that Jesus was considered to be God Himself.

However, at other times this Greek word is merely a polite form of address. Indeed, people, such as Philip the disciple of Jesus, are addressed with the Greek word kurios.

Consequently, we should not always assume *kurios* is a reference to the divine name. As always, the context must determine exactly what is meant by the use of the term.

QUESTION 27
What Was The Significance Of The Transfiguration Of Jesus?

One on the most important events in the life of Christ is what is known as His "Transfiguration." Because of its emphasis in the New Testament, it is necessary to have some understanding about what it was, as well as what it meant.

WHAT WAS THE TRANSFIGURATION OF JESUS?

The Transfiguration was the glorification of the human body of God the Son, Jesus Christ. On this occasion His body underwent a change in form, a metamorphosis, so that it shone as brightly as the sun. At the time of the Transfiguration, Jesus' earthly ministry was coming to a close. He had acknowledged that He was the Messiah, and had predicted His death and resurrection. Now He was to reveal, to a select few, His divine glory.

The Bible gives this account of what transpired in the following manner.

> Six days later, Jesus took with him Peter and James and his brother John and led them up a high mountain by themselves. There in their presence he was transfigured: his face shone like the sun and his clothes became as dazzling as light. And suddenly Moses and Elijah appeared to them; they were talking with him. Then Peter spoke to Jesus. 'Lord,' he said, 'it is wonderful for us to be here; if you want me to, I will

> make three shelters here, one for you, one for Moses and one for Elijah.' He was still speaking when suddenly a bright cloud covered them with shadow, and suddenly from the cloud there came a voice which said, 'This is my Son, the Beloved; he enjoys my favour. Listen to him.' When they heard this, the disciples fell on their faces, overcome with fear. But Jesus came up and touched them, saying, 'Stand up, do not be afraid.' And when they raised their eyes they saw no one but Jesus (Matthew 17:1-8 NLT).

Jesus told Peter, James, and John not to tell anyone about this event until after He had risen from the dead. Matthew writes.

> As they descended the mountain, Jesus commanded them, "Don't tell anyone what you have seen until I, the Son of Man, have been raised from the dead" (Matthew 17:9 NLT).

In telling these disciples to remain silent about this experience, Jesus again predicted that He would be raised from the dead.

YEARS LATER PETER RECALLED THE EVENT

Some years later, Simon Peter would write of being present at this event on the Mount of Transfiguration. He stated it as follows.

> When we told you about the power and the return of our Lord Jesus Christ, we were not telling clever stories that someone had made up. But with our own eyes we saw his true greatness. God, our great and wonderful Father, truly honored him by saying, "This is my own dear Son, and I am pleased with him." We were there with Jesus on the holy mountain and heard this voice speak from heaven (2 Peter 1:16-18 CEV).

Peter was there as an eyewitness and he wrote what he recalled of this event.

QUESTION 27

WHAT DOES THE TRANSFIGURATION OF JESUS REPRESENT?

The transfiguration represents a number of things. They include the following.

1. IT SHOWS JESUS IS THE SON OF GOD

The Transfiguration provides further evidence that Jesus Christ was the divine Son of God. It is not coincidental that this happened soon after Jesus had acknowledged Himself to be the Christ—the one who left heaven's glory to come to earth. Now we find that three of His disciples were to get a glimpse of that glory.

2. IT SHOWS HE FULFILLED THE LAW AND THE PROPHETS

The appearance of Moses and Elijah with Jesus is also highly significant. Indeed, the name Moses was equated with the Old Testament Law that God had given to the people. Jesus came and fulfilled the commandments of the law, and did the things the law could not do—to provide an answer for the problem of sin. The law pointed out the problem but it was Jesus Christ who gave the solution. John wrote.

> For the law was given by Moses, but grace and truth came by Jesus Christ (John 1:17 KJV).

It is also noteworthy that the great prophet Elijah appeared. He was an outstanding figure in the Old Testament. His appearance with Moses on the Mount of Transfiguration testified that Jesus fulfilled the writings of the prophets, as well as the law. The Law and the Prophets was another way of saying the entire Scripture.

3. THERE WAS A CONFIRMATION OF THE FATHER

The voice of God the Father gave further confirmation of the calling and Sonship of Jesus. He acknowledged that Jesus had pleased Him in the things which He had said and done. This testimony is especially important since Jesus came to earth to do the will of the Father.

4. IT REPRESENTED HIS COMING KINGDOM

The Transfiguration scene of Jesus is a representation of His coming kingdom in its fullness. Jesus Himself said to His disciples.

> I promise you that some of those standing here will not die before they see the Son of Man coming with his kingdom (Matthew 16:28 CEV).

The Transfiguration occurred with Jesus and three of His disciples—Peter, James, and John. Moses and Elijah miraculously appeared with Jesus. At the foot of the mountain were the remainder of Jesus' disciples, and the multitudes.

IS THIS A PICTURE OF THE DIFFERENT ASPECTS OF THE COMING KINGDOM?

When one considers the various individuals and groups involved, it seems to paint a marvelous picture of Jesus' coming kingdom. Consider the following characters that were involved.

JESUS HIMSELF

First, there is the Lord Jesus in His glorified body. He was glorified in front of these witnesses. Matthew writes.

> Jesus' appearance changed in front of them. His face became as bright as the sun and his clothes as white as light (Matthew 17:2 God's Word).

He will rule in His coming kingdom in His glorified body.

MOSES

Moses represented the saved that will enter God's kingdom through death. They died with a promise of a future life.

ELIJAH

Elijah never died. He represents those believers who enter the kingdom of God by the translation, or the rapture, of the church. Paul wrote about this event.

> Brothers and sisters, this is what I mean: Flesh and blood cannot inherit the kingdom of God. What decays cannot inherit what doesn't decay. I'm telling you a mystery. Not all of us will die, but we will all be changed. It will happen in an instant, in a split second at the sound of the last trumpet. Indeed, that trumpet will sound, and then the dead will come back to life. They will be changed so that they can live forever. This body that decays must be changed into a body that cannot decay. This mortal body must be changed into a body that will live forever (1 Corinthians 15:50-53 God's Word).

There will come a day when all of us will be changed from mortal to immortal, from perishable to imperishable. This is a wonderful promise of Scripture.

JESUS' DISCIPLES

Peter, James, and John in their natural bodies depict those Jewish believers who will enter the coming kingdom. There will be people alive when Christ returns. They will enter His kingdom here upon the earth.

THE MULTITUDE REPRESENTS VARIOUS NATIONS THAT WILL MAKE UP THE KINGDOM

The multitude of people, left at the base of the mountain, represent the various nations who will enter the kingdom of God in their natural or non-glorified bodies. The prophet Isaiah wrote of a day when this will occur.

> In that day the Root of Jesse will stand as a banner for the peoples; the nations will rally to him, and his place of rest will be glorious. In that day the Lord will reach out his hand a second time to reclaim the remnant that is left of his people from Assyria, from Lower Egypt, from Upper Egypt, from Cush, from Elam, from Babylonia, from Hamath and from the islands of the sea. He will raise a banner for the nations and gather the exiles of Israel; he will assemble the scattered people of Judah from the four quarters of the earth (Isaiah 11:10-12 NIV).

These people at the base of the mountain are seen as representative of these nations who are mentioned in Isaiah.

SOME BIBLE-BELIEVERS DO NOT ACCEPT THIS INTERPRETATION

We should note that there are many good Bible-believers who do not think the Scripture teaches that Jesus Christ will reign on earth for a literal one thousand years.

Consequently, they do not see the same significance of the various personages that were at the Transfiguration, or who were down the mountain. While they acknowledge the significance of the event, they do not interpret the details in the same manner.

SUMMARY TO QUESTION 27
WHAT WAS THE SIGNIFICANCE OF THE TRANSFIGURATION OF JESUS?

After Jesus acknowledged to His Twelve Disciples that He was indeed the promised Messiah, the gospels record that an extraordinary event took place. Jesus' body was transfigured, or changed, in the presence of the Old Testament prophets, Moses and Elijah, as well as in the presence of three of His disciples. This Transfiguration was the glorification of the human body of Jesus. It is significant for a number of reasons.

Those with Jesus saw Him in His glory as the Son of God. The appearance of Moses and Elijah also testified that Jesus was the One of whom the Law and Prophets spoke. The approving testimony of God the Father further confirmed the identity of Jesus as the promised Messiah.

There is something else. The Transfiguration also represents His coming kingdom. In the Transfiguration of Jesus, we seem to have the various elements of the coming kingdom represented.

First, there is the glorified King. With Him are His disciples—they represent the living believers who will enter His earthly kingdom upon His return.

Also included in this picture are those who will enter the kingdom of God through death. Moses is an example of this.

There are also those who will come into the kingdom through the transformation of their bodies at the rapture of the church. They will not see death—but will be changed when the Lord Jesus returns. Elijah is representative of these people.

There are also those people from the various nations who will also enter into the millennium in non-glorified bodies. They are represented by the multitudes who are at the base of the mountain.

These different groups are all represented through the transfiguration of Jesus. It must be noted that this is the viewpoint of those who believe that Christ will literally rule for a thousand-year period on the earth sometime in the future.

Some Bible-believers do not believe that we should be that specific in determining what the various parties will represent in the future.

Indeed, they do not think the Scripture teaches that Jesus Christ will literally rule for a thousand years upon His return. Hence they do not assume that we can find too many specific details in the account of the Transfiguration that refer to His future kingdom.

However, all agree that the Transfiguration is a wonderful picture of the King who was about to enter into His glory. The New Testament records that this is exactly what happened. Indeed, Jesus died but He also rose from the dead.

QUESTION 28

Did Jesus Perform Miracles?

One of the things that sets Jesus Christ apart from other religious leaders, and even other biblical prophets, were the unique miracles that He performed while here upon the earth. Since Jesus Himself appealed to these signs as proof that He was the promised Messiah, it is important that we understand what type of signs that He did perform, as well as their significance.

JESUS TESTIMONY TO HIS MIRACLES

To begin with, we discover that Jesus Himself appealed to His miracles as a testimony to His Divine character. We can make the following observations.

HIS RESPONSE TO JOHN THE BAPTIST

The Scripture records that John the Baptist sent his messengers to Jesus to ask if He were really the Messiah, the Christ. Jesus replied to this question by performing miracles. Matthew records.

> When John heard in prison what the Messiah was doing, he sent word by his disciples and said to him, "Are you the one who is to come, or are we to wait for another?" Jesus answered them, "Go and tell John what you hear and see: the blind receive their sight, the lame walk, the lepers are

cleansed, the deaf hear, the dead are raised, and the poor have good news brought to them (Matthew 11:2-5 NRSV).

This would remind them of various Old Testament passages that predicted the Messiah would be a miracle worker. For example, we read in Isaiah.

> Then the eyes of the blind shall be opened, and the ears of the deaf unstopped; then shall the lame man leap like a deer, and the tongue of the mute sing for joy (Isaiah 35:5,6 ESV).

Therefore, the people would have understood Jesus' miracles in light of the Old Testament prophecies concerning the credentials of the Messiah.

HIS DIRECT CLAIMS

On another occasion, Jesus told His disciples that His miracles proved He was sent from God the Father. John wrote.

> Do you not believe that I am in the Father and the Father is in me? The words that I say to you I do not speak on my own authority, but the Father who dwells in me does his works. Believe me that I am in the Father and the Father is in me, or else believe on account of the works themselves (John 14:10,11 ESV).

Therefore, the performing of miracles is Jesus' specific claim to substantiate His identity—it is not our claim.

JESUS PERFORMED TWO TYPES OF MIRACLES

As we look at the evidence of Jesus' miracles from the four gospels, we find that they can basically fit into two different categories—some of His miracles could be labeled as miracles of timing, while others were purely supernatural events.

In other words, some of the miracles attributed to Him were deeds that are contrary as to how the universe normally functions, while others were miracles of timing. We can make the following distinctions between these two types of miracles.

1. THERE WERE MIRACLES OF TIMING

In the first instance, the word miracle is used to describe an unusual or natural event that occurs at a precise time. This is usually in answer to prayer. Therefore, the miracle is in the timing—not in the event itself. There are examples of this type of miracle in the four gospels.

THE MIRACULOUS CATCH OF FISH

On two separate occasions, the gospels record that Jesus was involved in a miraculous catch of fish. Luke records one of these incidents. He wrote.

> When He had stopped speaking, He said to Simon, "Launch out into the deep and let down your nets for a catch." But Simon answered and said to Him, "Master, we have toiled all night and caught nothing; nevertheless at Your word I will let down the net." And when they had done this, they caught a great number of fish, and their net was breaking. So they signaled to their partners in the other boat to come and help them. And they came and filled both the boats, so that they began to sink (Luke 5:4-7 NKJV).

This miracle was in the timing. Catching a large amount of fish is not a miracle in-and-of-itself. It was the timing of this event that made it miraculous.

After Jesus' resurrection, John reported an incident between Jesus and several of His disciples on the Sea of Galilee. It reads as follows.

> Just as day was breaking, Jesus stood on the shore; yet the disciples did not know that it was Jesus. Jesus said to them,

"Children, do you have any fish?" They answered him, "No." He said to them, "Cast the net on the right side of the boat, and you will find some." So they cast it, and now they were not able to haul it in, because of the quantity of fish (John 21:4-6 ESV).

Again, there is nothing miraculous about throwing a net into the water and having it filled with fish. This event, however, was a miracle. Indeed, they had been fishing all night and had not caught a thing. But when Jesus told where to put their net, it immediately became full.

THE COIN IN THE MOUTH OF THE FISH

Another natural event, that is a miracle of timing, is the episode of the coin found in the mouth of the fish to pay the temple tax. Jesus told Peter to do the following.

> However, so that we don't create a scandal, go to the sea and throw in a hook. Take the first fish that you catch. Open its mouth, and you will find a coin. Give that coin to them for you and me (Matthew 17:27 God's Word).

Again, the miracle is not the event itself, but rather in the timing of the event. It is certainly possible to catch a fish that may have a coin in its mouth. However, the fact that Jesus told Peter that the first fish he would catch would have a coin in its mouth which would pay the temple tax was indeed a miracle.

THE PIGS RUNNING INTO THE SEA

The gospels record an account of pigs running into the sea. Again, this could also be considered a natural event. However, the pigs only did this after Jesus cast demons into them. Matthew records it this way.

> "All right, go!" Jesus commanded them. So the demons came out of the men and entered the pigs, and the whole herd

plunged down the steep hillside into the lake and drowned in the water (Matthew 8:32 NLT).

It is certainly possible for a herd of pigs to rush into the sea and drown because of natural causes. However, this herd did so immediately after the command of Jesus. This demonstrates that the episode was miraculous.

THE SERVANT HEALED BY JESUS

In another instance, John's gospel tells us of Jesus healing a man's son at a distance when He was not physically present. The incident occurred as follows.

> Go," Jesus replied, "your son will live." The man took Jesus at his word and departed. While he was still on the way, his servants met him with the news that his boy was living. When he inquired as to the time when his son got better, they said to him, "Yesterday, at one in the afternoon, the fever left him." Then the father realized that this was the exact time at which Jesus had said to him, "Your son will live." So he and his whole household believed. This was the second sign Jesus performed after coming from Judea to Galilee. (John 4:50-53 NIV).

We have here another example of a miracle of timing. The fact that the fever broke was not miraculous in-and-of itself. However, the miracle is that it broke at the exact time on the previous day when Jesus told the man that his son was healed.

THE EARTHQUAKE AT JESUS' DEATH

The Bible also says an earthquake occurred at the moment of Jesus' death on the cross. Matthew records it as follows.

> Once again Jesus shouted, and then he died. At once the curtain in the temple was torn in two from top to bottom. The earth shook, and rocks split apart (Matthew 27:50-51 CEV).

The miracle is that the timing of the earthquake coincided with Jesus' death. While earthquakes are not miracles, this one came at the precise time when Christ died. Again, the miracle is in the timing.

Events like these are not contrary to the laws of science and nature. Nonetheless, they are miracles of timing and place. Other New Testament events that could fall into this category include the cessation of the storm on the Sea of Galilee the moment Jesus commanded it to stop, and the withering of the fig tree when Jesus cursed it.

In sum, Jesus performed a number of miracles which were not contrary to the laws of nature—but they were miracles nonetheless.

2. THERE WERE EVENTS THAT WENT BEYOND NATURAL LAW

The Bible speaks of a second type of miracle performed by Jesus during His public ministry. This kind of miracle cannot be explained in terms of normal cause and effect. In other words, it is a totally supernatural event. We will provide two examples of this type of miracle.

JESUS WALKING ON WATER

Jesus walking on the water is an example of this type of totally supernatural miracle. Matthew records what happened.

> Now in the fourth watch of the night Jesus went to them, walking on the sea (Matthew 14:25 NKJV).

The normal laws of science certainly cannot explain this miracle—for it is physically impossible for people to walk on water. Yet Jesus Christ did this!

THE FEEDING OF THE FIVE THOUSAND

Another example of this kind of miracle is Jesus feeding the five thousand with a few loaves of bread and fish. When a multitude of people who had followed Jesus became hungry, Jesus took the food that was available—five loaves and two fish—and miraculously turned it into enough food to feed the great crowd. The Bible says.

> They all ate as much as they wanted, and they picked up twelve baskets of leftovers. About five thousand men had eaten from those five loaves, in addition to all the women and children! (Matthew 14:20,21 NLT).

Not only did everyone eat, they all were satisfied! Furthermore, the disciples gathered twelve baskets full of leftovers from the miracle. The normal laws of cause and effect cannot explain this event.

JESUS PERFORMED BOTH TYPES OF MIRACLES

Therefore, the evidence of miracles can either be from natural events or purely supernatural events. Both types of miracles are recorded in Jesus' public ministry. They give testimony to His ability to overrule the natural —the normal ways in which the universe functions. In other words, the laws of nature are under His control. He indeed is Lord of all.

SUMMARY TO QUESTION 28
DID JESUS PERFORM MIRACLES?

The New Testament says that Jesus Christ appealed to miracles to back up His claim as being the long-awaited Messiah. These signs would indicate that He was the One whom the Law and the Prophets spoke of.

These miracles of Jesus can be defined in two ways. They are either unusual events that occur at a precise time, or they are things that happen in a strictly supernatural way.

In the life of Jesus, we see both of these types of miracles performed. For example, the gospel records a miraculous catch of fish on more than one occasion. While there was nothing miraculous in catching a large number of fish, the fact that it occurred when Jesus said it would it would take place was what was miraculous.

There is also the example of Jesus healing the servant of a man while not being physically present. The man was healed at the exact time Jesus said that he was healed. These are a few of the examples of the miracles of timing which the gospels record.

However, Jesus' walking on water is a miracle of a different order— it is a totally supernatural miracle. The same is true for other miracles He performed such as the feeding of the five thousand. There is no natural explanation for these types of miracles. In doing these types of miracles Jesus showed that He was Lord of all.

In either case, the miracles are convincing evidence of Jesus' great power, and His control over the laws He established when He created the universe. This is why Jesus appealed to His miracles as signs He was the Messiah.

QUESTION 29

What Was The Purpose Of Jesus' Miracles?

The consistent testimony of the New Testament is that Jesus Christ performed a number of miraculous deeds—miracles. The word translated miracle can also mean, "sign." The question then arises as to "why" He perform these signs? What was their purpose?

THE SIGNS WERE TO CAUSE BELIEF IN HIM

The Apostle John testified as to why he recorded Jesus' miracles in his written gospel. He wrote the following.

> Jesus performed many other signs in the presence of his disciples, which are not recorded in this book. But these are written that you may believe that Jesus is the Messiah, the Son of God, and that by believing you may have life in his name (John 20:30,31 NIV).

According to John, Jesus' miracles were signs to the people that He was indeed the person whom He claimed to be. They were specifically performed, as well as recorded, to cause belief in Him.

THE MIRACLES TESTIFIED TO JESUS' IDENTITY

Thus, the miracles of Jesus were done as a testimony to the His identity. We find that these signs that Jesus performed convinced many that He was the Messiah. John writes.

> Now when he was in Jerusalem at the Passover Feast, many believed in his name when they saw the signs that he was doing (John 2:23 ESV).

Many people believed in Jesus as the Messiah after seeing the miraculous signs that He performed in their presence.

SOME DOUBTED THE MIRACLES WHICH JESUS PERFORMED

Yet even with all these miraculous signs, there were some who doubted.

We read of the following response when Jesus was speaking to the multitudes.

> "Father, glorify Your name." Then a voice came from heaven, saying, "I have both glorified it and will glorify it again." Therefore the people who stood by and heard it said that it had thundered. Others said, "An angel has spoken to Him" (John 12:28,29 NKJV).

Though it was actually the voice of God the Father who spoke, many believed they only heard thunder.

SOME DIDN'T BELIEVE THAT CHRIST HAD RISEN

After Jesus' resurrection, there were still some who did not believe that He had actually risen from the dead. We read of this in Matthew.

> When they saw Him, they worshiped Him; but some doubted (Matthew 28:17 NKJV).

Consequently, the evidence of Jesus' miracles did not cause everyone to believe. There were still people who rejected Him in spite of the overwhelming evidence.

AN IMPORTANT LESSON LEARNED: MIRACLES WILL NOT CONVINCE EVERYONE

This teaches us an important lesson. No amount of evidence will convince someone who does not wish to be convinced. Jesus testified to that fact when He compared the reasons the religious leaders rejected Him and John the Baptist. We read Him saying the following.

> For John the Baptist didn't drink wine and he often fasted, and you say, 'He's demon possessed.' And I, the Son of Man, feast and drink, and you say, 'He's a glutton and a drunkard, and a friend of the worst sort of sinners!' But wisdom is shown to be right by what results from it" (Matthew 11:18,19 NLT).

John the Baptist lived without worldly comforts. The people didn't believe his message because of his lifestyle of self-denial. Jesus ate and drank with people. He was rejected because He was eating and drinking! Unbelief is never satisfied.

Therefore, while the miracles of Jesus were convincing evidence that He was the One whom He claimed to be, there were still people who did not believe in Him. However, this occurred in spite of the evidence—not because of it.

SUMMARY TO QUESTION 29
WHAT WAS THE PURPOSE OF JESUS' MIRACLES?

The miracles of Jesus Christ were performed as signs to testify to His unique identity as the Messiah—the One sent from God. Indeed, only God could perform such miracles as Jesus did. By doing things on a scale that nobody else has ever done, including God's own prophets, Jesus set Himself apart from anyone else who has ever lived. His miracles left no doubt as to who He was.

Although the signs convinced many, there were still some who doubted. We discover that it was not so much that they could not believe in Jesus' signs, as they would not believe. These chose to ignore the evidence.

Jesus emphasized this in His illustration of why He and John the Baptist were rejected. John was rejected because he lived in self-denial while Jesus was rejected because He did not live a life of self-denial!

It illustrates the truth that those who do not wish to believe in Jesus will always find an excuse. However, no excuse will be accepted on Judgment Day. Jesus miracles made His identity clear to all.

QUESTION 30

Why Should Anyone Believe In The Miracles Of Jesus?

There is no doubt that the New Testament emphasizes the miraculous signs that Jesus Christ performed. The Bible says that they were given to demonstrate that He was the long-awaited Messiah. Spectacular miracles are indeed attributed to Jesus—signs that nobody has been able to do before or since.

However, since the time of Christ, there have been many people who have denied His miracles. For whatever reason, they have not believed the New Testament's account of His supernatural works.

The people in Jesus' day, however, had a chance to witness firsthand whether or not He performed miraculous deeds. The following are some of the reasons as to why the miracles attributed to Jesus should be believed.

1. THERE WAS A SUFFICIENT NUMBER OF MIRACLES

First, the number of miracles Jesus performed was sufficient for honest inquirers to believe in them. The four gospels record Jesus performing about thirty-five separate miracles. Most of the miracles that Jesus performed are recorded in more than one gospel. Two of His miracles, the feeding of the five thousand, and His resurrection from the dead, are found in all four gospels.

2. JESUS DID MANY MORE MIRACLES THAN ARE RECORDED IN THE GOSPELS

In addition, each gospel writer says that Jesus performed many more miracles than they recorded. We can make the following observations.

THE TESTIMONY OF MATTHEW

Matthew writes about how Jesus cured every disease and sickness with which He came into contact with.

> Jesus went throughout Galilee, teaching in their synagogues and proclaiming the good news of the kingdom and curing every disease and every sickness among the people (Matthew 4:23 NRSV).

There was no disease or illness which the Lord could not cure!

MARK

Mark noted a number of miracles Jesus performed. He said that everyone who came to Jesus was cured of their sicknesses.

> And wherever he went—into villages, towns or countryside—they placed the sick in the marketplaces. They begged him to let them touch even the edge of his cloak, and all who touched it were healed (Mark 6:56 NIV).

According to Mark, Jesus did miracles wherever He went.

LUKE

In his gospel, Luke also recorded how Jesus healed many people without giving the specifics. He wrote the following.

> Everyone was trying to touch Jesus, because power was going out from him and healing them all (Luke 6:19 CEV).

Again, we have the testimony of His many miracles.

JOHN

John wrote about many miracles of Jesus, that He too did not record. Indeed, he said that the things he did write about Jesus were only selective of the signs that He performed. John wrote.

> Jesus' disciples saw him do many other miraculous signs besides the ones recorded in this book (John 20:30 NLT).

Consequently, each of the four gospel writers makes it clear that Jesus performed many more miracles than they record. The vast number of miracles in which Jesus performed demonstrates that they were a regular part of His ministry.

3. THE MIRACLES WERE OF A SUFFICIENT VARIETY

The miracles of Jesus were also of a sufficient variety to demonstrate that He had miraculous power. Indeed, of the specific miracles recorded in the four gospels, we find the following: seventeen were bodily cures, six were healing of demonic possession, nine were miracles of nature, and there were three occasions where He raised someone from the dead.

THERE WERE VARIOUS ILLNESSES HEALED

Of the seventeen specific bodily healing miracles that are recorded in the four gospels there is a variety of different illnesses that Jesus healed. These include: leprosy, paralysis, fever, shriveled limbs, an amputated ear, blindness, deafness, muteness, and blood hemorrhaging.

In other words, Jesus was not limited in the types of healing He could perform. Indeed, He healed every type of malady in which He came into contact with.

HE HAS ULTIMATE AUTHORITY OVER LIFE AND DEATH

The gospels record that Jesus Christ also had the authority over life and death. The Bible records three specific cases of Jesus bringing a dead person back to life. They include: Jairus' daughter who had just died (Matthew 9:18-26), the widow of Nain's son who was in the coffin (Luke 7:11-15), and Lazarus who had been in the tomb for four days (John 11).

Hence, in these examples, Jesus showed His control over the three stages of death—those who had just died, those who were going to be buried, and those who were already in the tomb. The emphasis is that Jesus is Lord of all.

4. THE MIRACLES COVERED ALL POSSIBLE AREAS OF AUTHORITY

We find Jesus' authority as "Lord of all" further illustrated. As the Son of God, Jesus exercised authority over all realms.

For example, the Gospel of Matthew, in the eighth and ninth chapter, relates ten different areas over which Jesus demonstrated His authority. The point of recording these various miracles is to show that Jesus is Lord of every realm imaginable—He is Lord of all! The evidence is as follows.

MIRACLE NUMBER 1: JESUS IS LORD OVER INCURABLE DISEASE

After delivering the Sermon on the Mount, Jesus came down from the mountain and reached out to a man who was in a hopeless state—one who had contracted the dreaded skin disease of leprosy. At this time there was no known cure for it.

Therefore, a leper was considered to be one of the living dead. However, Jesus had compassion on this particular man and healed him instantaneously. Matthew records it this way.

> When Jesus came down from the mountainside, large crowds followed him. A man with leprosy came and knelt before him and said, "Lord, if you are willing, you can make me clean." Jesus reached out his hand and touched the man. "I

am willing," he said. "Be clean!" Immediately he was cleansed of his leprosy (Matthew 8:1-3 NIV).

In this instance, Jesus demonstrated authority over the realm of incurable disease.

We should also note that when Jesus spoke the words, this leper was cured immediately. The Bible does not tell the stage of this man's leprosy—it is possible that he may have already lost portions of his body to the disease. Whatever the case may be, when Jesus spoke to him, his health was restored completely and instantly. Miraculously, this individual had his life back. Consequently, this former leper could return to his to his family, as well as to the synagogue.

MIRACLE NUMBER 2: JESUS IS LORD OVER SPACE AND TIME

Jesus Christ also had the ability to heal someone without being physically present. A Roman centurion approached Jesus on behalf of his paralyzed servant. The centurion's faith was such that he believed the servant would be healed—if Jesus merely gave the word. In other words, there was no need for His actual presence. Jesus marveled at the man's faith. Matthew records what occurred at this particular episode.

> When Jesus heard this, he was so surprised that he turned and said to the crowd following him, "I tell you that in all of Israel I've never found anyone with this much faith! Many people will come from everywhere to enjoy the feast in the kingdom of heaven with Abraham, Isaac, and Jacob. But the ones who should have been in the kingdom will be thrown out into the dark. They will cry and grit their teeth in pain." Then Jesus said to the officer, "You may go home now. Your faith has made it happen" (Matthew 8:10-13 CEV).

Matthew then records that the servant of the centurion was indeed healed. Therefore, Jesus exhibited power to heal when He was not physically present—not even near the afflicted person! This demonstrates that He is Lord of space and time.

MIRACLE NUMBER 3: JESUS IS LORD OVER THE SABBATH (MAKING HIMSELF EQUAL WITH GOD)

Next, we are told that Jesus healed the mother-in-law of Simon Peter.

> Now when Jesus entered Peter's house, he saw his mother-in-law lying down, sick with a fever. He touched her hand, and the fever left her. Then she got up and began to serve them (Matthew 8:14.15 NET).

From the gospel of Mark, we learn that this took place on the Sabbath day.

> Now as soon as they left the synagogue, they entered Simon and Andrew's house, with James and John. Simon's mother-in-law was lying down, sick with a fever, so they spoke to Jesus at once about her. He came and raised her up by gently taking her hand. Then the fever left her and she began to serve them (Mark 1:29-31 NET).

Notice that Jesus performed this miracle after leaving the synagogue. This would have been for the Sabbath service. Therefore, He healed Peter's mother-in-law while it was still the day of the Sabbath.

The Jews believed that only God was allowed to work on the Sabbath day. Therefore, Jesus, by performing this miracle on the Sabbath was making Himself equal to God.

MIRACLE NUMBER 4: JESUS IS LORD OVER NATURE

Jesus Christ is not only the Lord over disease, and over the Sabbath, He is also the Lord over nature. When Jesus and His disciples were sailing on the Sea of Galilee, the gospels record an incident where a great storm arose which covered their boat with the water from the waves. The Bible tells us that Jesus then calmed the storm.

> So the disciples came and woke Him up, saying, "Lord, save us! We're going to die!" But He said to them, "Why are you

fearful, you of little faith?" Then He got up and rebuked the winds and the sea. And there was a great calm. The men were amazed and asked, "What kind of man is this? — even the winds and the sea obey Him!" (Matthew 8:25-27 HCSB).

When He calmed this raging storm, Jesus displayed His authority over nature— the realm of the visible world. He is Lord over it.

MIRACLE NUMBER 5: HE IS LORD OVER THE SUPERNATURAL REALM

As they completed this boat trip, we find that Jesus also had authority over the supernatural realm—the realm where unseen spirits exist.

The Bible says that after they got out of the boat, Jesus met two demon-possessed men who were terrorizing the countryside. When Jesus approached they cried out for His help.

> Suddenly they shouted, "Jesus, Son of God, what do you want with us? Have you come to punish us before our time?" (Matthew 8:29 CEV).

Jesus cast out demons into a herd of swine and the two men returned to normal. By doing this, Jesus showed authority in the area of the supernatural—the invisible realm.

Therefore, in one short boat trip on the Sea of Galilee, Jesus showed His authority over both the visible and invisible realm!

MIRACLE NUMBER 6: JESUS HAS AUTHORITY TO FORGIVE SINS

This account is found in Matthew 9:1-8. When Jesus healed a paralyzed man at Capernaum, He claimed that His authority extended to the forgiveness of sins. The Bible records the following as having happened.

> Just then some men brought to Him a paralytic lying on a mat. Seeing their faith, Jesus told the paralytic, "Have courage, son, your sins are forgiven" (Matthew 9:2 HCSB).

Only God can forgive sins—because all sin is ultimately committed against Him. By claiming the ability to forgive sins that were committed against God, Jesus made Himself equal with God. As we have seen, Jesus did not merely make claims, He backed them up with convincing evidence.

MIRACLE NUMBER 7: JESUS HEALS A HEMORRHAGING WOMAN (ANOTHER INCURABLE DISEASE)

While on His way to heal the daughter of a particular ruler, Jesus healed a woman who was hemorrhaging. Apart from the physical problems, this bleeding would have caused the woman a number of other problems. First, she would have been in a constant condition of ceremonial uncleanness (see Leviticus 15:25-33). Consequently, she could not worship in the synagogue; neither could she could have normal social relationships. In sum, under Jewish law, anyone who touched her also became unclean. Therefore, the woman had been treated almost as severely as a leper.

Like the synagogue ruler, this woman also sought out Jesus.

> And behold, a woman who had suffered from a discharge of blood for twelve years came up behind him and touched the fringe of his garment, for she said to herself, "If I only touch his garment, I will be made well." Jesus turned, and seeing her he said, "Take heart, daughter; your faith has made you well." And instantly the woman was made well (Matthew 8:20-22 ESV).

This particular miracle demonstrated that Jesus could heal an incurable female ailment.

MIRACLE NUMBER 8: HE IS LORD OVER LIFE AND DEATH

After the healing of this woman, we discover that Jesus demonstrated His authority was over life and death.

> While Jesus was still speaking, an official came and knelt in front of him. The man said, "My daughter has just now died! Please come and place your hand on her. Then she will live again." When Jesus went into the home of the official and saw the musicians and the crowd of mourners, he said, "Get out of here! The little girl isn't dead. She is just asleep." Everyone started laughing at Jesus. But after the crowd had been sent out of the house, Jesus went to the girl's bedside. He took her by the hand and helped her up (Matthew 9:18,23-25 CEV).

Even death was subject to His authority.

MIRACLE NUMBER 9: JESUS GIVES SIGHT TO THE BLIND

We also find that Jesus healed the blind.

> And as Jesus passed on from there, two blind men followed him, crying aloud, "Have mercy on us, Son of David." When he entered the house, the blind men came to him, and Jesus said to them, "Do you believe that I am able to do this?" They said to him, "Yes, Lord." Then he touched their eyes, saying, "According to your faith be it done to you." And their eyes were opened (Matthew 9:27-30 ESV).

Interestingly, we should note that they could see spiritually before they could see physically! They recognized that Jesus was the "Son of David" —the Messiah. They knew the genuine Messiah would be a miracle-worker. This would include opening the eyes of the blind.

MIRACLE NUMBER 10: JESUS IS LORD OVER THE NATURAL REALM AND THE SUPERNATURAL AT THE SAME TIME

The last miracle recorded in these two chapters consists of a man who had problems in both the natural and supernatural realm. Jesus had no problem healing him. Matthew writes.

> Just as they were going out, a demon-possessed man who was unable to speak was brought to Him. When the demon had been driven out, the man spoke. And the crowds were amazed, saying, "Nothing like this has ever been seen in Israel!" But the Pharisees said, "He drives out demons by the ruler of the demons!" (Matthew 9:32-34 HCSB).

Though this man was both demon-possessed and mute, Jesus had no difficulty dealing with both realms simultaneously.

CONCLUSION: JESUS SHOWED AUTHORITY IN EVERY CONCEIVABLE AREA

Therefore, in these two chapters in Matthew Jesus' miracles include the following.

1. Authority over incurable disease.

2. Being able to heal without being physically present.

3. Authority over the Sabbath.

4. Authority over nature.

5. Authority over the supernatural realm.

6. Authority over sins.

7. Authority over another incurable disease

8. Authority over life and death.

9. Authority over blindness

10. Authority over the natural and supernatural realm at the same time.

These ten specific miracles, recorded in these two chapters, prove convincingly that Jesus is Lord of all!

5. THE MIRACLES WERE DONE PUBLICLY AND WERE WELL-KNOWN

Another important fact concerning the miracles of Jesus is that they were done publicly. The Apostle Paul would later emphasize this when he spoke to a particular ruler.

> But Paul replied, "I'm not out of my mind, most excellent Festus. On the contrary, I'm speaking words of truth and good judgment. For the king knows about these matters. It is to him I am actually speaking boldly. For I am convinced that none of these things escapes his notice, since this was not done in a corner (Acts 26:25,26 HCSB).

The facts concerning the miracles of Jesus Christ were obviously well-known. If not, Paul could not make such a statement.

Indeed, when Jesus rose on Easter Sunday, He walked, supernaturally unrecognized, with two disciples on the road to Emmaus. When Jesus asked them what they were talking about, He received the following response.

> The one named Cleopas answered Him, "Are You the only visitor in Jerusalem who doesn't know the things that happened there in these days?" (Luke 24:18 HCSB).

Cleopas could not believe that this stranger would even ask the question. There is only one subject that everyone was talking about—Jesus! The events concerning the life and death of Jesus Christ were well-known to everyone.

6. THEY WERE DONE IN A STRATEGIC LOCATION

There is something else about Jesus' miracles which should be appreciated. The land of Israel was a strategic geographic place in the Roman Empire. Indeed, it was in the middle of a great crossroads where a large amount of travel occurred. This is the spot where Jesus performed His miraculous deeds—not on some barren fringe of the empire where no one could observe them. In other words, He performed His miracles where the maximum number of people could see for themselves if they were genuine.

7. THEY WERE PERFORMED BEFORE LARGE CROWDS

When Jesus performed His miracles, it was often done in the presence of the huge crowds. In fact, some passages emphasize that multitudes, even entire cities, saw the miracles of Jesus. We read in Matthew.

> Then great multitudes came to Him, having with them the lame, blind, mute, maimed, and many others; and they laid them down at Jesus' feet, and He healed them. So the multitude marveled when they saw the mute speaking, the maimed made whole, the lame walking, and the blind seeing; and they glorified the God of Israel (Matthew 15:30,31 NKJV).

Therefore, we find that the miracles happened in front of large crowds—as well as in a number of different places.

In addition, Matthew wrote of another occasion where large crowds followed Jesus. He wrote the following.

> When Jesus finished teaching, he left Galilee and went to the part of Judea that is east of the Jordan River. Large crowds followed him, and he healed their sick people (Matthew 19:1,2 CEV).

There had to be a reason why large crowds would follow Jesus everywhere. The gospels say it was because He was healing everyone who had a disease or illness!

Mark records that the entire city of Capernaum came out to see Jesus heal. He said Jesus healed all who came to Him.

> That evening after sunset the people brought to Jesus all the sick and demon-possessed. The whole town gathered at

the door, and Jesus healed many who had various diseases. He also drove out many demons, but he would not let the demons speak because they knew who he was (Mark 1:32-34 NIV).

Mark too testified that very large crowds followed Jesus wherever He went. He wrote the following to his readers.

> They crossed the sea, came to shore at Gennesaret, and anchored there. As soon as they stepped out of the boat, the people recognized Jesus. They ran all over the countryside and began to carry the sick on cots to any place where they heard he was. Whenever he would go into villages, cities, or farms, people would put their sick in the marketplaces. They begged him to let them touch the edge of his clothes. Everyone who touched his clothes was made well (Mark 6:53-56 God's Word).

The crowds came out to see Jesus because they knew He had the ability to heal every disease.

Luke also speaks of a great number of people being healed by Jesus. He gave the following description of the ministry of Jesus.

> When they came down the slopes of the mountain, the disciples stood with Jesus on a large, level area, surrounded by many of his followers and by the crowds. There were people from all over Judea and from Jerusalem and from as far north as the seacoasts of Tyre and Sidon. They had come to hear him and to be healed, and Jesus cast out many evil spirits. Everyone was trying to touch him, because healing power went out from him, and they were all cured (Luke 6:17-19 NLT).

Therefore, we have the consistent testimony of the gospel writers that Jesus healed large numbers of people wherever He went.

8. THEY DID NOT OCCUR IN ONE SPECIAL PLACE

This brings us to our next point. The ability of Jesus Christ to perform miracles went with Him wherever He went. Whether it was on the Sea of Galilee, in the city of Jerusalem, or in the town of Jericho, the miracle power was always present with Him.

In other words, there was no staging area where Jesus brought those who needed healing. Consequently, there was no way in which His followers could control the event or the outcome.

9. THERE WAS NO SPECIAL TIME OF DAY WHEN THEY WERE DONE

We also find that His miraculous deeds were performed at all times of the day—morning, noon, and night, and all seasons of the year—fall, winter, spring, and summer. There was nothing hindering the miracle power of Jesus.

We find Jesus walking on the water in the early morning hours, healing the servant's ear in the Garden of Gethsemane at night, and healing the infirmed in the temple during the day. There were no limitations on when, where, or how, He would heal.

10. THEY WERE PERFORMED BEFORE GENTILES

The miracles of Jesus Christ were not limited to His countrymen—the Jews. Indeed, we also find the Lord Jesus doing miracles for Gentiles as well (Mark 7:24-30; John 4:46-53).

These people were not looking for a Jewish Messiah. Yet Jesus also performed miracles on their behalf. This demonstrates that He is indeed the Savior of all humanity.

11. THEY WERE DONE WITHOUT PROPS

Jesus' miracles were performed without any props. There were no devices, as other religious figures have used, that helped Him when

He performed His miraculous deeds. In fact, many times Jesus merely spoke the word, and the miracle occurred. This demonstrated the authority which He had.

12. THE MIRACLES WERE DONE WITH RESTRAINT

Whenever Jesus performed a miracle, it was always done for a specific purpose. Indeed, the miracles were performed for two basic reasons—as signs to testify of God's existence and power, or to meet a specific need. They were never performed as a sideshow, or to merely attract attention.

For example, when Jesus was being tempted by the devil, He refused to use His miraculous powers to show off. The devil wanted Jesus to throw Himself down from the pinnacle of the temple and let the angels miraculously save Him. Yet, Jesus would not stoop to this type of supernatural sideshow. His miracles were done with restraint and always for a definite purpose.

13. JESUS DID ONLY BENEFICIAL MIRACLES

With only two exceptions, the cursing of the fig tree and casting of the demons into the herd of swine, the miracles of Jesus were curative in nature. They were done to help people—not to curse His enemies.

When two of Jesus' disciples wanted Him to destroy a Samaritan village by fire we find that they were rebuked. We read in Luke.

> When James and John heard about it, they said to Jesus, "Lord, should we order down fire from heaven to burn them up?" But Jesus turned and rebuked them (Luke 9:54,55 NLT).

The miraculous power of Jesus was never done vindictively, or in reaction to what someone said or did to Him.

14. THEY WERE NOT DONE FOR HIS OWN ADVANTAGE

Jesus' miracles were never done in His own interest but always in the interest of others.

For example, during His temptation by the devil, Christ would not turn stones into bread for Himself to eat. However, on another occasion, He multiplied the fish and bread for the five thousand—so they could eat something when they were hungry. He was always thinking of others.

In another instance, when Peter tried to stop Jesus' arrest in Gethsemane, Jesus corrected His well-intentioned sword play. He told Peter that it was well within His capability to perform a miracle if necessary.

> Then Jesus said to him, "Put your sword away! All who use a sword will be killed by a sword. Don't you think that I could call on my Father to send more than twelve legions of angels to help me now? (Matthew 26:52,53 God's Word).

Jesus did not stop His own arrest by performing some miracle—though He made it clear that He could have done this.

15. THEY MET GENUINE HUMAN NEEDS

Jesus performed miracles to meet real human needs—not merely to draw a large crowd. For example, when people were in a desert place and needed food, Jesus miraculously provided the food. The miracle met the particular need of the people at that time. In fact, we find that each miracle of Jesus was performed either as a sign of His authority, or to meet a genuine need. They were never performed as a sideshow or to attract attention.

16. THEY ARE IN CONTRAST TO THE MIRACLES IN APOCRYPHAL GOSPELS

After the New Testament was completed, a number of untrustworthy accounts about the life of Jesus were composed. Some of these attempted to fill in the gaps of Jesus' missing years. When they are read in comparison to the four gospels, the differences become immediately obvious.

One of these stories has Jesus making birds out of clay, and then making them fly. Another account of the boyhood of Jesus has Him turning the shell of a snail on the Sea of Galilee into the size of Mt. Tabor! Then suddenly the snail went back to its original form.

Some of these later stories paint Jesus as vindictive—one who uses His miraculous power to turn His friends into stones or animals.

In contrast, the four gospels never contain any of this type of nonsensical material. Therefore, we never find the types of miracles that are grotesque or childish. Nothing in the miracles of Jesus leads us to think of the absurd or the bizarre.

17. THEY WERE DONE WITH GREAT EASE

The miracles of Jesus were performed without ceremony or ostentatious behavior—they were done with great ease. There was no strain on Jesus' behalf to bring forth the miracle. He simply spoke and it was done.

Indeed, in almost all of the cases, the miracles occurred immediately after His simple word or gesture. In fact, they were so much a part of His ministry that He could easily move into the area of the miraculous without going through any outward display. This is further demonstration of the unique abilities which He possessed.

18. THEY WERE RECORDED BY EYEWITNESSES

We will emphasize again that the accounts given to us in the four Gospels were from eyewitnesses. The writers Matthew and John were observers of the miracles, and they reported what they saw occur.

Mark and Luke recorded the eyewitness testimony that was given to them. Therefore, the miracles of Jesus are well substantiated by people who were there. John the evangelist would later write the following about what they saw and heard.

> The one who existed from the beginning is the one we have heard and seen. We saw him with our own eyes and touched him with our own hands. He is Jesus Christ, the Word of life (1 John 1:1 NLT).

These miracles were reported by people who were there!

19. THE REACTION TO HIS MIRACLES IS EXACTLY WHAT WE WOULD EXPECT

Our next point is extremely important! The reaction to Jesus' miracles from those who observed them, is exactly what we would expect—if they had occurred. Those who witnessed the miracles of Jesus were not gullible people expecting miraculous deeds.

In fact, it must be recognized that the people living at the time of Jesus were just as skeptical of the miraculous as is modern humanity. When we look at the responses by the people to the miracles of Jesus we discover that this is the case.

THE DISCIPLES WERE THE FIRST UNBELIEVERS OF THE RESURRECTION

For example, the disciples of Jesus were the first unbelievers of His resurrection! When certain women returned from the tomb on Easter Sunday and told them that Jesus had risen, His disciples responded as follows.

> But they did not believe the women, because their words seemed to them like nonsense (Luke 24:11 NIV).

Jesus' disciples have the dubious distinction of being the first doubters of His resurrection from the dead!

QUESTION 30

In another example, when Jesus healed a man who had been blind from birth, the response of the crowd was amazement. The crowd said.

> Since the beginning of time, no one has ever heard of anyone giving sight to a person born blind (John 9:32 God's Word).

They were not used to seeing anything like this. The deed was something extraordinary to them.

THEY HAD NEVER SEEN THIS SORT OF THING BEFORE

On another occasion, Jesus healed a man who had been lame. When He performed this miracle, the people reacted just as we would expect anyone to act who witnessed a similar thing. Mark records the following reaction.

> Immediately he arose, took up the bed, and went out in the presence of them all, so that all were amazed and glorified God, saying, "We never saw anything like this!" (Mark 2:12 NKJV).

Notice the response "We never have seen anything like this!" Their words speak volumes. Miracles were not the norm. Indeed, neither they, nor anyone else, had never seen anything like this before!

On the Sea of Galilee Jesus performed another miracle like no one had ever seen—He calmed the raging wind and the waves in an instant. Luke writes.

> But as they sailed He fell asleep. And a windstorm came down on the lake, and they were filling with water, and were in jeopardy. And they came to Him and awoke Him, saying, "Master, Master, we are perishing!" Then He arose and rebuked the wind and the raging of the water. And they ceased, and there was a calm. But He said to them, "Where is your faith?" And they were afraid, and marveled, saying

to one another, "Who can this be? For He commands even the winds and water, and they obey Him!" (Luke 8:23-25 NKJV).

Again, we have the response of people who were amazed at what they witnessed.

These accounts illustrate that people of the first-century were just as amazed and puzzled as modern humankind would be when it comes to viewing the miraculous first hand. Indeed, their response is exactly what we would expect.

20. THE MIRACLES OF JESUS WERE NEVER DENIED

But we also discover that these same people, even though they were not used to seeing miracles, could not deny these supernatural deeds. The religious rulers, who were enemies of Jesus, sought to discredit Him. Instead of denying His miracles, they attributed them to the power of the devil. We read the following account in Matthew's gospel.

> Then a demon-possessed man, who was both blind and unable to talk, was brought to Jesus. He healed the man so that he could both speak and see. The crowd was amazed. "Could it be that Jesus is the Son of David, the Messiah?" they wondered out loud. But when the Pharisees heard about the miracle, they said, "No wonder he can cast out demons. He gets his power from Satan, the prince of demons" (Matthew 12:22-24 NLT).

The religious leaders, by arguing that Christ's miracles were a work of Satan, were acknowledging the fact that Jesus was a miracle worker. If they could have denied them, they certainly would have. However, the lack of denial on their part shows, from an unfriendly source, that the miracles attributed to Jesus did indeed occur. We can give two illustrations.

EVERYONE WAS AWARE OF HIS MIRACLES

On the Day of Pentecost, after the death, resurrection and ascension of Jesus, Simon Peter, in testifying to Christ's resurrection, appealed to the knowledge of His hearers. He made it clear that they were all aware that Jesus had performed miracles. He said.

> Men of Israel, listen to these words: This Jesus the Nazarene was a man pointed out to you by God with miracles, wonders, and signs that God did among you through Him, just as you yourselves know (Acts 2:22 HCSB).

He stated to that large audience that the miracles of Jesus were something that "they themselves" knew about. The fact that Peter was not immediately shouted down demonstrates that the people knew that he was telling the truth. Multitudes had seen Jesus perform many miracles. The certainty that Jesus performed miracles was never in question. The question was, "How did He do it?"

21. ALL EARLY REPORTS OF JESUS AGREE THAT HE PERFORMED MIRACLES

Another important point is this: for the first five centuries of the Christian era, every account of Jesus, whether coming from a believer or a non-believer, has Jesus performing miracles. No friend or foe, in the early centuries, ever denied His miraculous power. Indeed, they could not deny it—Jesus Christ truly worked miracles!

THE TESTIMONY IS SUFFICIENT

The testimony of Christ's miracles comes from several different groups of witnesses. They include those who benefited from the miracles, those who observed the miracles, and those who were skeptical.

A. THERE WERE THOSE WHO BENEFITED FROM THE MIRACLES

The first group that gives testimony to Jesus' miracles are those who directly benefited from His deeds. They give first-hand testimony with respect to what Jesus did for them.

B. THERE WERE THOSE WHO OBSERVED THE MIRACLES

Next, we have those who were not direct beneficiaries of the miracles but who saw them occur. This would include Jesus' disciples, as well as the multitudes. They too confirm His miracles.

C. THERE WERE THOSE WHO WERE UNBELIEVERS AND SKEPTICS

Not only were the miracles of Jesus done publicly with the multitudes present, they were also performed in front of unbelievers. Among those who watched Jesus perform healings were the unbelieving religious leaders (Matthew 12). They were there to find fault, not to believe. Jesus, therefore, was not merely preaching to the converted.

22. THEY WERE AN ESSENTIAL PART OF HIS MINISTRY

Miracles were not something that was an afterthought in the ministry of Jesus. They are interlocked with everything that He said or did. Certain teachings of Jesus would be meaningless without the miracle connected to it.

For example, the discourse in John's gospel about Jesus being "the bread of life" makes no sense whatsoever without the miracle that explains it. Apart from the miracle of the feeding of the five thousand, this discourse is unexplainable (John 5,6).

23. THE CIRCUMSTANTIAL EVIDENCE FOR JESUS' MIRACLES

We also have circumstantial testimony to Jesus' miracles. This is evidence from sources other than the four gospels. This can be listed as follows.

THE TESTIMONY OF THE BOOK OF ACTS

The Book of Acts testifies to Jesus' miraculous deeds as having literally occurred. On the Day of Pentecost, Peter said the following to the crowd that had gathered.

> Men of Israel, listen to these words: This Jesus the Nazarene was a man pointed out to you by God with miracles, wonders, and signs that God did among you through Him, just as you yourselves know. (Acts 2:22 HCSB).

Peter emphasized that the miracles of Jesus were common knowledge. In fact, they were such common knowledge that he could say to the crowd that Jesus performed miracles "as you yourselves know." He appealed to the knowledge of those who were present. They knew that Jesus was a miracle-worker. In fact, it is likely that some in that very crowd had actually been healed by Jesus.

THE TESTIMONY OF PAUL

The Apostle Paul emphasized that the miracle of the resurrection proved Jesus was whom He claimed to be. He wrote to the Romans.

> From Paul, a servant of Christ Jesus. God chose me to be an apostle, and he appointed me to preach the good news that he promised long ago by what his prophets said in the holy Scriptures. This good news is about his Son, our Lord Jesus Christ! As a human, he was from the family of David. But the Holy Spirit proved that Jesus is the powerful Son of God, because he was raised from death (Romans 1:1-4 CEV).

His resurrection proved His identity as God the Son. It separated Him from all other human beings before or since.

The New English Translation puts it this way.

> From Paul, a slave of Christ Jesus, called to be an apostle, set apart for the gospel of God that he promised beforehand through his prophets in the holy scriptures, concerning his Son who was a descendant of David with respect to the flesh, who was appointed the Son-of-God-in-power according to the Holy Spirit by the resurrection from the dead, Jesus Christ our Lord (Romans 1:1-4 NET).

Jesus was appointed the Son-of-God-in-power by coming back from the dead.

24. MIRACLES BY JESUS' DISCIPLES WHEN HE WAS STILL ON EARTH

Jesus' disciples also performed miracles. This includes miracles during the time of His public ministry, as well as after His ascension into heaven. While Jesus was here on earth, He gave His own disciples the power to perform miracles. Matthew records Jesus sending out His disciples with the same miraculous power that He had.

> Jesus called together his twelve disciples. He gave them the power to force out evil spirits and to heal every kind of disease and sickness (Matthew 10:1 CEV).

They were given the ability to do the same miraculous signs as their Lord. They performed these deeds to testify to Jesus' identity.

THERE WERE MIRACLES BY THE DISCIPLES AFTER JESUS HAD ASCENDED

After Jesus ascended into heaven, the disciples of Jesus still had the ability to perform miracles. The Book of Acts records some of their miracles which were done through the authority of Jesus. When Peter saw a lame man at the temple he said.

> "I don't have any money, but I'll give you what I do have. Through the power of Jesus Christ from Nazareth, walk!" Peter took hold of the man's right hand and began to help him up. Immediately, the man's feet and ankles became strong. Springing to his feet, he stood up and started to walk. He went with Peter and John into the temple courtyard. The man was walking, jumping, and praising God (Acts 3:6-8 God's Word).

After Peter healed this man, the religious leaders made the following admission about the fact that this man had been healed.

"What should we do with these men?" they asked each other. "We can't deny they have done a miraculous sign, and everybody in Jerusalem knows about it" (Acts 4:16 NLT).

Even the miracles of the apostles were undeniable. The religious leaders had to admit that they had the same miraculous ability as Jesus.

CONCLUSION: JESUS CHRIST WAS A MIRACLE-WORKER

The evidence is loud and clear. Jesus Christ worked miracles. Indeed, this is a fact which cannot be denied!

SUMMARY TO QUESTION 30
WHY SHOULD ANYONE BELIEVE IN THE MIRACLES OF JESUS?

There are a number of reasons as to why we should believe that the miracles attributed to Jesus actually occurred. We can summarize them as follows.

To begin with, there were a sufficient number of them. Indeed, the gospels list about thirty-five separate miracles which Jesus performed. They were also of a sufficient variety. He could heal any disease, any ailment. Nothing was too difficult for Him. The miracles of Jesus covered all possible areas of authority—His miracles were in the realm of nature as well as in the area of the unseen supernatural world.

These signs were also done publicly and in front of large crowds. Jesus went to where the people were rather than expecting them to come to Him. Thus, there was no special place in which the miracles occurred.

In addition, His miracle power went with Him wherever He went. Neither was there a special time when these miracles were performed. Wherever He went, whenever it was necessary, Jesus could perform a miracle. These signs were performed in front of Gentiles as well as Jews.

The miracles were beneficial to humanity. They met real needs. They were not done for Jesus' own advantage.

It is also important to note that eyewitnesses recorded the miracles. Those who observed them had same reaction as we would have. They were shocked and amazed by what they saw. Furthermore, His contemporaries never denied the miracles attributed to Jesus. This includes unbelievers as well.

There is also circumstantial evidence that Jesus performed miracles. In the Book of Acts, we have the testimony that Jesus performed miracles while here on earth. The Apostle Paul also confirmed the fact that Jesus did miracles.

In addition, Jesus' disciples had the ability to perform miracles. This ability was with them during Jesus' public ministry, as well as after His ascension.

The totality of the evidence shows that Jesus was indeed a worker of miracles. He did signs that only someone can perform if the power of God is with them.

QUESTION 31

What Objections Have Been Made To Jesus' Miracles?

Historically there have been many objections to Jesus' miracles. For a number of reasons, people have denied the miracles the New Testament attributes to Him. They include the following objections.

OBJECTION 1: MIRACLES, BY DEFINITION, ARE IMPOSSIBLE

One of the popular ways to deny miracles is simply to define them out the realm of possibility. Many people state as a fact that the idea of a miracle is impossibility. End of discussion. Everyone knows that unchangeable laws of cause and effect govern the universe. These laws have always existed, and they will always continue to exist. Therefore, miracles, by definition, are impossible.

RESPONSE

Of course, the problem with that position is that only God could know whether miracles are possible or not. Therefore, the denial of the possibility of miracles is something that is beyond the ability of humans.

THE ILLUSTRATION OF THE PLATYPUS

The fallacy of the outright rejection of the miraculous can be found in the illustration of the platypus. When explorers first came to eastern Australia, they came across a creature that should not have existed. It was a furry, semi-aquatic, egg-laying mammal with a duck's bill and webbed feet. It was named the platypus. The characteristics of this little rabbit-sized creature were so strange that some people in England considered it a hoax when the skin of a dead platypus was first brought to London.

THE DOUBTS HAD NOTHING TO DO WITH THE EVIDENCE

The reason the existence of the platypus was doubted had nothing to do with the evidence. For the evidence, as strange as it was, clearly pointed to the existence of this egg-laying mammal. The rejection came because it did not fit the scientist's particular view of the world of nature. Since no mammal was known to have laid eggs, zoologists were certain this creature could not exist. Eventually, all scientists came around to believe the platypus did exist—with all its bizarre characteristics.

THE SAME MISCONCEPTION IS WITH US TODAY

Since no one had ever seen a creature like this before, people assumed that it could not exist. This is the same misconception of many of those who reject miracles—since they have never seen a miracle they assume it cannot happen. Furthermore, no amount of evidence would convince them to change their mind.

Yet the platypus does exist, and miracles did happen—this is what the evidence testifies to. Therefore, we cannot rule out the possibility of miracles ahead of time. Indeed, we must examine the evidence.

OBJECTION 2: THE MIRACLES HAPPENED IN A PRE-SCIENTIFIC AGE

It is alleged that since the miracles recorded in the four gospels occurred some two thousand years ago, they should not be believed. These events took place before the age of modern science when people were ignorant about the way the universe functioned. We now know better. Consequently, the miracles which are attributed to Jesus should be rejected.

RESPONSE

Granted, the miracles of Jesus Christ were recorded before modern times—yet the testimony to their truthfulness remains. The eyewitnesses to the events in the life of Christ were just as skeptical as modern humanity. In addition, as we have mentioned, their reaction to the miraculous was the same as ours would have been—if we had seen the same events which they observed. In other words, they were just as surprised as we would be!

OBJECTION 3: THE MIRACLES WERE SELF-INDUCED

There are those who argue that the healing miracles recorded in the New Testament could have been self-induced. In the first century, before the advent of modern medicine, there was much ignorance regarding disease. Could not one easily argue that the healings of Jesus were self-induced because the illnesses were psychological rather than physical?

RESPONSE

This argument does not make sense for a number of reasons. They are as follows.

THEY ARE BEYOND NATURAL EXPLANATION

To begin with, a study of the Gospel accounts will put that question to rest. The healing miracles of Jesus were of such a nature as to be beyond any natural explanation.

For example, Jesus healed a man who was paralyzed (Mark 2:3-12) and another who was blind from birth (John 9:1-7). Lazarus was dead four days when Jesus brought him back to life (John 11). A young girl who was dead was brought back to life by Jesus (Luke 8:51-56). He healed ten lepers at once (Luke 17:11-19) and healed a man who was a deaf mute (Mark 7:31-37). These miracles were observed and recorded by eyewitnesses.

THEY COULD NOT ALL BE SELF-INDUCED

It stretches beyond the bounds of imagination to think that all these people, including the ones who had been dead, could only be ill in their minds and not in their bodies.

Furthermore, we are never told of Jesus ever refusing to heal a person because of lack of ability on His part. Unless one would want to argue that no legitimate disease was present in the first century, it seems clear that His healings were often and varied enough to prove valid.

OBJECTION 4: WHY AREN'T MIRACLES HAPPENING TODAY?

Another objection, which is similar to an earlier one, is that if miracles occurred long ago, we should expect them to occur today—if indeed they really did occur. Jesus' miracles should be duplicated by His followers today.

RESPONSE

This objection ignores the fact that miracles are found in clusters in Scripture, not on every page. Consequently, miracles were not the norm. Indeed, they only occurred at specific times.

But even if miracles were found on every page, we would say, "So what?" The issue is, "Did they happen in the life and ministry of Jesus as the eyewitnesses testify?" Indeed, it does not necessarily follow that if miracles occurred in biblical times then they must continue to happen today.

OBJECTION 5: THERE IS THE POSSIBILITY OF MISINTERPRETING THE EVENT

This objection deals with the frailty of us as humans. We all know that it is possible to watch an event and describe it in such a way as to misinterpret what actually happened. Since humans sometimes poorly report what they have seen, then why should we believe the biblical account of miracles?

RESPONSE

If we took this objection to its logical fulfillment, then there could be no accurate reporting of any event. All reports would be suspect and nothing could be believed. Yet experience tells us that humans can accurately report on events they witness. The evidence has to be weighed and evaluated for each incident.

EVEN THE UNBELIEVERS RECOGNIZED THE MIRACLES

Furthermore, there were skeptics present at most of Jesus' miracles. They would have been looking for alternative explanations. Yet, they too acknowledged Jesus' miraculous power. This gives further evidence that His miracles actually took place.

OBJECTION 6: THERE ARE CONTRADICTIONS BETWEEN THE ACCOUNTS

Often it is alleged that the gospel accounts of the miraculous deeds of Jesus are so hopelessly contradictory that they should not be believed. Thus, the miracles of Christ should be rejected.

RESPONSE

Yet this is not the case. The fact that there are minor differences in details only shows that the accounts are independent of one another. Indeed, there is agreement between them on the major points. Consequently, this provides another reason as to why Jesus' miraculous deeds should be accepted as actually occurring.

OBJECTION 7: WE FIND MIRACLE REPORTS IN OTHER RELIGIONS

What about the miracles in other religions? Since there are other religions who also report miraculous deeds occurring among them, why should they be rejected and the miracles of Jesus Christ believed?

RESPONSE

Three things should be considered when answering this question.

A. THERE WERE NOT THAT MANY MIRACLES

First, there are not as many miracles in the world religions as some people assume. Indeed, miracles are very rare in the accounts of the major religions of the world. The exception, of course, is the gospel accounts—where miracles are a central part of the message of Jesus Christ.

B. THE SO-CALLED MIRACLES WERE NOT DONE PUBLICLY

The public demonstration of Jesus with respect to His miracles is in contrast to other so-called miracle workers who did their work in private. There is no evidence that any religious leader has done public miracles that were attested to by unbelievers. Jesus, on the other hand, performed His miraculous deeds for all to see. This includes those who did not believe in Him. As we have stressed, even these unbelievers did not deny Jesus' miracles.

THERE IS NO REAL PURPOSE FOR THEM

The miracles attributed to those in other religions are not backed up by eyewitness testimony. Furthermore, they are all too often performed as a sideshow with no direct purpose in mind. Indeed, the so-called miracles of other religions do not touch humanity at its basic needs—as do the miracles recorded in the life and ministry of Jesus. This, and the lack of corroborative testimony to their actually occurring in these other religions, causes them to be rejected.

OBJECTION 8: THEY WERE RECORDED LONG AFTER THE FACT

Often it is objected that the miracles of the New Testament were written long after the events transpired. This gave time for legends to grow about Jesus. Supposedly this makes the miracle accounts untrue.

RESPONSE

This objection is what is untrue. Those who recorded the events were there when they took place! They were eyewitnesses to the miracles in the life of Christ. For example, the Apostle John testified that he wrote about what he personally knew about Jesus' life and ministry.

> The Word that gives life was from the beginning, and this is the one our message is about. Our ears have heard, our own eyes have seen, and our hands touched this Word (1 John 1:1 CEV).

These writers saw the miracles of Jesus with their own eyes.

In addition, they were written and circulated while other people who were familiar with Jesus' life and ministry were still alive. If the New Testament writers exaggerated what had taken place, these people would have corrected the record.

Furthermore, their accounts of what Jesus said and did are consistent with each other. Consequently, there is no reason to believe that their stories grew larger and larger with time.

CONCLUSION: JESUS WORKED MIRACLES

All the evidence we have points to the fact that Jesus Christ did indeed work miracles. Both believers and unbelievers testified to this fact. No one doubted His ability to perform supernatural deeds.

Indeed, the question they asked Jesus was not *if* He performed miracles—rather they wanted to know *how* did He do these supernatural works. The truth of His miracle working ability was beyond all doubt.

SUMMARY TO QUESTION 31
WHAT OBJECTIONS HAVE BEEN MADE TO JESUS MIRACLES?

Whenever the miracles of Jesus Christ are mentioned there are a number of objections that are usually brought up. The main objections can be summed up as follows.

To many, the idea of miracles is simply impossible. Consequently, there is no reason to refute something that everyone knows does not occur.

However, this assumes knowledge that none of us have. Nobody is in a position to say whether miracles can happen—or never have happened.

Another objection concerns the miracle of Jesus being done in a pre-scientific age. This supposedly makes them untrue. However, when they occurred has nothing to do with whether or not they occurred. To determine this, we must look at the evidence, and the evidence says that they did indeed take place. Jesus was a miracle-worker.

Some attempt to argue that the miracles were merely self-induced experiences—not genuine miracles. The problem with this view is that many of the biblical miracles, such as raising people from the dead, cannot be attributed to some mere psychological cause.

The fact they are not happening today has also been raised. Again, this has nothing to do as to whether or not they happened in the past. The evidence must be what determines this.

There is also the objection that the event was not really a miracle but only interpreted as such. Yet this does not take into account the nature of the events, or the eyewitness testimony. Indeed, there can be no purely natural explanation for the miracles of Jesus.

The gospel accounts of the miraculous deeds of Jesus supposedly have contradictions between them. Yet these can be harmonized if one will carefully examine all that is said. Furthermore, a closer examination will show that the sources are independent of one another. This gives us an additional reason to believe their testimony.

The miracles in other religions do not contradict the idea of Jesus' miracles. Indeed, they do not have the same type of attesting evidence as the signs and wonders attributed to Jesus.

Finally, it is objected that they were recorded long after the fact. However, this is untrue. Eyewitnesses testified to the gospel miracles. They wrote and circulated their accounts while other witnesses, both friendly and unfriendly, were still alive.

Consequently, the evidence points to the fact that the Bible is accurate in attributing miracles to Jesus Christ. None of the objections against Jesus' miracles has any merit.

QUESTION 32

Why Did Jesus Speak In Parables?

One of the methods Jesus employed in communicating His message was through parables. A parable is basically an earthly story with a heavenly meaning. When Jesus started telling parables to the people, His disciples asked the obvious question.

> And the disciples came and said to Him, "Why do You speak to them in parables?" (Matthew 13:10 NKJV).

They wanted to know why Jesus resorted to teaching this way.

JESUS GIVES A REVEALING ANSWER TO THEIR QUESTION

Jesus' answer to the question was quite revealing. Matthew records His response.

> He answered, "To you it has been given to know the secrets of the kingdom of heaven, but to them it has not been given. For to those who have, more will be given, and they will have an abundance; but from those who have nothing, even what they have will be taken away. The reason I speak to them in parables is that 'seeing they do not perceive, and hearing they do not listen, nor do they understand.' With them indeed is fulfilled the prophecy of Isaiah that says: 'You will indeed listen, but never understand, and you will indeed look, but

never perceive. For this people's heart has grown dull, and their ears are hard of hearing, and they have shut their eyes; so that they might not look with their eyes, and listen with their ears, and understand with their heart and turn—and I would heal them' (Matthew 13:11-15 NRSV).

Unwillingness on the part of the people to receive Jesus' message of the kingdom of God was the reason that He taught in parables. They heard the truths of the kingdom of God, but they were not understood. It was not because God was hiding the truth from them—it was because they did not want to hear.

THE PEOPLE HAD THE CHANCE TO BELIEVE

These facts points to a great truth. God has given the people every chance to accept the message of Jesus Christ. His ministry was attested by astonishing miracles. He offered the proper credentials as the Messiah, yet they still did not believe in Him. The realities of the kingdom, therefore, were not theirs to know. The people who believed in Jesus as the Messiah would understand the parables. They would comprehend the great truths of the kingdom of God.

THEY ARE TO BE UNDERSTOOD SPIRITUALLY

Some years later the Apostle Paul would echo the same truth. He wrote the following to the people at the church in Corinth.

> No, we speak of God's secret wisdom, a wisdom that has been hidden and that God destined for our glory before time began. None of the rulers of this age understood it, for if they had, they would not have crucified the Lord of glory. However, as it is written: "No eye has seen, no ear has heard, no mind has conceived what God has prepared for those who love him"— but God has revealed it to us by his Spirit. The Spirit searches all things, even the deep things of God. For who among men knows the thoughts of a man except the man's spirit within

him? In the same way no one knows the thoughts of God except the Spirit of God. We have not received the spirit of the world but the Spirit who is from God, that we may understand what God has freely given us. This is what we speak, not in words taught us by human wisdom but in words taught by the Spirit, expressing spiritual truths in spiritual words. The man without the Spirit does not accept the things that come from the Spirit of God, for they are foolishness to him, and he cannot understand them, because they are spiritually discerned (1 Corinthians 2:7-14 NIV).

The spiritual truth that Scripture reveals must be understood spiritually. Indeed, God has given His Holy Spirit to believers so they can discern spiritual truths.

MOST PEOPLE WERE NOT INTERESTED IN THE TRUTH

The truth of God is ultimately to be understood spiritually. The great majority of the people in Jesus' day were not interested in God's truth. Jesus clearly explained this.

> For this reason I speak to them in parables: Although they see they do not see, and although they hear they do not hear nor do they understand (Matthew 13:13 NIV).

Unfortunately, this is still true today. Most people do not want to hear God's truth. God is speaking but they are not listening.

SUMMARY TO QUESTION 32
WHY DID JESUS SPEAK IN PARABLES?

Jesus Christ spoke in parables during His public ministry. These parables are earthly stories with a heavenly meaning. He did so that His disciples would comprehend His teachings and that unbelievers would be without comprehension.

Indeed, those interested in understanding the truth of His message would understand while those not interested would remain without understanding. His message is still clear for anyone who wants to hear it.

QUESTION 33

Did Jesus Know The People Would Reject Him?

When God the Son, Jesus Christ, came to earth, and preached the arrival of the kingdom of God to the nation Israel, His message was rejected. The religious leaders brought Him to Pilate for crucifixion because they believed Him to be a blasphemer. They said.

> The Jews answered him, "We have a law, and according to our law He ought to die, because He made Himself the Son of God" (John 19:7 NKJV).

Although some had believed in Him, the nation as a whole rejected Him. Did Christ know this would occur? Was He aware that His message would not be heeded? If so, then was His offer of a kingdom a legitimate one?

The following points need to be made.

1. JESUS' SUFFERING AND GLORY WERE PREDICTED

The two comings of Christ were predicted in the Old Testament. The prophets spoke of both His suffering and His glory. Peter wrote.

> Some prophets told how kind God would be to you, and they searched hard to find out more about the way you would be saved. The Spirit of Christ was in them and was telling them how Christ would suffer and would

then be given great honor. So they searched to find out exactly who Christ would be and when this would happen (1 Peter 1:10,11 CEV).

At His First Coming, He was to suffer for the sins of the world. Jesus was well aware of what would happen to Him. He knew that His message would be rejected. This was all part of God's eternal plan.

2. JESUS OFTEN SPOKE OF HIS DEATH AND RESURRECTION

At the beginning of His public ministry, Jesus spoke of both His death and resurrection. We read of this in John's gospel.

> "What right do you have to do these things?" the Jewish leaders demanded. "If you have this authority from God, show us a miraculous sign to prove it." "All right," Jesus replied. "Destroy this temple, and in three days I will raise it up." "What!" they exclaimed. "It took forty-six years to build this Temple, and you can do it in three days?" But by "this temple," Jesus meant his body. After he was raised from the dead, the disciples remembered that he had said this. And they believed both Jesus and the Scriptures (John 2:18-22 NLT).

From the very beginning of His public ministry, Jesus was well aware that the people would reject Him. He knew that He would eventually die for the sins of the world.

3. HE MADE A LEGITIMATE OFFER OF A KINGDOM

Does this make His offer of a kingdom illegitimate? No. When Jesus came the first time, He promised the people that God's kingdom would take place—if they believed in Him. Yet, they rejected Him. The Bible says.

> He was in the world, and the world was made through Him, and the world did not know Him (John 1:10 NRSV).

Jesus knew they were going to reject Him. However, that did not make His offer invalid. If the people would have believed in Him, God's kingdom would have been established then and there. The offer was legitimate. But Jesus knew they would not believe.

4. HE HAS PROMISED TO COME AGAIN

Though the rightful King was crucified, Jesus Christ has promised to come again for those who believe in Him. He said to His disciples.

> Let not your heart be troubled; you believe in God, believe also in Me. In My Father's house are many mansions; if it were not so, I would have told you. I go to prepare a place for you. And if I go and prepare a place for you, I will come again and receive you to Myself; that where I am, there you may be also (John 14:1-3 NKJV).

Therefore, the kingdom will indeed be set up—but only when He comes again.

In sum, Jesus knew all along that He would be rejected by the people. He also knew that He would have to die. Yet, as the Bible so clearly tells us, His death was not the end!

SUMMARY TO QUESTION 33
DID JESUS KNOW THE PEOPLE WOULD REJECT HIM?

The people of Jesus' time rejected Him as their Messiah. Jesus knew ahead of time that this would happen. However, this does not make His offer of an immediate kingdom illegitimate. Had the people believed in Him, God's kingdom would have been immediately set up.

Yet, the people chose to reject Him and put Him to death, rather than accept Him as their Messiah. Knowing this, Jesus predicted His death and resurrection from the dead.

He will indeed set up His promised kingdom—when He comes the second time.

QUESTION 34

Was Jesus A Prophet?

A prophet is someone who speaks in the place of somebody else. In the Bible, it is a man or woman who speaks to the people on behalf of the one true God.

The New Testament makes it clear that Jesus Christ was the greatest of all the prophets, or spokesman, which God had sent to the world. Indeed, Jesus was One who spoke to the people on behalf of the true God. We see this demonstrated in a number of ways in the New Testament. The evidence is as follows.

1. JESUS CONFIRMED THAT HE WAS A PROPHET

The gospels confirm that Jesus believed that He was a prophet. Matthew records the following episode in Jesus' hometown of Nazareth.

> And they took offense at him. But Jesus said to them, "Prophets are not without honor except in their own country and in their own house" (Matthew 13:57 NRSV).

Jesus acknowledged that He was a prophet in His hometown. This is despite the fact that His own people rejected Him.

2. THE PEOPLE KNEW HE WAS A PROPHET

The people considered Jesus to be a prophet. When Jesus asked His disciples whom the people thought He was, they made the following reply.

"Well," they replied, "some say John the Baptist, some say Elijah, and others say Jeremiah or one of the other prophets" (Matthew 16:14 NLT).

The people of that day realized that Jesus of Nazareth spoke for God in a unique way.

The crowds in Jerusalem also testified that Jesus was a prophet. They recognized that He was sent from God to speak to them. The Bible says.

> The crowds were saying, "This is the prophet Jesus from Nazareth in Galilee" (Matthew 21:11 NRSV).

Again, Jesus is seen as a prophet by the great crowds.

3. JESUS WAS THE PROPHET MOSES WROTE ABOUT

In the Old Testament, we find that Moses predicted that a prophet like himself would one day come. He wrote.

> The LORD your God will raise up for you a prophet like me from among your own brothers. You must listen to him. This is what you requested from the LORD your God at Horeb on the day of the assembly when you said, 'Let us not continue to hear the voice of the LORD our God or see this great fire any longer, so that we will not die! (Then the LORD said to me, 'They have spoken well. I will raise up for them a prophet like you from among their brothers. I will put My words in his mouth, and he will tell them everything I command him. I will hold accountable whoever does not listen to My words that he speaks in My name' (Deuteronomy 18:15-19 HCSB).

Some people in the crowed thought Jesus could be that prophet which Moses wrote about. We read the following in John's gospel about this perception which the people had.

> When the crowd heard Jesus say this, some of them said, "He must be the Prophet!" (John 7:40 CEV).

It is clear that the crowd recognized that Jesus spoke for God in a unique way.

4. THE WOMAN IN SAMARIA KNEW JESUS WAS A PROPHET

A woman that Jesus met in the city of Samaria perceived Jesus as a prophet. John's gospel records the following.

> "Sir," the woman replied, "I see that You are a prophet" (John 4:19 HCSB).

Jesus told her things about herself that only a prophet of God would know. She recognized His unique calling.

5. THE BLIND MAN THAT JESUS HEALED RECOGNIZED HE WAS A PROPHET

A certain blind man that Jesus healed realized that He was a prophet. The religious leaders questioned him about his miraculous healing. We read about this in John's gospel. The conversation went as follows.

> They asked the man, "What do you say about this one who healed your eyes?" "He is a prophet!" the man told them (John 9:17 CEV).

It was obvious to this man that Jesus was at least a prophet.

6. THE TESTIMONY OF PETER: JESUS WAS THE PROPHET

After Jesus' death, resurrection and ascension, His message began to go out into the entire world through His spokesmen. Simon Peter, one of Jesus disciples, testified that Jesus was indeed the prophet which Moses had written about. After Peter performed a certain miracle, he said the following to the religious authorities.

Moses said, 'The Lord your God will raise up a Prophet like me from among your own people. Listen carefully to everything he tells you' (Acts 3:22 NLT).

Peter publicly testified to the prophetic status of Jesus. He made it clear that Jesus, the One whom had been recently crucified, was the special prophet that God had promised to send into the world.

7. THE MARTYR STEPHEN TESTIFIED TO JESUS' PROPHETIC STATUS

The martyr Stephen also testified that Jesus was "the" prophet. He cited the same passage in the Old Testament that predicted the coming of a special prophet.

> Moses himself told the people of Israel, 'God will raise up a Prophet like me from among your own people' (Acts 7:37 NLT).

Stephen was stoned to death for his testimony of Jesus.

GOD'S FINAL WORD TO HUMANITY IS THROUGH JESUS

Consequently, the New Testament makes it clear that Jesus was a prophet. He was sent from God to speak to the people. However, Jesus was different from all other prophets which came before Him or after Him—in that He was God Himself who became a human being.

The writer to the Hebrews stated it this way.

> Long ago God spoke to the fathers by the prophets at different times and in different ways. (In these last days He has spoken to us by [His] Son, whom He has appointed heir of all things and through whom He made the universe (Hebrews 1:1-2 HCSB).

God has indeed spoken to us through Jesus, His Son.

SUMMARY TO QUESTION 34
WAS JESUS A PROPHET?

The Old Testament predicted that the coming Messiah would be a special prophet. In a unique way, He would be one that would speak to the people from God. The gospels make it clear that Jesus was indeed that particular prophet.

We find a number of different people testifying to the fact that Jesus was indeed a prophet.

There was a certain woman from Samaria who attested that Jesus knew everything about her. She concluded that He was a prophet.

When Jesus healed a man who had been born blind, this person also concluded that Jesus was a prophet of God. Jesus Himself testified to His prophetic status.

The gospels tell us that when the crowds saw the miracles of Jesus they asked the question as to whether He could be that "special prophet" which Moses wrote about.

Simon Peter left no doubt about this. On the Day of Pentecost, when he spoke to the people after Jesus' death, resurrection and ascension, he made it clear that Jesus was indeed the prophet Moses wrote about. Soon thereafter the martyr Stephen testified to the same thing.

Therefore, it is the united testimony of the New Testament that Jesus was a prophet of God—the special prophet whom Moses said would appear.

In sum, God's final word to the human race was through Jesus Christ—as well as the specially chosen prophets which He selected to spread His message once He had ascended into heaven.

QUESTION 35

In What Ways Did Jesus Fulfill The Prophetic Ministry?

From the evidence found in Scripture, we discover that Jesus Christ was a prophet. In other words, He was sent from God to speak to the people.

In the Bible, a prophet had a twofold function. First, they spoke forth the word of God to the people. Second, the prophet would, at times, foretell the future.

Jesus, in His prophetic ministry, fulfilled the role of a prophet in each of these respects. The New Testament says the following about the prophetic ministry of Jesus.

1. JESUS SPOKE GOD'S WORDS

The words of Jesus were prophetic. In other words, He spoke forth God's Word. Matthew wrote of how Jesus taught the people.

> Then he began to teach them by saying (Matthew 5:2 NIV).

Jesus taught the truth of God to the people of His day.

The Bible says that the crowds were amazed at His teaching. At the end of the Sermon on the Mount, Matthew records the following response of the crowd.

When Jesus finished speaking, the crowds were surprised at his teaching. He taught them like someone with authority, and not like their teachers of the Law of Moses (Matthew 7:28,29 CEV).

The people realized that Jesus had unique authority. Indeed, He was in a class by Himself.

2. JESUS' OWN TESTIMONY TO THE POWER OF HIS WORDS

Jesus Himself testified to the power of His words. He made the following claim about them to the multitudes.

> It is the Spirit who gives eternal life. Human effort accomplishes nothing. And the very words I have spoken to you are spirit and life (John 6:63 NLT).

His words were the words of life.

We read in the Book of Revelation that Jesus' voice was loud like a trumpet blast.

> It was the Lord's Day, and I was worshiping in the Spirit. Suddenly, I heard a loud voice behind me, a voice that sounded like a trumpet blast. It said, "Write down what you see, and send it to the seven churches: Ephesus, Smyrna, Pergamum, Thyatira, Sardis, Philadelphia, and Laodicea" (Revelation 1:10,11 NLT).

Jesus' voice spoke powerful words—the words of the Lord.

3. THE EXTENT OF JESUS' PROPHETIC MINISTRY WAS FROM HIS BAPTISM TO THE CROSS

The prophetic ministry of Jesus began at the river Jordan. After His baptism, the Holy Spirit came upon Him. He then began to proclaim the message of God's coming kingdom. The Gospel of Matthew says the following.

QUESTION 35

> Jesus was going all over Galilee, teaching in their synagogues, preaching the good news of the kingdom, and healing every disease and sickness among the people. Then the news about Him spread throughout Syria. So they brought to Him all those who were afflicted, those suffering from various diseases and intense pains, the demon-possessed, the epileptics, and the paralytics. And He healed them. Large crowds followed Him from Galilee, Decapolis, Jerusalem, Judea, and beyond the Jordan (Matthew 4:23-25 HCSB).

His prophetic ministry ended when He offered Himself as a sacrifice for the sins of the world upon Calvary's cross.

4. JESUS, LIKE SOME PROPHETS, PERFORMED MIRACULOUS DEEDS

While not all of God's prophets performed miraculous deeds, many of them did. Jesus performed miracles as part of his prophetic ministry. Jesus said.

> But I have a greater testimony than John's because of the works that the Father has given Me to accomplish. These very works I am doing testify about Me that the Father has sent Me (John 5:36 HCSB).

Jesus compared Himself to John the Baptist. However, He said His testimony was greater than that of John because of the miracles He performed.

In fact, Jesus emphasized that His miraculous deeds demonstrated that He was the One that He claimed to be. Jesus said the following to those who questioned His identity.

> I have told you, and you refused to believe me. The things I do by my Father's authority show who I am (John 10:25 NLT).

The proof of His claims was in His miraculous deeds.

5. THE PEOPLE WERE HELD RESPONSIBLE

Jesus said the people were responsible to believe because they had seen His miracles. John records Jesus saying the following about this.

> If I hadn't done such miraculous signs among them that no one else could do, they would not be counted guilty. But as it is, they saw all that I did and yet hated both of us—me and my Father (John 15:24 NLT).

The fact that these people saw Jesus' signs and wonders made them responsible to act upon what they saw and heard.

On the Day of Pentecost, Peter reminded the people of Jesus miracles. He made the following statement to the crowd.

> Men of Israel, listen to these words: This Jesus the Nazarene was a man pointed out to you by God with miracles, wonders, and signs that God did among you through Him, just as you yourselves know (Acts 2:22 HCSB).

They were familiar with the fact that Jesus was a miracle worker. In fact, Peter said that Christ was a miracle-worker "as you yourselves know."

6. HE WAS A MATCHLESS EXAMPLE

Jesus was a spokesman for God by providing a matchless example. In fact, the Lord said that His behavior was to serve as an example for others to follow.

> For I have given you an example, that you should do as I have done to you (John 13:15 NKJV).

Jesus is our example.

Peter would later write about the example that Jesus left for us. He put it this way.

After all, God chose you to suffer as you follow in the footsteps of Christ, who set an example by suffering for you. Christ did not sin or ever tell a lie (1 Peter 2:21-22 CEV).

We are to behave like Christ. He has given us the pattern which we are to follow.

7. HE WAS SILENT WHEN NECESSARY

Jesus not only spoke forth the Word of God—He was also silent when necessary. Pontius Pilate attempted to have Jesus respond to the charges that were placed against Him.

> "Don't you hear their many charges against you?" Pilate demanded (Matthew 27:13 NLT).

Jesus heard the charges, yet He did not respond to Pilate. Rather, Jesus remained silent. We also read in Matthew's gospel.

> But Jesus did not say anything, and the governor was greatly amazed (Matthew 27:14 CEV).

Later, Peter wrote about this silence of Jesus in the face of the false accusations made against Him.

> Although he was abused, he never tried to get even. And when he suffered, he made no threats. Instead, he had faith in God, who judges fairly (1 Peter 2:23 CEV).

This is another illustration of how we are to behave. Instead of always trying to defend ourselves against false accusations, we should allow the Lord to be our defender.

8. JESUS SENT THE HOLY SPIRIT TO TESTIFY OF HIMSELF

Jesus also fulfilled the role of a prophet by sending the Holy Spirit. He made the following promise to His disciples.

> But the Counselor, the Holy Spirit and the Father will send Him in My name and will teach you all things and remind you of everything I have told you (John 14:26 God's Word).

The Holy Spirit, sent from Jesus, will testify to Jesus' words and deeds.

Jesus made a further promise about the role of the Spirit. John also records Jesus' words.

> I will send you the Spirit who comes from the Father and shows what is true. The Spirit will help you and will tell you about me (John 15:26 CEV).

Today, the Holy Spirit carries on the prophetic ministry of Jesus Christ. He is the One who proclaims the word of Christ by speaking through the believers.

In sum, we find that Jesus Christ was a prophet who fulfilled the prophetic ministry that the Lord had given Him. This took place from the time of His baptism until His final words on the cross.

SUMMARY TO QUESTION 35
IN WHAT WAYS DID JESUS FULFILL THE PROPHETIC MINISTRY?

Jesus Christ was a prophet. In other words, He was God's spokesmen to the people. Jesus fulfilled the prophetic ministry in a number of ways.

As a prophet, He publicly spoke the words of God to the people. He was thus God's representative on the earth.

His prophetic ministry extended from the time of His baptism at the Jordan River, until He died on Calvary's cross. In other words, from the moment He appeared publicly, until His death, He was God's spokesman to the world.

Unlike some prophets, Jesus also performed miraculous deeds. While other prophets performed miracles, Jesus' miracles were unique. Indeed, He did things nobody else has ever done before or since.

In addition, His words and His life give a matchless example to all. We are to mold our lives after His.

There is something else which we must appreciate. Jesus was God's spokesman while He was here on the earth, yet, there were times when He was remained silent. He did not defend Himself to Pontius Pilate. We can learn a valuable lesson from this. There are times when we too are to remain silent and let the Lord be our defender.

Today, the Holy Spirit, whom Jesus sent, carries on His prophetic ministry. His message is continuously being told in all parts of our world.

QUESTION 36

Did Jesus Make Predictions That Have Come True During His Lifetime?

Jesus Christ personally fulfilled prophecies from the Old Testament in His own life and ministry. Yet He did much more than this. Indeed, He Himself predicted events that were to come to pass at some time in the future.

Therefore, one of the ministries of Jesus was that of a prophet—He was a spokesman for the God of the Bible. The following observations need to be made about Jesus' prophetic ministry.

THERE ARE PROPHECIES OF JESUS THAT HAVE BEEN FULFILLED IN HIS LIFETIME

One of the marks of a true prophet of God is that he or she must make predictions which can be fulfilled in their own lifetime. This way the people would know whether or not that person truly had the prophetic gift. We read.

> You may say to yourself, 'How can we recognize a message the LORD has not spoken?' When a prophet speaks in the LORD's name, and the message does not come true or is not fulfilled, that is a message the LORD has not spoken. The prophet has spoken it presumptuously. Do not be afraid of him (Deuteronomy 18:21-22 HCSB).

Jesus qualified. We are going to look at a number of specific predictions that Jesus made—as well as their fulfillment. Each of these occurred during His lifetime.

PREDICTION 1: HE WILL BE BETRAYED BY ONE OF HIS DISCIPLES: JUDAS ISCARIOT

To begin with, we find that Jesus predicted that He would be betrayed by one of His own disciples. Matthew record Jesus making this prediction during the Last Supper.

> While they were eating, He said, "I assure you: One of you will betray Me." Deeply distressed, each one began to say to Him, "Surely not I, Lord?" (Matthew 26:21, 22 HCSB).

This prediction involves a number of factors. First, He will be betrayed. Second, it will be by someone who is one of His own disciples.

In addition, Jesus predicted which one, among His Twelve disciples, would betray Him—Judas Iscariot. John records what took place.

> After saying these things, Jesus was troubled in his spirit, and testified, "Truly, truly, I say to you, one of you will betray me." The disciples looked at one another, uncertain of whom he spoke. One of his disciples, whom Jesus loved, was reclining at table close to Jesus, so Simon Peter motioned to him to ask Jesus of whom he was speaking. So that disciple, leaning back against Jesus, said to him, "Lord, who is it?" Jesus answered, "It is he to whom I will give this morsel of bread when I have dipped it." So when he had dipped the morsel, he gave it to Judas, the son of Simon Iscariot. Then after he had taken the morsel, Satan entered into him. Jesus said to him, "What you are going to do, do quickly" (John 13:21-27 ESV).

This prediction was indeed literally fulfilled by Judas Iscariot. Luke records what happened.

QUESTION 36

> But even as he said this, a mob approached, led by Judas, one of his twelve disciples. Judas walked over to Jesus and greeted him with a kiss. But Jesus said, "Judas, how can you betray me, the Son of Man, with a kiss?" (Luke 22:47,48 NLT).

As Jesus predicted, one of His own disciples, Judas Iscariot, betrayed Him.

PREDICTION 2: ALL OF HIS DISCIPLES WOULD DESERT HIM AT HIS BETRAYAL

Jesus also predicted that all His disciples would leave Him when He was betrayed. He said.

> "Tonight all of you will desert me," Jesus told them. "For the Scriptures say, 'God will strike the Shepherd, and the sheep of the flock will be scattered.' But after I have been raised from the dead, I will go ahead of you to Galilee and meet you there" (Matthew 26:31,32 NLT).

Notice that Jesus said that "all" of them would abandon Him. If one of them stayed behind, the prophecy would not have been fulfilled.

This prediction was literally fulfilled when Jesus was arrested. Matthew records what took place.

> But all this has happened so that the prophetic Scriptures would be fulfilled. Then all the disciples deserted Him and ran away (Matthew 26:56 HCSB).

None of them remained with Him. Again, the words of Jesus are fulfilled.

PREDICTION 3: PETER WOULD DENY HIM ON THREE OCCASIONS THAT VERY NIGHT

Jesus also predicted that on three different occasions, Peter would deny knowing Him. Furthermore, Jesus said that this would take place that very night. Matthew records Jesus' prediction.

> Peter told Him, "Even if everyone runs away because of You, I will never run away!" "I assure you," Jesus said to him, "tonight—before the rooster crows, you will deny Me three times!" (Matthew 26:33,34 HCSB).

While Peter predicted that he would never leave Jesus, we find that Jesus made a different prediction. That very night he would deny knowing His Lord.

As Jesus had predicted, this was literally fulfilled. Matthew records the fulfillment.

> Peter began to curse and swear, "I don't know that man!" Right then a rooster crowed, and Peter remembered that Jesus had said, "Before a rooster crows, you will say three times that you don't know me." Then Peter went out and cried hard (Matthew 26:74,75 CEV).

That same night, Peter denied knowing His Lord. When he realized what he had done, Peter cried intensely.

PREDICTION 4: HE WOULD SUFFER BECAUSE OF THE RELIGIOUS RULERS

Jesus said that He would suffer as a result of the religious rulers. This prediction was first given while on the way to Jerusalem.

> From that time Jesus began to show to His disciples that He must go to Jerusalem, and suffer many things from the elders and chief priests and scribes, and be killed, and be raised the third day (Matthew 16:21 NKJV).

Again we have a specific prophecy. His suffering would take place at the hands of the religious rulers.

On the night of His arrest, the religious rulers allowed Him to be beaten by those who were guarding Him.

The men who were guarding Jesus made fun of him and beat him. They put a blindfold on him and said, "Tell us who struck you!" They kept on insulting Jesus in many other ways (Luke 22:63-65 CEV).

These cowards humiliated Jesus—just as He had predicted.

PREDICTION 5: HE WOULD DIE IN THE CITY OF JERUSALEM

Although a number of attempts had been made on His life outside of the city of Jerusalem, Jesus predicted that His death must take place there and there alone. Matthew records the specific prophecy which Jesus gave.

> From that time on Jesus began to explain to his disciples that he must go to Jerusalem and suffer many things at the hands of the elders, chief priests and teachers of the law, and that he must be killed and on the third day be raised to life (Matthew 16:21 NIV).

Jerusalem was the only place where our Lord would meet His death. And Jesus died in the city of Jerusalem just as He predicted. The Bible makes this clear.

> Some women were looking on from a distance. They had come with Jesus to Jerusalem. But even before this they had been his followers and had helped him while he was in Galilee. Mary Magdalene and Mary the mother of the younger James and of Joseph were two of these women. Salome was also one of them (Mark 15:40,41 CEV).

Though there were a number of attempts to kill Him before this time, Hs death was to be in the predicted place, Jerusalem.

PREDICTION 6: HE WOULD DIE BY MEANS OF CRUCIFIXION

Jesus predicted the exact manner of His death—crucifixion. We read.

> When Jesus had finished teaching, he told his disciples, "You know that two days from now will be Passover. That is when the Son of Man will be handed over to his enemies and nailed to a cross" (Matthew 26:1-2 CEV).

This was the manner of death by which Jesus predicted that He would die.

Jesus died by crucifixion—as He predicted. Mark writes.

> They nailed Jesus to a cross and gambled to see who would get his clothes. It was about nine o'clock in the morning when they nailed him to the cross. On it was a sign that told why he was nailed there. It read, "This is the King of the Jews." The soldiers also nailed two criminals on crosses, one to the right of Jesus and the other to his left (Mark 15:26-28 CEV).

As He had predicted, the Lord Jesus died upon the cross at Calvary.

PREDICTION 7: HE WOULD DIE DURING THE PASSOVER

Jesus also predicted His death would occur during the Passover celebration. He said.

> When Jesus had finished teaching, he told his disciples, "You know that two days from now will be Passover. That is when the Son of Man will be handed over to his enemies and nailed to a cross." At that time the chief priests and the nation's leaders were meeting at the home of Caiaphas the high priest. They planned how they could sneak around and have Jesus arrested and put to death. But they said, "We must not do it during Passover, because the people will riot" (Matthew 26:1-2 CEV).

We should note that while Jesus predicted that He would die during the Passover, the religious leaders insisted that His death should not take place during that time.

If His death took place at any other time, then Jesus would have been a false prophet. However, as He predicted His death took place at the Passover celebration. We read about this in John's gospel.

> It was the day of Preparation of Passover Week, about the sixth hour. "Here is your king," Pilate said to the Jews. But they shouted, "Take him away! Take him away! Crucify him!" "Shall I crucify your king?" Pilate asked. "We have no king but Caesar," the chief priests answered. Finally Pilate handed him over to them to be crucified. So the soldiers took charge of Jesus (John 19:14-16 NIV).

The exact time of crucifixion was predicted and fulfilled by the Lord Jesus—not after the Passover as the religious leaders had planned. Among other things, this makes it clear that Jesus was in control of all things.

PREDICTION 8: HIS RESURRECTION FROM THE DEAD ON THE THIRD DAY

Jesus also predicted His resurrection from the dead. He said it would happen exactly three days after His death. We read this prediction in the early chapters of John's gospel.

> "What right do you have to do these things?" the Jewish leaders demanded. "If you have this authority from God, show us a miraculous sign to prove it." "All right," Jesus replied. "Destroy this temple, and in three days I will raise it up." "What!" they exclaimed. "It took forty-six years to build this Temple, and you can do it in three days?" But by "this temple," Jesus meant his body. After he was raised from the dead, the disciples remembered that he had said this. And they believed both Jesus and the Scriptures (John 2:18-22 NLT).

This prediction occurred some three years before the event took place.

Jesus again predicted His resurrection as He drew near to the city of Jerusalem.

> From then on, Jesus began telling his disciples what would happen to him. He said, "I must go to Jerusalem. There the nation's leaders, the chief priests, and the teachers of the Law of Moses will make me suffer terribly. I will be killed, but three days later I will rise to life" (Matthew 16:21 CEV).

Jesus repeated this prediction again and again.

After Jesus' crucifixion, the people remembered Jesus' prophecy.

> On the next day, which followed the Day of Preparation, the chief priests and Pharisees gathered together to Pilate, saying, "Sir, we remember, while He was still alive, how that deceiver said, 'After three days I will rise'" (Matthew 27:62,63 NKJV).

The chief priests, and the teachers of the Law, were the ones who arrested Jesus and brought Him to Pilate for execution. They remembered that He had predicted His resurrection.

Yet three days after His crucifixion, Jesus was alive again as He had predicted. The angel at His tomb on that first Easter made it clear to those who arrived.

> He isn't here! He has been raised from the dead, just as he said would happen. Come, see where his body was lying (Matthew 28:6 NLT).

Jesus was crucified on Good Friday and came back from the dead on Easter Sunday morning—three days by Jewish reckoning. Again, His predictions were literally fulfilled.

JESUS QUALIFIED AS A PROPHET

These predictions, as well as their fulfillment, testify that Jesus Christ had the ability to accurately predict the future. Indeed, we find many things which He predicted, were accurately fulfilled during His lifetime. This left no doubt in the minds of the people that Jesus of Nazareth was a true prophet of God.

SUMMARY TO QUESTION 36
DID JESUS MAKE PREDICTIONS THAT HAVE COME TRUE DURING HIS LIFETIME?

We find that Jesus Christ not only fulfilled prophecy in His own life, He also made predictions that have been miraculously fulfilled. This is important to realize—for a true prophet of God must make predictions which were fulfilled in their own lifetime. In doing so, the people would realize that this person had been sent from God. Jesus certainly met these qualifications.

Indeed, there are at least eight major predictions that Jesus made during His public ministry which have been fulfilled exactly as they were given. They include the following.

First, Jesus said that He would be betrayed. This betrayal would happen by one of His own disciples, Judas Iscariot. Thus, there are three elements in this prediction—betrayal, betrayal by one of His own, and Judas would be that betrayer.

This was literally fulfilled when Judas Iscariot handed Jesus over to the religious rulers in the Garden of Gethsemane.

Second, Jesus also said that all of the disciples would leave Him at His betrayal—He would be left alone. Again, we find this prediction literally fulfilled when He was betrayed.

Next, Jesus told Simon Peter that would deny Him at three different times before the rooster crowed. Thus, we have the prediction that Peter would deny Jesus that very night. We find that this took place exactly as Jesus has predicted.

Jesus also predicted He would suffer because of the religious rulers. The gospels record that this prediction was also fulfilled.

On a number of occasions, He predicted His death would occur in the city of Jerusalem. While attempts were made on His life outside of Jerusalem, Jesus, as predicted, died in Jerusalem.

Jesus said that He would die by means of crucifixion. Again, while there were attempts to stone Him or throw Him off of a cliff, these attempts failed. As predicted, Jesus died in the city of Jerusalem by means of crucifixion.

His death would occur during the feast of the Passover. This is another specific prediction. It would take place during the time of the Passover celebration. As is true with the other predictions, this was literally fulfilled.

Death would not hold Him for Jesus predicted that He would be raised from the dead. Furthermore, His resurrection would occur the third day after His death. Again, this prediction was literally fulfilled.

These predictions, along with their fulfillments in His own lifetime, make it clear that Jesus qualified as a true prophet of God. This being the case, the people could believe everything else which He said.

QUESTION 37

Did Jesus Make Predictions That Have Come True After His Lifetime?

Jesus Christ personally fulfilled prophecies written about Him when He came to earth. In addition, He made predictions which were fulfilled in His lifetime. These facts demonstrate that Jesus was the One that He claimed to be—God the Son.

However, there is something else about Jesus' prophetic ministry which must be considered. He predicted things which would take place long after He left this earth. We find that these predictions were also literally fulfilled. The only way that these predictions and fulfillments can be rationally explained is that Jesus Christ did indeed know what was going to occur in the future.

We can list the following predictions which Jesus made which were fulfilled after His lifetime.

PREDICTION 1: HIS WORDS WOULD BE EVERLASTING

First, Jesus made an astounding prediction about His words. He said they would be everlasting. Matthew records Jesus saying.

> Heaven and earth will disappear, but my words will remain forever (Matthew 24:35 NLT).

He clearly predicted that His words would be everlasting—they would remain forever.

We need to appreciate the amazing nature of this prophecy. Here was a man who lived in the first century A.D. with only a small group of followers, whose country was subject to the bondage of Rome. There were no modern means of mass communication, or storage of a person's words.

Yet Jesus made the statement that His words were eternal—they will never pass away. Although it seemed improbable at the time, it has occurred exactly as He predicted. The words of Jesus are still with us today, read and believed by untold millions. It has happened just as He said.

PREDICTION 2: THE STORY OF MARY OF BETHANY WOULD BE REMEMBERED

Mary of Bethany poured oil on the body of Jesus in anticipation of His coming death. The disciples rebuked her for wasting the oil, but Jesus said she had done a good thing. He said.

> You will always have the poor among you, but I will not be here with you much longer. She has poured this perfume on me to prepare my body for burial. I assure you, wherever the Good News is preached throughout the world, this woman's deed will be talked about in her memory (Matthew 26:11-13 NLT).

Jesus predicted that her story would be told wherever the "Good News," the "Gospel," was preached. As He predicted, the story of Mary of Bethany, and her anointing of Jesus before His death, is still told today wherever the Gospel is preached. The fact that you are reading about it right now continues to fulfill Jesus' prophecy.

PREDICTION 3: THE COMING OF THE HOLY SPIRIT

Jesus predicted the coming of the Holy Spirit. Before His death, He made the following promise to His disciples.

QUESTION 37

> But the Counselor, the Holy Spirit, whom the Father will send in my name, will teach you all things and will remind you of everything I have said to you (John 14:26 NIV).

After Jesus left the world, the Holy Spirit would come down and represent Him in a special way to believers. This was fulfilled on the Day of Pentecost. The Bible says.

> On the day of Pentecost all the Lord's followers were together in one place. Suddenly there was a noise from heaven like the sound of a mighty wind! It filled the house where they were meeting. Then they saw what looked like fiery tongues moving in all directions, and a tongue came and settled on each person there. The Holy Spirit took control of everyone, and they began speaking whatever languages the Spirit let them speak (Acts 2:1-4 CEV).

The Holy Spirit came as Jesus predicted. He gave Jesus' disciples power to spread His Word—as well as work miracles.

PREDICTION 4: THE DESTRUCTION OF THE CITY OF JERUSALEM WITHIN ONE GENERATION

After the Jewish nation rejected Jesus, He pronounced judgment upon them. The Lord predicted that the city of Jerusalem would be destroyed. Forty years before it occurred, Jesus gave specifics to its destruction.

> Before long your enemies will build ramparts against your walls and encircle you and close in on you. They will crush you to the ground, and your children with you. Your enemies will not leave a single stone in place, because you have rejected the opportunity God offered you (Luke 19:43,44 NLT).

Jesus predicted that their enemies would build ramparts against the walls of the city of Jerusalem and crush the inhabitants.

Jesus also predicted Jerusalem would be surrounded by armies. He said.

> But when you see Jerusalem surrounded by armies, then know that its desolation has come near (Luke 21:20 NET).

These events would occur in the same generation that Jesus was speaking. Matthew records Jesus predicted the following.

> I assure you: This generation will certainly not pass away until all these things take place (Matthew 24:34 HCSB).

At the time when Jesus made this prediction, there was no imminent threat to the city of Jerusalem. However, in A.D. 70, as Christ had predicted, the city of Jerusalem was surrounded and destroyed by the armies of Titus the Roman.

The reason Jesus gave for the fall of the city was the peoples' rejection of Him as Messiah, "because you did not know the time of your visitation" (Luke 19:44). Jesus' words were literally fulfilled.

PREDICTION 5: THE TEMPLE IN JERUSALEM WOULD BE DESTROYED WITHIN ONE GENERATION

Another prediction of Jesus that was literally fulfilled concerns the destruction of the Temple in Jerusalem. Jesus specified the manner of its destruction.

> As Jesus was leaving the Temple grounds, his disciples pointed out to him the various Temple buildings. But he told them, "Do you see all these buildings? I assure you, they will be so completely demolished that not one stone will be left on top of another!" (Matthew 24:1,2 NLT).

Jesus said that the Temple would be demolished.

As was true with the city of Jerusalem, these events would occur in the same generation that Jesus was speaking. Matthew records Him saying.

> Truly, I say to you, this generation will not pass away until all these things take place. Heaven and earth will pass away, but my words will not pass away (Matthew 24:34,35 ESV).

This happened exactly as predicted. When Titus the Roman destroyed the city of Jerusalem in A.D. 70, he also destroyed the Temple. Interestingly, Titus had determined that the Temple was to be left standing. However, in spite of his intentions, the Temple was burnt to the ground. The prediction of Jesus came true.

PREDICTION 6: THE PEOPLE WOULD BE SCATTERED

When Jesus predicted the destruction of the city of Jerusalem and the Temple, He made clear the fate that awaited the Jewish people. The people will be scattered from their land and taken captive by other nations.

> They will be brutally killed by the sword or sent away as captives to all the nations of the world. And Jerusalem will be conquered and trampled down by the Gentiles until the age of the Gentiles comes to an end (Luke 21:24 NLT).

This occurred just as He had predicted. When the city and Temple were destroyed, the people were scattered to the ends of the earth. Those who were not killed when the city was captured were sold into slavery.

PREDICTION 7: THE HOLY LAND WOULD BE RULED BY GENTILES

Jesus also predicted the nation Israel would be dominated for a long period of time by the Gentile (non-Jewish) peoples.

> Some of them will be killed by swords. Others will be carried off to foreign countries. Jerusalem will be overrun by foreign nations until their time comes to an end (Luke 21:24 CEV).

The land remained under Gentile domination for two thousand years. Except for a few short years in the second century, the Jews had no rule over Jerusalem until 1967. The prediction that the nation would be subject to Gentile rule has been literally fulfilled.

PREDICTION 8: THE JEWISH PEOPLE WOULD BE PERSECUTED

The people would not only be scattered, Jesus also predicted that the Jewish race would be persecuted. He said.

> But Jesus turned and said to them, "Daughters of Jerusalem, don't weep for me, but weep for yourselves and for your children. For the days are coming when they will say, 'Fortunate indeed are the women who are childless, the wombs that have not borne a child and the breasts that have never nursed.' People will beg the mountains to fall on them and the hills to bury them (Luke 23:28-30 NLT).

History records that the Jewish people have indeed gone through terrible persecution. This occurred just as Jesus predicted. From the ghettos of the Middle Ages, to the Holocaust of World War II, the Jews have been a persecuted race, like no other people in history. Jesus' predictions have again come true.

PREDICTION 9: THOUGH PERSECUTED, THE NATION WILL SURVIVE

Though scattered and persecuted, Jesus also predicted the Jewish people would not perish. While the nation was to suffer terribly, Jesus made it clear they will still survive.

> They will be brutally killed by the sword or sent away as captives to all the nations of the world. And Jerusalem will be conquered and trampled down by the Gentiles until the age of the Gentiles comes to an end (Luke 21:24 NLT).

They would be persecuted *until* the times of the Gentiles would be fulfilled. Once this period of Gentile rule was over, the Jews would again have self-rule. Against all odds of history, the Jews returned to their land, became a modern state, and have Jerusalem again as their capital. Jesus' words are again fulfilled.

CONCLUSION: JESUS' WORDS ARE TO BE BELIEVED

From these predictions of Jesus that have been miraculously fulfilled we can come to only one conclusion —Jesus Christ accurately predicted the future. Whatever He says, on any subject, should be believed. This includes His claims to be the Savior of the world—the one way to reach the one true God. Jesus proved that He had the right to make these claims.

SUMMARY TO QUESTION 37
DID JESUS MAKE PREDICTIONS THAT HAVE COME TRUE AFTER HIS LIFETIME?

Jesus Christ made predictions of events which would take place after He left the earth. This being the case, there is not any possible way, humanly speaking, that He could have anything to do with the fulfillment. The fact that each and every one of them has literally come true shows that Jesus is indeed God Himself! Indeed, for only God could predict the future which such amazing accuracy.

First, He predicted that His words would never pass away—they would last forever. This prediction has indeed come true as millions upon millions of people read His words every day.

In addition, Jesus predicted that the story of Mary of Bethany, and her anointing of Him before His death, would be told and retold. He was also correct on that prediction.

He predicted the coming of the Holy Spirit on the Day of Pentecost. This was literally fulfilled.

Jesus also said that the city of Jerusalem would be destroyed within a generation. The Temple in Jerusalem would also be destroyed within one generation. Each of these predictions was literally fulfilled.

Then Jesus said that the Jewish people would be scattered. While they were scattered, Gentiles would rule the Holy Land. The Jewish people would be persecuted during this time. Again, these predictions of Jesus have been fulfilled in a literal manner.

Finally, Jesus predicted that, although persecuted, the nation of Israel would survive. This has miraculously come to pass.

Each of these predictions has been literally fulfilled just as Jesus predicted. Moreover, none of them have been unfulfilled. This fact demonstrates beyond any doubt that Jesus was indeed a genuine prophet of God.

Consequently, everything else He said must be believed as being true. This includes His claims to be the only hope of humanity—the Savior of the world.

PART THREE
The Betrayal, Trial, And Death Of Jesus
The Last Days Of Christ

This section examines some of the key elements of the public ministry of Jesus. Although His public life was for a period of a few short years, He has influenced the course of this world as none other.

In this first section we will find out why He came to this world, His relationship to the Law of Moses, His miraculous deeds, and His relationship to Bible prophecy.

QUESTION 38

What Was The Chronology Of The Events Surrounding The Death Of Christ?

It is important to have an idea of the basic chronology of the events surrounding the death of Jesus Christ. The truth of the message of the gospel of Christ is rooted in historical events. Just as the Fall of Adam and Eve in the Garden of Eden was an historical event, so were the events surrounding Jesus' betrayal, death, resurrection, and ascension.

We will briefly summarize the main points of His betrayal, trial, death, and burial as we begin to look at the significance of these events.

THE LAST SUPPER

The final night of Jesus' earthly life began with the celebration of the Last Supper with His intimate disciples. Jesus, in an act of humility, washed the feet of His Twelve disciples (John 13:1-20).

While they were eating the Last Supper, Jesus announced that one of them would betray Him.

> After saying these things, Jesus was troubled in his spirit, and testified, "Truly, truly, I say to you, one of you will betray me" (John 13:21 ESV).

This surprise declaration certainly shocked the disciples.

After they had finished eating, Jesus introduced a new ordinance that His followers would observe—the Lord's Supper. Luke records the following.

> Then He took a cup, and after giving thanks, He said, "Take this and share it among yourselves. For I tell you, from now on I will not drink of the fruit of the vine until the kingdom of God comes." And He took bread, gave thanks, broke it, gave it to them, and said, "This is My body, which is given for you. Do this in remembrance of Me." In the same way He also took the cup after supper and said, "This cup is the new covenant [established by] My blood; it is shed for you" (Luke 22:17-20 HCSB).

Jesus then gave them the Upper Room Discourse. This contained teaching on a number of important subjects—He was continuing to teach these disciples up until the very end.

THE GARDEN OF GETHSEMANE

Jesus and His eleven disciples left the upper room and headed toward the Mount of Olives. Judas Iscariot had left earlier in the evening to arrange the betrayal of Jesus. While He was walking along the way to Gethsemane, Jesus prayed for a number of things to God the Father. This prayer is recorded in John 17.

Once they reached the Garden of Gethsemane, Jesus withdrew a short distance from His disciples. Jesus prayed again. He specifically addressed God the Father about the events that He would soon experience. Matthew writes what occurred.

> Going a little farther, he fell with his face to the ground and prayed, "My Father, if it is possible, may this cup be taken from me. Yet not as I will, but as you will." Then he returned to his disciples and found them sleeping. "Could you men not keep watch with me for one hour?" he asked Peter.

"Watch and pray so that you will not fall into temptation. The spirit is willing, but the body is weak." He went away a second time and prayed, "My Father, if it is not possible for this cup to be taken away unless I drink it, may your will be done." When he came back, he again found them sleeping, because their eyes were heavy. So he left them and went away once more and prayed the third time, saying the same thing (Matthew 26:39-44 NIV).

When Jesus had finished praying, He awoke His disciples. His arrest was about to occur. The powers of darkness had arrived.

THE ARREST OF JESUS AND TRIALS OF JESUS

The traitor Judas arrived with religious leaders and a large group of soldiers. Although a large crowd came to arrest Jesus, He offered no resistance. Instead He asked them why they came after Him like some kind of criminal. Jesus was then arrested and taken away.

A number of trials occurred during the night and early morning. Jesus appeared before the High Priest, the Sanhedrin, Pontius Pilate, Herod, and then He was sent back to Pilate. Although Pilate admitted that he found Jesus innocent, he still presented Him to the crowd to suggest how Jesus should be punished. The crowd said to crucify Him. Pilate gave in to the crowd and ordered Jesus to be crucified. Evil had triumphed.

JESUS DIED BY CRUCIFIXION

The New Testament reports that the soldiers beat Jesus before leading Him away to be crucified. The accusation against Him would have been written out and tied around His neck while He was carrying His cross to the place of crucifixion. This would let everyone know the crime for which He was being executed. The accusation was then nailed above the cross. Jesus' crime was published in three languages. It read as follows.

This is Jesus of Nazareth, the King of the Jews.

According to the New Testament, Jesus was on the cross for about six hours. When the soldiers came to break His legs to hasten His death, they found that He had already died.

JESUS WAS BURIED

Jesus was taken down from the cross by friendly hands. He was anointed with spices and then buried in the tomb of a rich man. This ended the earthly life of Jesus Christ.

From a human perspective it looked like everything was over. It seemed as if the religious leaders had won, and that Jesus and His disciples had been defeated.

THAT IS NOT THE END OF THE STORY!

However, the New Testament records the good news that this was not the end—it was just the beginning! Something happened on Easter Sunday that changed the world forever—Jesus Christ had risen from the dead!

SUMMARY TO QUESTION 38
WHAT WAS THE CHRONOLOGY OF THE EVENTS SURROUNDING THE DEATH OF CHRIST?

The basic chronology of the death of Christ was as follows. On the last night of His earthly life, after washing the disciples' feet, Jesus predicted that one of them would betray Him that very night.

After they ate a meal together Jesus instituted a new ordinance—the Lord's Supper. Jesus then gave His disciples their final teaching session before His death—known as the Upper Room Discourse.

Jesus and His eleven disciples then went to the Garden of Gethsemane. The traitor Judas had long since left to bring the religious leaders to Gethsemane to arrest Jesus. Jesus was arrested and taken away.

After going through a number of trials He was sent to Pontius Pilate. Pilate pronounced Jesus of Nazareth innocent but still ordered Him to be crucified. Jesus was crucified. He was on the cross some six hours when He died. He was taken down from the cross by loving hands, anointed with spices, and then buried in the tomb of a rich man. At that time the religious leaders assumed they had defeated Jesus.

However, they were about to learn of an incredible event—an event that would literally change the world. Jesus of Nazareth did not stay dead!

QUESTION 39

Why Was Jesus Betrayed By Judas Iscariot?

One of the darkest moments in all of recorded history is the betrayal of Jesus Christ by one of His disciples, Judas Iscariot. There are a number of lessons to be learned from this hideous deed of Judas.

JESUS PREDICTED HIS DEATH

When the disciples came to Jerusalem for the last time, Jesus made it clear that His death would be occurring in a few days. Matthew writes.

> When Jesus had finished saying all this, He told His disciples, "You know that the Passover takes place after two days, and the Son of Man will be handed over to be crucified" (Matthew 26:1-2 HCSB).

Here we have the specific prediction of Jesus Christ that His death would be during the time of the Passover—not before, not afterward.

Realizing this, Judas went to the chief priests for the purpose of betraying Jesus to them. Matthew records the following.

> Then one of the twelve, who was called Judas Iscariot, went to the chief priests and said, "What will you give me if I betray him to you?" They paid him thirty pieces of silver. And from that moment he began to look for an opportunity to betray him (Matthew 26:14-16 NRSV).

Judas has agreed to betray Jesus for a certain amount of money. Consequently, he was looking for a time in which he could fulfill his agreement.

On the night when Jesus and the disciples celebrated the Last Supper, Judas plotted with the religious rulers to take them to Jesus in the Garden of Gethsemane. It was there in the garden that Jesus was betrayed and arrested.

WHY DID JUDAS BETRAY JESUS?

The question which always comes up concerns the "why." Why did he do it? If Jesus clearly demonstrated that He was the Son of God, then why did one of His own disciples betray Him? There have been a number of views put forth to explain why Judas did this.

1. IT WAS FOREORDAINED: BUT JUDAS STILL HAD CHOICE

One view says that Judas was foreordained as a traitor, and could do nothing about it. In fact, the Bible says that Jesus knew from the beginning that Judas would betray Him. He said to His disciples.

> Yet there are some of you who do not believe. For Jesus had known from the beginning which of them did not believe and who would betray him (John 6:64 NIV).

Jesus also said the following.

> Jesus replied, "Didn't I choose you, the twelve, and yet one of you is the devil?" (John 6:70 NET).

Though Jesus knew ahead of time that Judas would betray Him, it does not mean He caused Judas to do it. Indeed, the Bible makes it clear that Judas acted on his own accord. He was not just a pawn, or puppet, in God's hands. Judas willingly chose to betray Jesus.

2. WAS JUDAS A FANATICAL BELIEVER?

Another view argues that Judas was a fanatical believer in Jesus who wanted to force His hand by betraying Him. Handing Jesus over to the religious leaders would supposedly force Jesus to set up His Messianic kingdom.

But this view does not square with the facts. Judas asked the chief priests for money for the betrayal—which is hardly in keeping with such "pure" spiritual motives. Moreover, the Gospels refer to Judas as a thief a betrayer and the devil—hardly the designation one would expect for a fanatical believer.

3. WAS JUDAS A SUPERPATRIOT?

Others have considered Judas a superpatriot who wanted to use Jesus as a means to revolt against their Roman oppressors.

But this does not fit the facts for the reasons mentioned above. There is no indication that Judas had any other motive but greed.

4. HE WAS A THIEF

This brings us to the likely explanation. Judas was a thief whose ambition was to have power and money. The gospel of John gives us some insight into his character.

> Then Mary took a twelve-ounce jar of expensive perfume made from essence of nard, and she anointed Jesus' feet with it and wiped his feet with her hair. And the house was filled with fragrance. But Judas Iscariot, one of his disciples—the one who would betray him—said, "That perfume was worth a small fortune. It should have been sold and the money given to the poor." Not that he cared for the poor—he was a thief who was in charge of the disciples' funds, and he often took some for his own use (John 12:3-6 NLT).

By aligning himself close to Jesus, Judas believed that He would receive a prominent place in the kingdom. When Jesus talked about dying, Judas realized the kingdom was not going to come immediately.

Therefore, he gained what he could by betraying Jesus. Judas did not ever truly believe in Jesus. He never referred to Jesus as Lord but rather as "master" or "teacher." Judas is an example of one who follows Jesus for all the wrong reasons. Jesus gave Judas' epitaph.

> For I, the Son of Man, must die, as the Scriptures declared long ago. But how terrible it will be for my betrayer. Far better for him if he had never been born (Matthew 26:24 NLT).

Judas was indeed a tragic figure—but a tragic figure of his own making. Indeed, he willingly chose to betray the One who would die for the sins of the world—including the sin of the person betraying Him. This will forever be how this person is remembered.

SUMMARY TO QUESTION 39
WHY WAS JESUS BETRAYED BY JUDAS ISCARIOT?

One of the most well-known events in the life of Jesus Christ is His betrayal by Judas Iscariot for thirty pieces of silver. The fact of the betrayal by Judas is beyond all doubt. The question is this: why did Judas do something like this?

Jesus had predicted His betrayal by one of His disciples. He then specifically said that Judas would be that disciple. Different motives have been ascribed to Judas for doing this terrible deed. They include the following.

It has been contended that Judas was some fanatical believer who wanted Jesus to immediately set up His kingdom. However, there is no evidence of this whatsoever. The fact that Judas wanted money for turning Jesus over to the religious leaders refutes the idea of any pure motive.

Some have argued that he was a superpatriot who was attempting to force Jesus to revolt against the Romans. Again, we have the problem of Judas taking the money for betraying Jesus.

While people continue to make excuses for Judas as to why he betrayed Jesus, there are no excuses. Judas was called a thief, the betrayer, and the devil by John in his gospel. This man who betrayed Jesus never really believed in Him as his Lord.

The truth is that the betrayal of Jesus was for Judas' own benefit. He thought that he could profit by this horrible deed.

The fact that Jesus knew that Judas would betray Him does not remove the responsibility from Judas. He betrayed Jesus because he chose to. Jesus Himself stated that it would have been better if Judas had not been born.

QUESTION 40

Why Did The Religious Leaders Want To Kill Jesus?

The New Testament records that the religious leaders hated Jesus Christ to the point that they arrested Him, tried Him, and brought Him to Pilate for a sentence of death. What was it that made them so angry at Jesus that they wanted to see Him dead?

THERE ARE MANY REASONS THEY WANTED JESUS DEAD

There were a number of things about Jesus that infuriated the religious leaders. These included the following.

1. The claims that He made.

2. The deeds that He did.

3. His threat to their religious system.

4. His threat to their way of life.

5. The people with whom He socialized.

6. The lack of respect He had for their religious traditions.

These six things caused outraged among the religious rulers. Consequently, they wanted to see Jesus dead. We will consider each of these reasons.

1. JESUS' CLAIMS OUTWEIGHED THEIR AUTHORITY

When Jesus claimed to be the Messiah it meant that His authority outweighed their authority. The religious leaders did not believe His claims and were angry that some of the people did. They said the following.

> Has any of the rulers or of the Pharisees believed in him? No! But this mob that knows nothing of the law—there is a curse on them (John 7:48,49 NIV).

The religious leaders assumed that the reason multitudes believed in Jesus was due to their ignorance. Add to this, the attention Jesus was getting brought out the leaders' hatred and jealousy. Simply put, the jealousy of the religious leaders caused them to want Jesus dead.

2. HIS DEEDS OUTRAGED THE RELIGIOUS RULERS

The deeds of Jesus also angered the religious leaders. After seeing Jesus heal a demon-possessed man, some of the multitude questioned if Jesus could be the Messiah. Matthew records the following.

> And all the people were amazed, and said, "Can this be the Son of David?" But when the Pharisees heard it, they said, "It is only by Beelzebul, the prince of demons, that this man casts out demons" (Matthew 12:23,24 ESV).

The miracle was undeniable—for the man was blind and mute as well as demon-possessed. Rather than believe Jesus to be the Messiah, these religious rulers attributed Jesus' power to the devil.

Therefore, their "official" explanation was that Jesus' power came from Satan. This was another cause for which they wanted Him dead.

3. JESUS WAS A THREAT TO THEIR RELIGIOUS SYSTEM

Jesus was also a threat to their religious system. He pointed out the hypocrisy that was connected with their practice. The Bible records that on two different occasions He came into the temple precincts and drove out the moneychangers. John records the following incident.

> It was time for the annual Passover celebration, and Jesus went to Jerusalem. In the Temple area he saw merchants selling cattle, sheep, and doves for sacrifices; and he saw money changers behind their counters. Jesus made a whip from some ropes and chased them all out of the Temple. He drove out the sheep and oxen, scattered the money changers' coins over the floor, and turned over their tables. Then, going over to the people who sold doves, he told them, "Get these things out of here. Don't turn my Father's house into a marketplace!" Then his disciples remembered this prophecy from the Scriptures: "Passion for God's house burns within me" (John 2:13-17 NLT).

Christ claimed that He had greater authority over the temple than these religious rulers. This angered them to the point that they wanted Him dead.

4. JESUS WAS A THREAT TO THEIR WAY OF LIFE

There were political reasons that the religious leaders wanted Jesus dead. There was an unstable situation between the Jews and the Romans. The thought of a Messiah who may lead an uprising against Rome was not something these people wanted. We read of the opinion of the High Priest Caiaphas.

> Then one of them, named Caiaphas, who was high priest that year, spoke up, "You know nothing at all! You do not realize that it is better for you that one man die for the people than that the whole nation perish" (John 11:49,50 NIV).

He was afraid the Romans would intervene if Jesus gained the support of the people. This, among other reasons, is why he insisted that Jesus must die.

5. THE PEOPLE WITH WHOM HE SOCIALIZED OUTRAGED THE RELIGIOUS RULERS

The religious leaders were filled with pride and arrogance. They were particularly proud that they did not socialize with "sinners." They did not believe that the genuine Messiah would socialize with such a crowd. When one Pharisee saw Jesus allow a woman to wash His feet, he was outraged. Luke writes.

> Now when the Pharisee who had invited Him saw this, he spoke to himself, saying, "This man, if He were a prophet, would know who and what manner of woman this is who is touching Him, for she is a sinner" (Luke 7:39 NKJV).

The fact that Jesus would allow this to happen further convinced these religious leaders that He was not the Messiah.

Jesus noted their opinion of Him.

> The Son of Man came eating and drinking, and they say, 'Look, a glutton and a drunkard, a friend of tax collectors and sinners!' Yet wisdom is vindicated by her deeds (Matthew 11:19 NRSV).

The religious rulers believed themselves to be righteous by avoiding sinners. When Jesus kept company with these individuals, it infuriated the proud Pharisees and other religious rulers.

6. JESUS HAD A LACK OF RESPECT FOR THEIR TRADITIONS

As much as anything, the lack of respect that Jesus had for their religious traditions incensed the religious leaders. Jesus ignored these traditions, which they observed so minutely. He knew they were human-made rules that had not come from God.

And it was Jesus' disregard for their traditions concerning the Sabbath that caused the most outrage. God had commanded the Sabbath to be a day of rest from labors and a time to worship Him. The religious leaders added all types of restrictions to the Sabbath—making it difficult, if not impossible to observe.

Jesus was grieved and angry at the way they had perverted the Sabbath observance. He asked the religious leaders a number of specific questions. Mark records this particular episode in the following manner.

> Then he turned to his critics and asked, "Is it legal to do good deeds on the Sabbath, or is it a day for doing harm? Is this a day to save life or to destroy it?" But they wouldn't answer him. He looked around at them angrily, because he was deeply disturbed by their hard hearts. Then he said to the man, "Reach out your hand." The man reached out his hand, and it became normal again! (Mark 3:4,5 NLT).

Jesus then healed a man in their presence on the day of the Sabbath. This healing on the Sabbath was more than they could endure. They concluded that the genuine Messiah would not dare do such a thing. Their response was immediate.

> The Pharisees went out and immediately conspired with the Herodians against him, how to destroy him (Mark 3:6 NRSV).

They were convinced that Jesus had to die.

THEY HAD NO GODLY OR RIGHTEOUS MOTIVE

In sum, it was not for anything godly or righteous that the religious leaders wanted to put Jesus to death. It was their hypocrisy, pride and arrogance that caused them to bring Jesus before Pilate to be crucified. They did not want to hear the truth of God.

SUMMARY TO QUESTION 40
WHY DID THE RELIGIOUS LEADERS WANT TO KILL JESUS?

The New Testament says that the religious leaders wanted Jesus Christ dead for a number of reasons—but none of the reasons were righteous. These unrighteous reasons can be listed as follows.

First, the claims that Jesus made demonstrated that His authority was greater than theirs. The religious leaders could not accept this. They could not believe that He was the genuine Messiah so they rejected His claims.

The miraculous deeds that He did, demonstrated His superior authority. These religious leaders could not deny the miracles. Since they rejected the idea that Jesus was the Messiah, they concluded that His miracles were done by the power of the devil.

Jesus was also a threat to their religious system. He went the temple and condemned their current practices. By doing this, He claimed that His authority was greater than theirs. They could not accept this claim.

These religious leaders also considered Jesus a threat to their way of life. They assumed that the great following that He had gathered would cause the Romans to come and remove them from their land. Thus, Jesus had to die to save the nation from becoming extinct.

The people with whom Jesus socialized offended the pride of the religious leaders. Indeed, these men could not comprehend how the real Messiah would mingle with "sinners," as Jesus did. Hence, they concluded He was not the Promised One.

Above all, it was the lack of respect for their religious traditions that caused them to desire to kill Him. This is particularly true of Jesus' attitude toward the Sabbath. When Jesus broke their human-made traditions by healing on the Sabbath, this was more than they could stand. Immediately they began to plot His death.

All of these things contributed to their evil desire to want Jesus dead. Yet, as noted, none of the reasons were godly. Indeed, by rejecting Jesus Christ these religious leaders rejected their only hope of salvation from sin.

QUESTION 41

Was The Death Of Jesus Planned Ahead Of Time?

Was the death of Jesus Christ something that happened without any planning? Or was it merely an afterthought among the Jews to kill Jesus?

To the contrary, the death of Jesus had been planned for some time. From the New Testament, we learn the following.

THERE WERE A NUMBER OF ASSASSINATION ATTEMPTS ON JESUS

There were a number of attempts to kill Jesus before His eventual crucifixion in Jerusalem. They include the following.

1. THE SLAUGHTER OF THE INNOCENTS

There was an attempt on Jesus' life as soon as He was born. We read about this episode in Matthew's gospel.

> When Herod found out that the wise men from the east had tricked him, he was very angry. He gave orders for his men to kill all the boys who lived in or near Bethlehem and were two years old and younger. This was based on what he had learned from the wise men (Matthew 2:16 CEV).

This attempt by the evil king Herod failed. He wanted to put to death any potential king that may oppose him. However, it was not to be.

2. AN EARLY ATTEMPT IN JERUSALEM

On an earlier trip to Jerusalem, before He died for the sins of the world, the religious leaders attempted to kill Jesus. John records what happened as follows.

> Then they picked up stones to throw at him, but Jesus hid himself and went out from the temple area (John 8:59 NET).

Jesus would not allow Himself to be killed on this occasion. There was a specific time when He was to die and His time had not yet come.

3. THERE WAS AN ATTEMPT ON HIS LIFE AT NAZARETH

In the city of Nazareth, the place where Jesus was raised, the people tried to throw Him over a large cliff. Luke records this episode.

> When they heard these things, all in the synagogue were filled with wrath. And they rose up and drove him out of the town and brought him to the brow of the hill on which their town was built, so that they could throw him down the cliff. But passing through their midst, he went away (Luke 4:28-30 ESV).

Again, it was not His time to die. Therefore, He was able to somehow pass through their midst without being killed.

4. THE ARGUMENT OVER THE SABBATH ISSUE

Jesus' breaking of the religious leaders' traditions regarding the Sabbath, and His claim of equality with God the Father, caused them to want to kill Him. John records how they became more intent on killing Jesus. He wrote.

> For this reason the Jews tried all the harder to kill him; not only was he breaking the Sabbath, but he was even calling God his own Father, making himself equal with God. Jesus

gave them this answer: "I tell you the truth, the Son can do nothing by himself; he can do only what he sees his Father doing, because whatever the Father does the Son also does" (John 5:18,19 NIV).

Their desire to kill Him continued to grow.

5. HEROD WANTED TO KILL JESUS

The Bible also says that King Herod plotted to kill Jesus.

> At that very hour some Pharisees came and said to him, "Get away from here, for Herod wants to kill you" (Luke 13:31 ESV).

He could not tolerate Jesus. He thought that he was the only king.

6. THE PLOT IN JERUSALEM

There was a plot to kill Jesus when He came to Jerusalem on His last visit. Matthew records the plotting of the religious leaders.

> Then the chief priests and the elders of the people gathered in the palace of the high priest, who was called Caiaphas, and they conspired to arrest Jesus by stealth and kill him (Matthew 26:3,4 NRSV).

They wanted to kill Him—but they were not going to do it during the Passover. They did not want to cause a major uproar among the people. However, they were never in charge of when Jesus was going to die.

7. THE PREDICTION OF CAIAPHAS

The High Priest Caiaphas spoke of the necessity of Jesus' death. We read of his unwitting prediction of Jesus' death in John's gospel.

> Then one of them, Caiaphas, who was high priest that year, said, "You know nothing at all! You do not realize that it is

more to your advantage to have one man die for the people than for the whole nation to perish." (Now he did not say this on his own, but because he was high priest that year, he prophesied that Jesus was going to die for the Jewish nation, and not for the Jewish nation only, but to gather together into one the children of God who are scattered.) So from that day they planned together to kill him (John 11:49-53 NET).

Without realizing it, he correctly predicted the reason for Jesus' death—to die for the nation.

HIS DEATH WAS PART OF GOD'S ETERNAL PLAN

The death of Jesus Christ was part of the eternal plan of God. On the day of Pentecost, fifty days after Jesus' death, the Apostle Peter declared that the death of Christ had been planned by God for all eternity. He said to the crowd that had gathered.

> You that are Israelites, listen to what I have to say: Jesus of Nazareth, a man attested to you by God with deeds of power, wonders, and signs that God did through him among you, as you yourselves know—this man, handed over to you according to the definite plan and foreknowledge of God, you crucified and killed by the hands of those outside the law. But God raised him up, having freed him from death, because it was impossible for him to be held in its power (Acts 2:22-24 NRSV).

This tells us that the death of Jesus Christ was not an accident, or an afterthought, in the plan of God. In fact, it had been planned by God for all eternity.

Indeed, as Jesus Himself stated, He came to earth to die for the sins of the world.

> Just as the Son of Man did not come to be served but to serve, and to give his life as a ransom for many (Matthew 20:28 NET).

On another occasion, the Lord said.

> Now my soul is greatly distressed. And what should I say? 'Father, deliver me from this hour'? No, but for this very reason I have come to this hour... Now is the judgment of this world; now the ruler of this world will be driven out. And I, when I am lifted up from the earth, will draw all people to myself." (Now he said this to indicate clearly what kind of death he was going to die.) (John 12:27, 31-33 NET)

It is clear that Christ came to this earth to be a sacrifice for our sins.

SUMMARY TO QUESTION 41
WAS THE DEATH OF JESUS PLANNED AHEAD OF TIME?

The death of Jesus Christ was not a spontaneous tragedy or an historical mistake—it was in the predetermined program of God—planned before the foundation of the world. Indeed, it is a crucial element in God's eternal plan to save humanity from their sins.

The New Testament tells us that a number of attempts were made on Jesus' life before His death on the cross.

This began as soon as He was born when the evil King Herod, known also as Herod the Great, ordered the slaughter of the innocents in Bethlehem.

On one of His first visits to Jerusalem the religious leaders picked up stones to kill Jesus.

At Jesus' hometown in Nazareth, when He claimed an Old Testament prophecy was fulfilled by Him, there was also an attempt to murder Him.

When Jesus broke the human-made traditions which the religious leaders added to the Sabbath, they were constantly looking for a convenient time to kill Him.

The High Priest Caiaphas predicted the necessity of the death of Jesus. Unwittingly he predicted the purpose of Jesus' death—to save the nation of Israel.

King Herod, the son of Herod the Great, also wanted Jesus dead. Yet, like his father, he was unable to do this.

However, Jesus' time had not yet come. On a human level, it was part of a pre-determined plot by the religious leaders of Jesus' day to put Him to death. Yet as we have emphasized, it was part of God's eternal plan. Consequently, we can truly say that the death of Jesus Christ was a planned event.

QUESTION 42

Did Jesus Receive A Fair Trial?

The trial of Jesus Christ is the most famous in history—none even comes close. Actually it was in two phases—one Jewish and one Roman. Each of these trials contained a number of parts. They can be broken down in the following manner.

THE JEWISH TRIALS

After His arrest, Jesus first went before Annas, the former High Priest. We read about this in the Gospel of John.

> The Roman officer and his men, together with the temple police, arrested Jesus and tied him up. They took him first to Annas, who was the father-in-law of Caiaphas, the high priest that year. This was the same Caiaphas who had told the Jewish leaders, "It is better if one person dies for the people" (John 18:12-14 CEV).

Though he was the former high priest, Annas was actually the power behind the office.

Jesus was then brought to Caiaphas, the son-in-law, of Annas. Matthew records this episode in the following manner.

> Those who had arrested Jesus took him to Caiaphas the high priest, in whose house the scribes and the elders had gathered (Matthew 26:57 NRSV).

Jesus now appears before the present high priest, Caiaphas. A number of religious rulers from the Sanhedrin, the Jewish ruling authority, were also at his house to interrogate Jesus.

Matthew explains what occurred when Jesus appeared before these religious leaders. We find that they are the ones who determined that He should die.

> Then the high priest tore his clothes and said, "He has spoken blasphemy! Why do we need any more witnesses? Look, now you have heard the blasphemy. What do you think?" "He is worthy of death," they answered (Matthew 26:65,66 NIV).

These religious leaders were convinced that Jesus' death was necessary.

THE ROMAN TRIALS

Jesus was then brought to the Roman Governor Pontius Pilate. After examining Jesus for a time, Pilate discovered that Jesus was from Galilee. Consequently, he sent Him to Herod, the ruler of Galilee who was in Jerusalem for the Passover. Luke writes.

> And when he learned that he belonged to Herod's jurisdiction, he sent him over to Herod, who was himself in Jerusalem at that time (Luke 23:7 ESV).

Herod had wanted to see Jesus. However, Jesus did not say a word to him. Eventually, the frustrated king sent Jesus back to Pilate. Again, Luke records what happened.

> Even Herod with his soldiers treated him with contempt and mocked him; then he put an elegant robe on him, and sent him back to Pilate (Luke 23:11 NRSV).

Jesus was sent back to Pilate after Herod and his soldiers had treated the Lord with contempt.

It was Pontius Pilate, the prefect of Judea, who sentenced Jesus to death. Luke records it in the following manner.

> Wanting to release Jesus, Pilate appealed to them again. But they kept shouting, "Crucify him! Crucify him!" For the third time he spoke to them: "Why? What crime has this man committed? I have found in him no grounds for the death penalty. Therefore I will have him punished and then release him." But with loud shouts they insistently demanded that he be crucified, and their shouts prevailed. So Pilate decided to grant their demand (Luke 23:20-24 NIV).

Pilate wanted to set Jesus free but gave in to the loud shouting of the crowd. Therefore, he knowingly sentenced an innocent man to death.

DID JESUS RECEIVE A FAIR TRIAL?

This briefly sums up the various trials Jesus experienced. The question is whether Jesus received a fair trial. Among believers there are two basic responses to this issue.

One view is that the religious leaders kept the letter of the law, but not the spirit when they condemned Him. The trial was legal. The other perspective is that there were a number of illegal things occurred. This is the traditional way of looking at His trial.

WAS IT BAD LAW?

It has been argued that the trial of Jesus is the classic example of following the law in a bad way. The religious leaders, it is contended followed the letter of the law but not the spirit of the law. While they may have done everything correct in a technical way, they did not follow the clear intention of the law.

THE TRIAL WAS ILLEGAL

Traditionally Christians have argued that the trial of Jesus consisted of one illegal act after another by the Sanhedrin—the Jewish ruling authority. Some of the main problems with the trial of Jesus include the following.

1. THERE WAS NO POSSIBILITY OF A FAIR TRIAL

First, the Sanhedrin should have never held the trial. They had plotted to kill Jesus weeks ahead of time.

WE READ THE FOLLOWING IN THE GOSPEL OF JOHN

> So the chief priests and the Pharisees called a meeting of the council. They asked, "What are we doing? This man is performing a lot of miracles. If we let him continue what he's doing, everyone will believe in him. Then the Romans will take away our position and our nation." One of them, Caiaphas, who was chief priest that year, told them, "You people don't know anything. You haven't even considered this: It is better for one man to die for the people than for the whole nation to be destroyed." Caiaphas didn't say this on his own. As chief priest that year, he prophesied that Jesus would die for the Jewish nation. He prophesied that Jesus wouldn't die merely for this nation, but that Jesus would die to bring God's scattered children together and make them one. From that day on, the Jewish council planned to kill Jesus (John 11:47-53 God's Word).

Since they had already plotted to kill Jesus, there was no way they could fairly judge Him. Indeed, Caiaphas the High Priest, the one presiding over the trial, is the one who said that it was necessary for Jesus to die for the entire nation. Consequently, the verdict was decided before the trial was even held.

2. A CAPITAL TRIAL AT NIGHT WAS ILLEGAL

When a person's life was at stake, it was illegal to try that person at night. By holding the first trial of Jesus at night, the Sanhedrin broke their own law. Therefore, the entire process of putting Jesus on trial was illegal.

3. THEY SHOULD NOT HAVE LOOKED FOR WITNESSES AFTER THE TRIAL STARTED

According to Jewish law, a trial could only start after the witnesses had previously come forward to testify. First, the witnesses were found, and then the trial was to occur.

Yet the Bible is clear that they looked for witnesses after the trial started. Since they had already determined the verdict ahead of time, they sought witnesses to seal the verdict. Again, we find no fairness whatsoever.

4. THEY SHOULD NOT HAVE LOOKED FOR FALSE WITNESSES

There was something even worse. Not only should the Sanhedrin have not looked for witnesses, they certainly should not have looked for false witnesses! Yet, the Bible says they were deliberately looking for false evidence. Matthew writes.

> The chief priests and the whole council wanted to put Jesus to death. So they tried to find some people who would tell lies about him in court (Matthew 26:59 CEV).

Theirs was a shameless attempt to subvert justice.

5. THE FALSE WITNESSES SHOULD HAVE BEEN PUNISHED

There is another problem. Since the Sanhedrin knew the testimony of the witnesses was false, these witnesses should have been punished.

> But they could not find any, even though many did come and tell lies. At last, two men came forward and said, "This man claimed that he would tear down God's temple and build it again in three days" (Matthew 26:60,61 CEV).

There is no indication that these false witnesses were ever punished. Yet Jewish law calls for false witnesses to be punished.

6. ANY JUDGMENT SHOULD HAVE BEEN DELAYED TILL NEXT DAY

In cases where a person's life was at stake, the punishment was supposed to be delayed until the next day. However, the Sanhedrin immediately pronounced judgment against Jesus. Matthew records the following happening.

> Early the next morning all the chief priests and the nation's leaders met and decided that Jesus should be put to death (Matthew 27:1 CEV).

They could not wait to put Him to death.

7. THERE WAS NOT SUPPOSED TO BE A TRIAL ON THE DAY BEFORE THE SABBATH OR BEFORE HOLY DAYS

The timing of the trial was also illegal. Punishment in a capital case could not be rendered until the next day. This made it illegal to try someone on the day before the Sabbath or before some holy day. The Sanhedrin could not legally meet during the Sabbath day, or a holy day. Yet, they illegally met the night before the Passover, the holiest day of the year, to try Jesus.

8. THEY NEVER CONSIDERED JESUS' TESTIMONY

There is also the problem of Jesus' testimony. When Jesus was put under oath He acknowledged that He was the Messiah—the promised Deliverer that the Law and the Prophets spoke of. This admission of Jesus was what caused the Sanhedrin to call for His death.

However, they never stopped for one moment to consider the possibility that Jesus was telling the truth! There was not the slightest interest among the members of the Sanhedrin to attempt to find out whether Jesus may indeed be the promised Messiah. No evidence was allowed to be presented on Jesus' behalf, and no witnesses were called to back up His claims. Nothing. As soon as He made the claim, under oath, they assumed Him guilty of blasphemy. His side was never heard.

9. THEY COULD NOT AGREE ON THE CHARGES

The Sanhedrin could not agree on what crime Jesus committed. They judged Him guilty because of blasphemy. The High Priest said.

> "You have heard his blasphemy! What is your decision?" All of them condemned him as deserving death (Mark 14:64 NRSV).

However, they brought Him before Pilate, the Roman governor, because supposedly He was inciting the people against Caesar. Luke writes.

> They began to accuse him, saying, "We found this man perverting our nation, forbidding us to pay taxes to the emperor, and saying that he himself is the Messiah, a king" (Luke 23:2 NRSV).

They charged Jesus with something they knew was untrue.

10. PILATE DECLARED HIM INNOCENT THREE DIFFERENT TIMES

There is something else that is truly pitiful. Pontius Pilate actually declared Jesus innocent three different times! These are all recorded in the gospel of Luke. We read.

> Pilate told the chief priests and the crowd, "I don't find him guilty of anything" (Luke 23:4 CEV).

This is the first admission of Pilate.

When Jesus had returned, after seeing Herod, Pilate again declared Him innocent. Luke states it as follows.

> Then Pilate called together the leading priests and other religious leaders, along with the people, and he announced his verdict. "You brought this man to me, accusing him of leading a revolt. I have examined him thoroughly on this point in your presence and find him innocent. Herod came to the same conclusion and sent him back to us. Nothing this man has done calls for the death penalty" (Luke 23:13-15 NLT).

Pilate declared that after examining Jesus he found Him innocent.

After trying, in vain, to release Jesus Pilate again testified to His innocence. We read the description that Luke gives.

> A third time he said to them, "Why? What has this man done wrong? I have found in Him no grounds for the death penalty. Therefore I will have Him whipped and [then] release Him" (Luke 23:22 HCSB).

Finally, Pilate sentenced a man, whom he knew to be innocent, and declared to be innocent, to the horrible death by crucifixion.

CONCLUSION TO THE TRIAL OF JESUS

When all the facts are weighed, it becomes clear that those who tried Jesus on that night were not interested in giving Him a fair trial. The verdict had been determined ahead of time. They only went through the motions of the appearance of a fair trial. Jesus was illegally and wrongfully tried. Although Pilate declared Him innocent, Jesus was still put to death. This was a mockery of justice.

SUMMARY TO QUESTION 42
DID JESUS RECEIVE A FAIR TRIAL?

The four gospels tell us that Jesus Christ went through a number of trials—Jewish and Roman—before He was put to death. There is a question as to whether or not Jesus received a fair trial. Some have argued that the trial of Jesus was legal but not ethical. It was the textbook example of using the law in a bad way.

The traditional view among Christians, however, is that the trial of Jesus was illegal in a number of ways.

First, there was no possibility of him receiving a fair trial because the verdict had already been determined in advance. His fate had already been decided by these religious rulers.

It was also illegal to try someone at night for a capital crime. Yet Jesus was tried at night.

According to Jewish law, witnesses were needed to *start* the trial. The trial did not begin and then a search would get underway to look for witnesses. However, it was only after Jesus' trial began that they started looking for witnesses. Furthermore, the witnesses used at Jesus' trial were false! Not only should their testimony have been rejected, they themselves should have been punished.

Because judgment in capital cases had to be delayed until the next day, no trial should have been held before the Sabbath day. Yet again we find them breaking their own law.

Most important, Jesus admission to being the Messiah was never seriously considered. As soon as He admitted His identity, they charged Him with blasphemy and declared Him guilty. There was not the least bit of effort to determine if Jesus' claims may have been true.

The farce continued. The religious rulers could not agree among themselves on the charges. They considered Jesus was worthy of death because He committed blasphemy. Yet they told Pilate that He was guilty of attempting to overthrow Rome.

Finally, Pilate, the judge, admitted on three different occasions that Jesus was innocent of all the charges. However, he still ordered a known innocent man to be crucified.

Therefore, when all the facts are considered, we conclude that Jesus' trial was the greatest injustice in all of history.

QUESTION 43

Why Did Jesus Die On The Cross?

Scripture testifies to the fact that Jesus Christ died on a cross after being betrayed to the religious rulers by one of His own disciples, Judas Iscariot. But the immediate reason Jesus died was because of the envy of the Jews. Pontius Pilate recognized this when the Jewish religious leaders brought Jesus to him. We read.

> Now at the festival the governor was accustomed to release a prisoner for the crowd, anyone whom they wanted. At that time they had a notorious prisoner, called Jesus Barabbas. So after they had gathered, Pilate said to them, "Whom do you want me to release for you, Jesus Barabbas or Jesus who is called the Messiah?" For he realized that it was out of jealousy that they had handed him over (Matthew 27:15-18 NRSV).

Their envy toward Jesus was due to the fact that He had drawn a large following by claiming to be the long-awaited Messiah. His miracles verified His claims. Jesus also criticized their corrupt religious system. Because of this, they decided to kill Him.

WHY JESUS DIED

There are more significant reasons, however, why Jesus died on Calvary's cross. They include the following.

1. JESUS' DEATH WAS NECESSARY IN GOD'S PLAN

The Bible makes it clear that the death of Jesus Christ was necessary in the eternal plan of God. Jesus Himself said.

> Just as Moses lifted up the snake in the wilderness, so the Son of Man must be lifted up (John 3:14 HCSB).

Jesus spoke of the necessity of Himself being lifted up, or crucified.

The Scripture says Christ's death was part of God's eternal purpose. We read the following in Hebrews.

> Then Christ said, "And so, my God, I have come to do what you want, as the Scriptures say." The Law teaches that offerings and sacrifices must be made because of sin. But why did Christ mention these things and say that God did not want them? Well, it was to do away with offerings and sacrifices and to replace them. That is what he meant by saying to God, "I have come to do what you want." So we are made holy because Christ obeyed God and offered himself once for all (Hebrews 10:7-10 CEV).

Jesus had come into the world for the purpose of dying on the cross. His death was in the will of God the Father.

Indeed, Jesus explicitly said that His purpose for coming into the world was to die. Matthew records Him saying.

> Just as the Son of Man did not come to be served, but to serve, and to give His life—a ransom for many (Matthew 20:28 HCSB).

His purpose was to die for the sins of the world.

2. JESUS WAS THE LAMB OF GOD

At His baptism, when John the Baptist saw Jesus coming, he declared Jesus to be the "Lamb of God."

> The next day he saw Jesus coming toward him and declared, "Here is the Lamb of God who takes away the sin of the world!" (John 1:29 NRSV).

Jesus' coming into the world was as the "Lamb of God." Indeed, His appearance in our world was for the purpose to take away the sins of everyone.

3. JESUS PAID THE PENALTY FOR SIN

The death of Jesus Christ was the payment for sin. It was the ransom, or price, paid to God to satisfy His holy demands. The Bible pictures humans as sinners who have rebelled against God. Christ's death on the cross paid the penalty for the sin of humankind. Jesus died in our place as our substitute, receiving the punishment that was due us.

The Bible says that Jesus Himself paid the penalty for our sins. Paul wrote to the Romans.

> He was handed over to die because of our sins, and he was raised from the dead to make us right with God (Romans 4:25 NLT).

Jesus died for our sins—not His. Indeed, He had no sin.

The writer to the Hebrews also declared that Jesus Christ died to take away sins. We read.

> So Christ died only once to take away the sins of many people. But when he comes again, it will not be to take away sin. He will come to save everyone who is waiting for him (Hebrews 9:28 CEV).

His death took away the sins of the world.

The Apostle Paul also wrote to the Corinthians about how Jesus Christ died for our sins.

> For I handed on to you as of first importance what I in turn had received: that Christ died for our sins in accordance with the scriptures (1 Corinthians 15:3 NRSV).

Because of Christ's death, believers will not have to suffer eternally for their sins.

There is something else. The penalty that Jesus paid for sin was not only for the human race—it was also for everything in the universe that had been marred by sin. Paul wrote.

> Because the creation itself also will be delivered from the bondage of corruption into the glorious liberty of the children of God (Romans 8:21 NKJV).

Everything in the universe which has been marred by sin will now be set free. The demands of a holy God were satisfied by Jesus' death on the cross.

4. JESUS' DEATH BOUGHT OUR FREEDOM

As we study the life of Christ, we often come into contact with the term, "redemption." The word, "redeem" means "to purchase." When Jesus Christ died for our sins, He paid the price for them with His own blood. Peter wrote.

> For you know that God paid a ransom to save you from the empty life you inherited from your ancestors. And the ransom he paid was not mere gold or silver. He paid for you with the precious lifeblood of Christ, the sinless, spotless Lamb of God (1 Peter 1:18,19 NLT).

It was His death which bought our freedom from sin.

The Bible also speaks of Christ redeeming us from the curse of the law. Paul wrote the following to the Galatians.

But Christ rescued us from the Law's curse, when he became a curse in our place. This is because the Scriptures say that anyone who is nailed to a tree is under a curse (Galatians 3:13 CEV).

Jesus became a curse for us so that we might be saved from our sins.

WE WERE BOUGHT OUT OF THE SLAVE MARKET

We find that the New Testament uses two terms that shed light upon the full meaning of redemption, *agorazo* and *lutro*. The word *agorazo*, along with its variation, *exagorazo*, has the idea of buying a slave out of the market, and then taking him home.

This term speaks of Christ buying us out of the slave market of the world. The price Jesus paid, with His own blood, was sufficient to buy every slave out of the market. His purchase also means that slave would never be sold again.

We have all been slaves to sin, but if we allow Him to be our Master, then we need never be sold again—for He becomes our eternal Master. This is certainly great news!

The word *lutro* has the idea of, "to buy and give freedom." When Jesus Christ bought us from the marketplace of the world, he not only gave us our freedom, He made us part of His family. Those who receive by faith the benefits of the sacrifice which Jesus Christ has provided, become children of God. We are now part of His eternal family. Paul wrote.

> God's Spirit makes us sure that we are his children. His Spirit lets us know that together with Christ we will be given what God has promised. We will also share in the glory of Christ, because we have suffered with him. (Romans 8:16,17 CEV).

When redemption is properly understood, it means that Jesus Christ bought humanity out of the slave market of the world. The price He paid was His own blood. When He bought us, He gave us our freedom. We cannot be sold again as slaves. We have become part of His family and participants in His rightful inheritance. All this is obtainable if we choose to place our faith in the sacrifice that He made on our behalf. This is indeed "good news!"

5. JESUS' DEATH SHOWED THE LOVE OF GOD

The death of Jesus Christ upon the cross also demonstrated that God loves sinful humanity. The Scripture speaks of His death as an act of love toward humankind. John wrote.

> God loved the people of this world so much that he gave his only Son, so that everyone who has faith in him will have eternal life and never really die (John 3:16 CEV).

It was the love of God the Father for this world that caused Him to send God the Son to die for our sins.

Paul wrote about the love God demonstrated for us in Jesus Christ. He put it this way.

> But God demonstrates His own love toward us, in that while we were still sinners, Christ died for us (Romans 5:8 NKJV).

It was love that motivated God the Son, Jesus Christ, to come to earth and to die on the cross for our sins.

6. HE WAS AN EXAMPLE TO THE BELIEVER

The Bible tells us the love of God, that was demonstrated by Jesus, should serve as an example for how we should treat one another.

> So now I am giving you a new commandment: Love each other. Just as I have loved you, you should love each other. Your love for one another will prove to the world that you are my disciples (John 13:34,35 NLT).

We are to show our love for God by loving each other.

In sum, there were a number of reasons as to why God the Son came into our world to die upon a cross. It is important that we understand these reasons.

SUMMARY TO QUESTION 43
WHY DID JESUS DIE ON THE CROSS?

Although the immediate reason for the death of Jesus Christ was the envy of the Jewish religious rulers, the Bible lists a number of other reasons as to why Christ died. They include the following.

First, it was in the eternal plan of God—it was not an afterthought. Scripture emphasizes the necessity of Jesus' death. Indeed, Jesus Himself spoke of the need for His own death.

We find that Jesus' death was necessary to complete the plan of redemption for this sinful world. He had to die so that others could live.

Therefore, Jesus Christ died on the cross for the sins of the world. Indeed, He was the perfect sacrifice for our sin. In other words, his sacrifice was acceptable to God.

The death of Jesus Christ was also a visible demonstration of the love of God for sinful humanity. It was that love which led God the Father to send God the Son into our world.

Jesus' death should serve as an example for the believers. In fact, we are told to pattern our lives after His life. Consequently, believers are to love one another in the same manner as Jesus has loved us.

This is a brief summation as to why the death of Jesus Christ was necessary from a biblical point of view.

QUESTION 44

Why Was Jesus Crucified Rather Than Stoned To Death?

At the time of Jesus, those who committed crimes worthy of capital punishment were stoned to death. Crucifixion was not the Jewish form of execution. Crucifixion was the Roman form of punishment.

Why then did the religious leaders take Jesus Christ to Pilate in order to have Him crucified? Why didn't they stone Him like they eventually did with the martyr Stephen? Several observations can be made as we seek to answer this question.

1. THERE IS A CURSE ASSOCIATED WITH CRUCIFIXION

One of the reasons may have been the curse associated with crucifixion. The Old Testament speaks of those being cursed who hang upon a tree. We read.

> If a man guilty of a capital offense is put to death and his body is hung on a tree, you must not leave his body on the tree overnight. Be sure to bury him that same day, because anyone who is hung on a tree is under God's curse. You must not desecrate the land the LORD your God is giving you as an inheritance (Deuteronomy 21:22,23 NIV).

By having Jesus crucified, the religious leaders may have thought that this would end any talk about Him being the Messiah—since the Messiah certainly would not have been cursed.

Paul would later write to the Galatians about the curse that Christ bore on our behalf. He put it this way.

> Christ paid the price to free us from the curse that God's laws bring by becoming cursed instead of us. Scripture says, "Everyone who is hung on a tree is cursed" (Galatians 3:13 God's Word).

Jesus became a curse on our behalf so that we could be set free from sin.

However, the curse associated with death by means of crucifixion could have been the motivation of the religious leaders to have Jesus die in this manner.

2. ONLY THE LOWEST MEMBERS OF SOCIETY WERE CRUCIFIED

Another reason may have been the way the Romans used crucifixion. A Roman citizen was never crucified—they were put to death by the quick method of beheading. Only slaves, political rebels, and the lowest criminals were put to death by crucifixion. The cross was a symbol of shame for the Romans. The Roman writer Cicero wrote.

> Even the word 'cross' must remain far, not only from the lips of the citizens of Rome, but also from their thoughts their eyes their ears.

The religious leaders may have wanted Jesus to die a particularly shameful death.

3. THE NEW TESTAMENT WRITERS DO NOT EMPHASIZE HIS SUFFERING

The New Testament writers did not emphasize the physical suffering of Jesus upon the cross. The suffering that Jesus went through was more than physical agony. Indeed, His death paid the penalty for the world's sins. In doing so He was, in some way unknown to us, separated from God the Father. The Bible says.

At about three o'clock, Jesus called out with a loud voice, "Eli, Eli, lema sabachthani?" which means, "My God, my God, why have you forsaken me?" (Matthew 27:46 NLT).

There was a separation between God the Father and God the Son in those hours that Jesus was upon the cross. During that time the penalty for our sins was placed upon Him.

Therefore, as far as Christians are concerned, the symbol of the cross does not have so much to do with the physical suffering of Jesus. Instead, it represents the "good news" that salvation has been obtained for those who come to God in faith.

SUMMARY TO QUESTION 44
WHY WAS JESUS CRUCIFIED RATHER THAN BEING STONED TO DEATH?

Jesus Christ was put to death by the terrible method of crucifixion. Although we are not told why the religious leaders did not organize a group of people to stone Him, it is likely due to the curse associated with crucifixion. The Old Testament speaks of those who die in this manner as being "cursed."

Crucifixion was reserved for the slaves, political rebels and the worst criminals. The religious leaders may have wanted to make it clear to everyone that Jesus could not have been the promised Messiah— because of the manner in which He died. Certainly God would not allow His "Chosen One" to die such a horrible death. Thus, they may have assumed a death by crucifixion would end all talk of Jesus being the Messiah.

When the New Testament writers spoke of Jesus' death, it was not to emphasize the horrible suffering that He endured on our behalf. Rather it was to proclaim the victory that Jesus won in paying the penalty for sin. He did indeed become a curse for us—the innocent died for the guilty.

Consequently, the fact that Jesus was crucified emphasizes that awfulness of our sin—the penalty of which was placed upon Him. Realizing this should cause us to hate sin all the more—as well as to love Jesus all the more. Indeed, He died so that each of us could live.

QUESTION 45

What Is The Significance Of The Words Jesus Spoke While On The Cross?

The Gospels record that during the six hours Jesus Christ was hanging on the cross He made seven different statements. These statements are of tremendous significance because they are the last words of Jesus before His death. They demonstrate that Jesus was consistent in His life, and in His message, until the very end. His words were as follows.

1. "FATHER, FORGIVE THEM, FOR THEY KNOW NOT WHAT THEY DO" (LUKE 24:34).

This first of seven sayings of Jesus shows that He was thinking of others until the end of His life. Even while experiencing the horrible pain of crucifixion, He was praying for the very people who caused His suffering. Christ came to earth for the purpose of forgiving sinners and He loved them, and forgave them up until the end. It was because of humanity's sin that Jesus was on the cross—suffering on behalf of that sin.

2. "TODAY YOU WILL BE WITH ME IN PARADISE" (LUKE 23:43).

Not only did Jesus forgive those who crucified Him, He also forgave one of the criminals crucified next to Him. When the criminals were put on the cross, both of them cursed Jesus. However, as time elapsed, one of the criminals had a change of heart. Luke records the following.

One of the criminals hanging beside him scoffed, "So you're the Messiah, are you? Prove it by saving yourself—and us, too, while you're at it!" But the other criminal protested, "Don't you fear God even when you are dying? We deserve to die for our evil deeds, but this man hasn't done anything wrong." Then he said, "Jesus, remember me when you come into your Kingdom" (Luke 23:39-42 NLT).

It was at this juncture that Jesus made His second statement from the cross promising to forgive the repentant criminal. Again, we see Jesus' concern for others. His example later led the Apostle Paul to exhort the Philippian church in the following manner.

Do nothing from selfish ambition or conceit, but in humility regard others as better than yourselves (Philippians 2:3 NRSV).

Jesus was always concerned with the needs of others.

3. "WOMAN, BEHOLD YOUR SON" (JOHN 19:26).

As Jesus continued to suffer on the cross, His mind was still upon others. He saw His mother standing near the Apostle John and said, "Woman, behold your son." He then looked at John and said, "Behold your mother!"

By doing this, He was entrusting the care of His mother to John. The law required the firstborn son to take care of his parents, and Jesus was obeying the law of God up until the end. Early in His ministry, Jesus emphasized His respect for the law when He made the following statement recorded in the Sermon on the Mount.

Don't suppose that I came to do away with the Law and the Prophets. I did not come to do away with them, but to give them their full meaning (Matthew 5:17 CEV).

He honored and obeyed the law of God throughout His life—He also honored the law while suffering His death.

4. "MY GOD, MY GOD, WHY HAVE YOU FORSAKEN ME?" (MATTHEW 27:46).

The fourth saying of Jesus from the cross is probably the most difficult for us to understand. The sinless Son of God who had been, from all eternity, in an intimate relationship with His Father, is now spiritually separated from Him. The penalty of the sins of the world was put upon Jesus.

Consequently, there was, for the first time, a separation between the Father and the Son. The Bible records something happened between them that we can only understand through the eye of faith. Paul wrote.

> For God was in Christ, reconciling the world to himself, no longer counting people's sins against them. This is the wonderful message he has given us to tell others (2 Corinthians 5:19 NLT).

The Father was placing the penalty of the sins of the world upon the Son in order that everything in the universe, that had been affected by sin, could again be made right with God. Jesus was suffering the pain and separation that we deserve. Paul also wrote.

> For God made Christ, who never sinned, to be the offering for our sin, so that we could be made right with God through Christ. (2 Corinthians 5:21 NLT).

In order for this to occur, the Father had to forsake the Son and punish Him on our behalf.

5. "I THIRST" (JOHN 19:28).

The fifth statement that Jesus made from the cross reminds us again that He suffered as a human being. The Bible says.

> After this, when Jesus knew that everything had now been finished, he said, "I'm thirsty." He said this so that Scripture could finally be concluded (John 19:28 God's Word).

Jesus lived as a human, and suffered as a human, in order that He could identify with suffering humanity. From this statement, we observe that Jesus suffered the full physical effect of crucifixion. There was no easing up, for the weight of our sins was placed upon Him.

6. "IT IS FINISHED" (JOHN 19:30).

The sixth statement from Jesus while on the cross was a cry of victory. The Greek text reads *tetelestai*, "It is finished." What was finished? As we consider the life and ministry of Jesus we can think of several things that His death made complete.

THE WAY OF SALVATION FROM SIN WAS NOW COMPLETE

First, Jesus had to finish the task the Father had sent Him to earth to accomplish—namely to provide salvation for humankind. By living His entire life without sin, Jesus was able to become the perfect sacrifice for the sins of the world.

The way of salvation had now been made complete. No more animal sacrifices were necessary. They had only pointed to the ultimate sacrifice Jesus had now offered. His was the supreme sacrifice that satisfied the righteous demands of a holy God.

JESUS FULFILLED THE PREDICTIONS REGARDING THE PROMISED MESSIAH

The second thing that was accomplished by Jesus on the cross was a fulfillment of prophecy. The predicted Messiah had come as God promised He would. Prophecies of the Word of God, which are always accurate, had again come to pass. The Savior was promised and now Christ the Savior had come! He accomplished the promised salvation.

JESUS ACCOMPLISHED VICTORY OVER THE DEVIL

A third matter that was accomplished by Jesus' death on the cross was the victory over the devil. The Scripture says that one of the purposes for Jesus' coming was to destroy the works of the devil. John wrote.

> But when people keep on sinning, it shows that they belong to the devil, who has been sinning since the beginning. But the Son of God came to destroy the works of the devil (1 John 3:8 NLT).

The death of Jesus Christ finished that task. The dominion over the earth that humanity, through his sin, had handed over to the devil, was now won back. The authority of Satan had been vanquished—the victory had been won. When Christ comes back again He will take hold of the victory that He won over the devil on Calvary's cross.

JESUS' OWN SUFFERING WAS FINISHED

A fourth and final reason that Jesus said, "It is finished" is with regard to His own suffering. Jesus spent over thirty years upon the earth living among sinful humanity, suffering from the self-imposed limitations of that existence. He had now endured the final six hours of that suffering on a cross. This was now finished. He would no longer have to suffer the limits of space and time. It was finished!

7. "FATHER, INTO YOUR HANDS I COMMEND MY SPIRIT" (LUKE 23:46).

This is the final statement that we have from Jesus before His death. Everything had been completed and now it was time to dismiss His spirit. Jesus had previously made the statement that He would willingly lay down His life for His sheep.

> Therefore My Father loves Me, because I lay down My life that I may take it again. No one takes it from Me, but I lay it down of Myself. I have power to lay it down, and I have power to take it again. This command I have received from My Father (John 10:17,18 NKJV).

From this, we realize that Jesus had to purposely dismiss His spirit—it could not be taken from Him. Unless He desired to die, He would not have had to. Because He was a willing victim, however, He chose to die. Upon making His final statement, Jesus died.

SUMMARY TO QUESTION 45
WHAT IS THE SIGNIFICANCE OF THE WORDS JESUS SPOKE WHILE ON THE CROSS?

The seven statements Jesus Christ made from the cross of Calvary have far-reaching significance for us today. They once again remind us that His death, besides being a fact of history, was much more than that. It was the supreme sacrifice that secured our salvation. His final words show us that we can have the utmost confidence in Him as our Savior.

The first statement was consistent with Jesus' entire life—He always thought about others. He asked the Father to forgive the sin of those who crucified Him.

The second statement also shows concern for others. He told a criminal that he would be with Him in paradise.

The third statement is another example of Jesus thinking about others. He entrusted His mother to John. In doing so, Jesus obeyed the Law of Moses until the end.

The fourth statement was recognition that He was forsaken by God the Father when the penalty of the sins of the world was placed upon Him. Our sins could now be forgiven because Jesus took the penalty on Himself.

The fifth statement makes us again aware of the human Jesus—He was thirsty. The pain and torment of the cross was not lessened.

The sixth statement was one of victory—Jesus' mission had been finished! Salvation from sin had now been accomplished, the works of the devil had now been destroyed, and Jesus' own suffering was now over.

The last statement allowed His spirit to return to the Father. Jesus willingly gave up His life.

These seven statements are an important reminder of Jesus' Person as well as His mission. He accomplished all that He set out to do and He did it for us.

QUESTION 46

Who Was Responsible For The Death Of Jesus?

There is an age-old question concerning the responsibility for Jesus' death. Who is to blame for the terrible crime of executing Jesus? Actually there are a number of different people to blame. They are as follows.

1. THE JEWISH RELIGIOUS RULERS WERE RESPONSIBLE

The Jewish religious rulers certainly deserve their share of the blame. They hated Jesus without any just, or righteous, cause. Their hatred caused them to arrest Jesus, find false witnesses at His trial, and then condemn him as guilty. They also brought false charges against Him in front of the Roman governor Pontius Pilate. We read.

> Then the assembly rose as a body and brought Jesus before Pilate. They began to accuse him, saying, "We found this man perverting our nation, forbidding us to pay taxes to the emperor, and saying that he himself is the Messiah, a king" (Luke 23:1,2 NRSV).

These religious leaders undoubtedly had their share of responsibility. They are the ones who instigated the entire process.

2. THE JEWISH PEOPLE WERE RESPONSIBLE

The Jewish people were also responsible for Jesus' death. John wrote about the lack of acceptance by His own people when He came into the world.

> He came into his own world, but his own nation did not welcome him (John 1:11 CEV).

The promised Messiah was rejected by those who should have received Him.

In another place, Jesus said the people of the city of Jerusalem were responsible for rejecting Him. He said the following concerning it.

> O Jerusalem, Jerusalem, the city that kills the prophets and stones God's messengers! How often I have wanted to gather your children together as a hen protects her chicks beneath her wings, but you wouldn't let me (Matthew 23:37 NLT).

The people from this Holy City did not accept the One whom they had been waiting for.

At His trial before Pontius Pilate, the crowd shouted to crucify Jesus. Matthew records their response to the attempt of Pilate to release Him.

> But the chief priests and leaders persuaded the crowd to ask for the release of Barabbas and the execution of Jesus. The governor asked them, "Which of the two do you want me to free for you?" They said, "Barabbas." Pilate asked them, "Then what should I do with Jesus, who is called Christ?" "He should be crucified!" they all said. Pilate asked, "Why? What has he done wrong?" But they began to shout loudly, "He should be crucified!" (Matthew 27:20-23 God's Word).

The people of the Jewish nation had their own share of responsibility. They rejected Jesus, and Jesus, in turn, rejected them.

3. PONTIUS PILATE WAS RESPONSIBLE

Pontius Pilate has his share of the blame in the death of Jesus Christ. As he told Jesus, he had the authority to release Him or crucify Him. John wrote.

Therefore, when Pilate heard that saying, he was the more afraid, and went again into the Praetorium, and said to Jesus, "Where are You from?" But Jesus gave him no answer. Then Pilate said to Him, "Are You not speaking to me? Do You not know that I have power to crucify You, and power to release You?" (John 19:8-10 NKJV).

Pilate did not accept the Sanhedrin's verdict of Jesus being guilty of any crime. To the contrary, Pilate testified to his innocence. John writes.

> Pilate went out again and said to them, "Look, I am bringing him out to you to let you know that I find no case against him" (John 19:4 NRSV).

Still, he gave the command for Jesus to be executed. John records the decision made by this weak politician.

> Then Pilate gave Jesus to them to be crucified. So they took Jesus and led him away (John 19:16 NLT).

Pilate was unquestionably responsible, to some degree, for Jesus' death. He knew of Jesus' innocence—yet he still ordered His death.

4. THE ENTIRE HUMAN RACE WAS RESPONSIBLE

Ultimately, it was the entire human race that is responsible for Jesus' death on the cross. The penalty for the sins of all of us was placed upon Jesus when He was on Calvary's cross. The Apostle Paul wrote.

> For God made Christ, who never sinned, to be the offering for our sin, so that we could be made right with God through Christ (2 Corinthians 5:21 NLT).

While there was the immediate blame with the Jewish religious rulers, the Jewish people and Pontius Pilate, the real blame should be placed where it deserves to be placed—all of us. It was for our sins that caused Jesus to die on Calvary's cross.

SUMMARY TO QUESTION 46
WHAT WAS RESPONSIBLE FOR THE DEATH OF JESUS?

The death of Jesus was a horrible crime. Blame can be rightly placed upon a number of people, as well as individuals. For one thing, the Jewish religious leaders have their share of the blame. For a number of years, they wanted Jesus dead. They hated Him and condemned Him without any righteous reason whatsoever.

The Jewish people were to blame as well. They rejected His claim to be the Messiah—though Jesus had the necessary credentials and provided the proper evidence.

Pontius Pilate also deserves blame. He ordered Jesus executed after declaring Him innocent of all charges. He was not guiltless.

However, the blame has to be ultimately placed upon the entire human race. It was for our sins that Jesus went to His death on Calvary's cross. Therefore, all of us were ultimately responsible for the death of Jesus Christ.

APPENDIX 1

What Day Of The Week Was Jesus Crucified: Wednesday, Thursday, Or Friday?

All Bible-believers agree that on Easter Sunday morning, the first day of the week, Jesus Christ had risen from the dead. The Bible says.

> After the Sabbath, at dawn on the first day of the week, Mary Magdalene and the other Mary went to look at the tomb (Matthew 28:1 NIV).

Mark explains it in this manner.

> When the Sabbath was over, Mary Magdalene, Mary the mother of James, and Salome bought aromatic spices so that they might go and anoint him. And very early on the first day of the week, at sunrise, they went to the tomb (Mark 16:1-2 NET).

As the Bible goes on to tell us, these women found the tomb empty on that Sunday morning—for the Lord has risen from the dead! All four gospels tell the same story—Jesus rose on Sunday—the first day of the week.

However, one of the most often-asked questions about Jesus' death on the cross concerns the day in which He was crucified. There have been those who advocated that it happened on Wednesday of Holy Week, others contend it was Thursday, while the traditional view says it took place on Friday. Do we know what day it was?

When all the evidence is in, it will become clear that the only day that fits the facts is Friday. We can make the following observations.

FIRST LINE OF EVIDENCE: JESUS WAS CRUCIFIED THE DAY BEFORE THE SABBATH

To begin with, all four gospels report that Jesus was crucified on "the day before the Sabbath" or the "day of preparation." The evidence is as follows.

MATTHEW

Matthew tells us that the religious leaders came to Pilate the day after Jesus was crucified. This would have been Saturday.

> The next day (which is after the day of preparation) the chief priests and the Pharisees assembled before Pilate (Matthew 27:62 NET).

MARK

Mark records the fact that Jesus was buried on the day of preparation—the day before the Sabbath began. This would have been Friday—since the Sabbath began at sundown on Friday.

> Now when evening had already come, since it was the day of preparation (that is, the day before the Sabbath), Joseph of Arimathea, a highly regarded member of the council, who was himself looking forward to the kingdom of God, went boldly to Pilate and asked for the body of Jesus (Mark 15:42 NET).

Mark goes on to tell us that Jesus was buried before sundown began on Friday.

> After Joseph bought a linen cloth and took down the body, he wrapped it in the linen and placed it in a tomb cut out of the rock. Then he rolled a stone across the entrance of the

tomb. Mary Magdalene and Mary the mother of Joses saw where the body was placed (Mark 15:46-47 NET).

Since it was against Jewish law to do physical work, or to travel on the Sabbath, the day before was called the Preparation Day—the day which prepared for the Sabbath.

LUKE

Luke also tells us that the women left Jesus' tomb because the Sabbath was about to begin with the sun going down.

> It was the day of Preparation, and the Sabbath was beginning. The women who had come with him from Galilee followed and saw the tomb and how his body was laid. Then they returned and prepared spices and ointments. On the Sabbath they rested according to the commandment (Luke 23:54-56 ESV).

JOHN

Like the other gospel writers, John tells us that the Sabbath was the next day.

> Then, because it was the day of preparation, so that the bodies should not stay on the crosses on the Sabbath (for that Sabbath was an especially important one), the Jewish leaders asked Pilate to have the victims' legs broken and the bodies taken down (John 19:31 NET).

The Scripture tells us that Sabbath was a high day—an especially important day—because it coincided with the Passover festival. Hence, those who were crucified were taken down from the cross before the Sabbath day began.

To sum up this first line of evidence, these passages from the four gospels could only mean that Jesus was crucified on Friday—the day of preparation for the Sabbath. Since, the Jewish day began at sundown, the Sabbath would have begun on Friday night. Therefore, Jesus was crucified during the day on Friday.

Also, in the religious vocabulary of the Jews, this term "the day of preparation," had become a technical designation for Friday. Add to this, the Greek word translated here as "preparation," (Pa-ra-ske-vee) is the word for Friday in modern Greek!

SECOND LINE OF EVIDENCE: HE WOULD BE RAISED "ON THE THIRD DAY"

Next, the Bible says that Jesus, after His death, would rise, or had risen, "on the third day." In fact, this is stated, in various ways, some twelve times in the New Testament.

THE PREDICTIONS BY JESUS

First, we have the gospel writers recording Jesus predicting that He would come back from the dead "on the third day" after His death.

> From that time on Jesus began to show his disciples that he must go to Jerusalem and suffer many things at the hands of the elders, chief priests, and experts in the law, and be killed, and on the third day be raised (Matthew 16:21 NET).

Later Jesus made the same prediction.

> As they were gathering in Galilee, Jesus said to them, "The Son of Man is about to be delivered into the hands of men, and they will kill him, and he will be raised on the third day." And they were greatly distressed (Matthew 17:23 ESV).

We find this same prediction repeated again by Jesus.

> Look, we are going up to Jerusalem, and the Son of Man will be handed over to the chief priests and the experts in the law. They will condemn him to death, and will

turn him over to the Gentiles to be mocked and flogged severely and crucified. Yet on the third day, he will be raised (Matthew 20:18,19 NET).

In total, Matthew records Jesus, on three separate occasions, predicting His resurrection will be "on the third day."

MARK

If Jesus was raised "on the third day," then why do we find the expression "after three days" from Mark?

They went out from there and passed through Galilee. But Jesus did not want anyone to know, for he was teaching his disciples and telling them, The Son of Man will be betrayed into the hands of men. They will kill him, and after three days he will rise (Mark 8:31 NET).

How could Jesus have been raised "on the third day" as well as "after three days?"

RESPONSE: AFTER THREE DAYS AND ON THE THIRD DAY ARE INTERCHANGEABLE EXPRESSIONS

We have a couple of responses to this.

First, Mark himself elsewhere records Jesus' prediction that His resurrection will take place on "the third day."

For He taught His disciples and said to them, "The Son of Man is being betrayed into the hands of men, and they will kill Him. And after He is killed, He will rise the third day" (Mark 9:31 NKJV).

Since the same writer, Mark used two different expressions "the third day" and "after three days" to describe when Jesus would rise from the dead, we can conclude that both phrases mean the same thing.

We should note that some manuscripts of Mark have "after three days" in 9:31. Hence, many English translations would read this way. However, we feel the evidence is stronger for the reading "the third day."

Whatever the case may be, we discover that these two phrases are used interchangeably in Scripture.

Indeed, we find in Matthew's gospel, that the religious leaders said the following to Pilate the day after the Lord was crucified.

> The next day (which is after the day of preparation) the chief priests and the Pharisees assembled before Pilate and said, "Sir, we remember that while that deceiver was still alive he said, 'After three days I will rise again.' So give orders to secure the tomb until the third day" (Matthew 27:62-64 NET).

The phrase "after three days" was equivalent to "until the third day." Otherwise surely the Pharisees would have asked for a guard of soldiers until the "fourth day." Consequently, we find that these two phrases were used interchangeably.

Later, we will give another example of these two phrases being used interchangeably from the Old Testament.

FURTHER TESTIMONY TO THE THIRD DAY

The predictions of Jesus resurrection "on the third" day were common knowledge. In fact, the false witnesses at His trial gave a jumbled account of this prediction.

> We heard him say, 'I will destroy this temple that is made with hands, and in three days I will build another, not made with hands.' (Mark 14:58 ESV).

We know from John's gospel that Jesus was speaking of the temple of His body—that He would raise it up "in three days."

> So the Jews said to him, "What sign do you show us for doing these things?" Jesus answered them, "Destroy this temple, and in three days I will raise it up." The Jews then said, "It has taken forty-six years to build this temple, and will you raise it up in three days?" But he was speaking about the temple of his body. When therefore he was raised from the dead, his disciples remembered that he had said this, and they believed the Scripture and the word that Jesus had spoken (John 2:18-22 ESV).

Note that Jesus said that "in three days" I will raise it up. This is another way of saying "on the third day."

LUKE

Luke also records Jesus predicting that He will rise on the third day.

> The Son of Man must suffer many things and be rejected by the elders, chief priests, and experts in the law, and be killed, and on the third day be raised (Luke 9:22 NET).

On Easter Sunday morning, the angels reminded the women who came to the tomb that Jesus had predicted that He would be raised from the dead on the third day after His death. They said the following.

> He is not here, but has been raised! Remember how he told you, while he was still in Galilee, that the Son of Man must be delivered into the hands of sinful men, and be crucified, and on the third day rise again." Then the women remembered his words (Luke 24:6-8 NET).

Later, on the day of His resurrection, Easter Sunday, we find two disciples discussing with the risen Christ exactly what had taken place in the previous days.

> But we had hoped that he was the one who was going to redeem Israel. Not only this, but it is now the third day since these things happened (Luke 24:21 ESV).

Notice, that on Easter Sunday, these two said, "it is now the third day since these things happened." Again we find that Sunday was considered to be the third day after His death on the cross.

THE BOOK OF ACTS

When Peter preached to the household of the gentile Cornelius, he made the following statement about Jesus.

> They killed him by hanging him on a tree, but God raised him up on the third day and caused him to be seen (Acts 10:40 NET).

Jesus was raised "on the third day."

When the Apostle Paul wrote his first letter to the Corinthians, he stated that Jesus rose from the grave "on the third day according to the Scriptures."

> For I passed on to you as of first importance what I also received - that Christ died for our sins according to the scriptures, and that he was buried, and that he was raised on the third day according to the scriptures (1 Corinthians 15:3,4 NET).

To summarize, the fact that Jesus rose "on the third day" rules out any other day but Friday as the day He was crucified. Indeed, if He had been crucified on Thursday, His resurrection would have occurred on the "fourth day" after His death, and if on Wednesday it would have been on the "fifth day."

The third day, Sunday, means that Friday was counted as the first day and Saturday the second day.

THE VERDICT

When we put all of these references together, we find twelve separate times in the New Testament we are told that Jesus will come back from the dead, or had come back from the dead, on the third day after His crucifixion.

To summarize, Jesus was crucified from approximately 9am to 3pm on Good Friday. He died about 3pm. This was day one.

At sundown on Friday, the second day began. Sundown on Saturday would have marked the beginning of the "third day."

It was on this third day, Easter Sunday, when the tomb was found empty and Christ appeared to a number of witnesses as having risen from the dead. Therefore, we conclude that Jesus died on Good Friday and arose from the dead on Easter Sunday.

OBJECTION: WHAT ABOUT JESUS' PREDICTION OF THREE DAYS AND THREE NIGHTS?

While it seems clear that Jesus died on Good Friday, and rose on Easter Sunday, there one matter that we must deal with. Indeed, probably the biggest objection to a Friday crucifixion and a Sunday resurrection is the prediction that Jesus made about the time that He would spend in the grave. Matthew records Jesus saying the following.

> An evil and adulterous generation asks for a sign, but no sign will be given to it except the sign of the prophet Jonah. For just as Jonah was in the belly of the huge fish for three days and three nights, so the Son of Man will be in the heart of the earth for three days and three nights (Matthew 12:39-41 NET).

According to this statement of Jesus, He would be in the grave three days and three nights—seventy-two hours. Therefore, it is claimed that it is impossible to have a Friday crucifixion and a Sunday resurrection.

RESPONSE: ANY PART OF A DAY IS CONSIDERED AN ENTIRE DAY

The answer to this objection can be simply stated—the Jews living at the time of Christ did not reckon time as we do. For them, any part of a day was considered to be an entire day. In other words, they counted the day on which any period began as one day, and they did the same with the day on which the period ended.

Consequently, we have Friday, Saturday, Sunday—three days. To the Jewish way of reckoning time, it did not matter that neither the Friday, nor the Sunday, was a complete day.

To support this idea of the way they reckoned time, we can cite Rabbi Eleazar ben Azariah, who lived around A.D. 100.

> A day and night are an Onah ['a portion of time'] and the portion of an Onah is as the whole of it" (from *Jerusalem Talmud*: Shabbath ix. 3).

According to his statement, Rabbi Azariah stated that any portion of a twenty-four-hour period could be considered the same "as the whole of it."

Therefore, at the time of Christ, Jesus' statement that He would be in the grave "three days and three nights" does not mean three complete days and three complete nights. Three days and three nights was an idiomatic expression.

Hence, as the Jews reckoned time, three days and three nights could have meant three full days, or any parts of three different days. From Scripture we have determined that Jesus was indeed in the grave for parts of three days—Friday, Saturday, and Sunday.

EXAMPLES OF THIS USAGE FROM OTHER PARTS OF SCRIPTURE

In addition, we have a number of examples from Scripture as to how the expression "three days and three nights" does not require three literal nights, and the expression "three days" does not require three complete days.

JOSEPH

The patriarch Joseph put his brothers in prison for three days.

> And he put them all together in custody for three days (Genesis 42:17 ESV).

However, we are told that he spoke to them on the third day.

> On the third day Joseph said to them, "Do this and you will live, for I fear God" (Genesis 42:18 ESV)

The context informs us that he released them on that same day—namely the third day. Therefore, the three days did not consist of three full days and three full nights.

REHOBOAM

We find that King Rehoboam asked certain people to come back to him "after" three days.

> So he said to them, "Come back to me after three days." And the people departed (2 Chronicles 10:5 NKJV)

Later we read.

> So Jeroboam and all the people came to Rehoboam the third day, as the king said, "Come to me again the third day" (2 Chronicles 10:12 ESV)

This is another illustration of what we discovered in the gospels. The phrase "after three days" means the same thing as "on the third day."

SAMUEL

We also the find the phrases "three days and three nights" and "three days ago" used interchangeably in an episode recorded in 1 Samuel.

> And they gave him a piece of a cake of figs and two clusters of raisins. So when he had eaten, his strength came back to him; for he had eaten no bread nor drunk water for three days and three nights (1 Samuel 30:12 NKJV).

This man had not eaten any food or had any water for "three days and three nights."

Yet, we discover that this does not mean a literal seventy-two hours.

> Then David said to him, "To whom do you belong, and where are you from?" And he said, "I am a young man from Egypt, servant of an Amalekite; and my master left me behind, because three days ago I fell sick (1 Samuel 30:13 NKJV).

The man had fallen sick three days ago—the day before yesterday. Consequently, it was for two nights, not three.

ESTHER

Queen Esther asked her uncle Mordecai to have the Judeans in Susa fast for three days and three nights before she would visit the king.

> Go, gather all the Jews to be found in Susa, and hold a fast on my behalf, and do not eat or drink for three days, night or day. I and my young women will also fast as you do. Then I will go to the king, though it is against the law, and if I perish, I perish" (Esther 4:16 ESV).

Yet we are told that Esther then visited the king "on the third day."

> On the third day Esther put on her royal robes and stood in the inner court of the king's palace, in front of the king's quarters, while the king was sitting on his royal throne inside the throne room opposite the entrance to the palace (Esther 5:1 ESV).

From studying the Scripture, we can conclude that expressions such "three days," "the third day," "on the third day," "after three days," and "three days and three nights" are all used to signify the same period of time.

THE OLD TESTAMENT APOCRYPHA

We also find this expression, three days and three nights, used in the Old Testament apocrypha—books written between the testaments that the Roman Catholic Church accepts as Holy Scripture. In the Book of Tobit, we read the following.

> At these words she went into an upper chamber of her house: and for three days and three nights did neither eat nor drink (Tobit 3:12 Douay)

We are told that this woman did not eat for "three days and three nights."

However, we are also told she ended her prayer "on the third day."

> But continuing in prayer with tears besought God, that he would deliver her from this reproach. And it came to pass on the third day, when she was making an end of her prayer, blessing the Lord (Tobit 3:13 Douay).

Again we find that the expression "three days and three nights" does not necessarily equal seventy-two hours or three nights.

THE TESTIMONY OF AN EARLY CHURCH FATHER

In addition to the biblical evidence, as well as from the Old Testament Apocrypha, and Jewish writings at the time of Christ, we also find that the early Christians understood the phrase "three days and three nights" to simply mean any part of three days.

Theodore of Heraclea, who lived from approximately A.D. 328-355, wrote the following.

> Christ says he will spend "three days and three nights in the heart of the earth." He is referring to the end of Friday, all of Saturday and the beginning of Sunday [of the passion week], in keeping with the way people understood the beginning and ending of days. For we too commemorate the third day of those who have died, not when three days and three nights, completed in equal measure, have gone by. But we reckon as a single, complete day that day on which the person died, regardless of what hour the death occurred. We count as another day that on which we take our leave of the departed in hymns before the tombs. Following this same kind of sequence, then, the Lord announced that he would spend a full three days and nights under the earth. A clear indication of this is the fact that the women arrived at that very time, in order to fulfill those things that the law prescribed to be done for the dead upon the third day (Theodore of Heraclea, Fragment 90).

Consequently, when all the evidence is considered, it becomes clear that the traditional date of Friday is indeed the day that Jesus Christ was crucified for our sins.

SUMMARY TO APPENDIX 1
WHAT DAY OF THE WEEK WAS JESUS CRUCIFIED: WEDNESDAY, THURSDAY OR FRIDAY?

One question that is often-asked about the crucifixion of Jesus Christ concerns which day of the week it took place. While Friday is the traditional view, there have been those who have advocated a Wednesday or Thursday crucifixion. However, the overwhelming evidence is that Jesus was crucified on Good Friday.

APPENDIX 1

The case for a Friday crucifixion is based upon two solid facts.

First, all four gospels state that Jesus was crucified on the day of preparation—the day before the Sabbath. Since the Sabbath day started at sundown on Friday, the day before the Sabbath would be Friday. In fact, the day of Preparation had become a technical term among the Jews for Friday.

Our second line of evidence notes that some twelve times in the New Testament, Jesus' resurrection is said to have taken place on "the third day" after His death. This includes Jesus' predictions that He would rise on the third day, as well as statements after His resurrection that it did indeed occur on the third day.

Since the Jews reckoned any part of a day as an entire day, this could only mean that He was crucified on Friday.

The chronology would then be as follows: the Lord died about 3pm on the day before the Sabbath, Friday. This would have been "day one." The Sabbath began at sundown on Friday. According to Jewish reckoning, this would have been "day two." Sundown on Saturday would have begun the third day.

When the women came to the tomb on Easter Sunday morning, on the "third day," they found the tomb empty. Furthermore, they were told by certain angels at the tomb that Christ had risen from the dead "on the third day"—just as He had predicted.

Consequently, a Friday crucifixion and a Sunday resurrection is the only explanation that fits all of the facts.

Some object to this because Jesus predicted that He would be in the grave for "three days and three nights." However, as we observed, this is an idiomatic way of saying three days according to the way Jews reckoned time.

Indeed, this "three days and three nights" was a recognized figure of speech, a Semitic idiom, for any portion of three calendar days. Thus, Jewish people regarded even a part of a day as "a day and a night."

In other words, this particular phrase did not require that seventy-two hours must have elapsed between the death of Jesus Christ and His resurrection from the dead—since the Jews reckoned any part of a day to be as a whole day.

Add to this, the Old Testament consistently counted any part of a day as an entire day. Furthermore, the Old Testament Apocrypha also gives us an example of how the phrase "three days and three nights" can be understood without three literal nights taking place.

We also cited an early church father, Theodore of Heraclea, who explained the three days and three nights in the same manner as we have just done.

In sum, it seems clear from the totality of the evidence that Jesus Christ died for our sins on Good Friday.

ABOUT THE AUTHOR

Don Stewart is a graduate of Biola University and Talbot Theological Seminary (with the highest honors).

Don is a best-selling and award-winning author having authored, or co-authored, over seventy books. This includes the best-selling *Answers to Tough Questions*, with Josh McDowell, as well as the award-winning book *Family Handbook of Christian Knowledge: The Bible*. His various writings have been translated into over thirty different languages and have sold over a million copies.

Don has traveled around the world proclaiming and defending the historic Christian faith. He has also taught both Hebrew and Greek at the undergraduate level and Greek at the graduate level.